My Faraway Country Myanmar

Linda Lewin

For my father
and all my travelling companions
xx

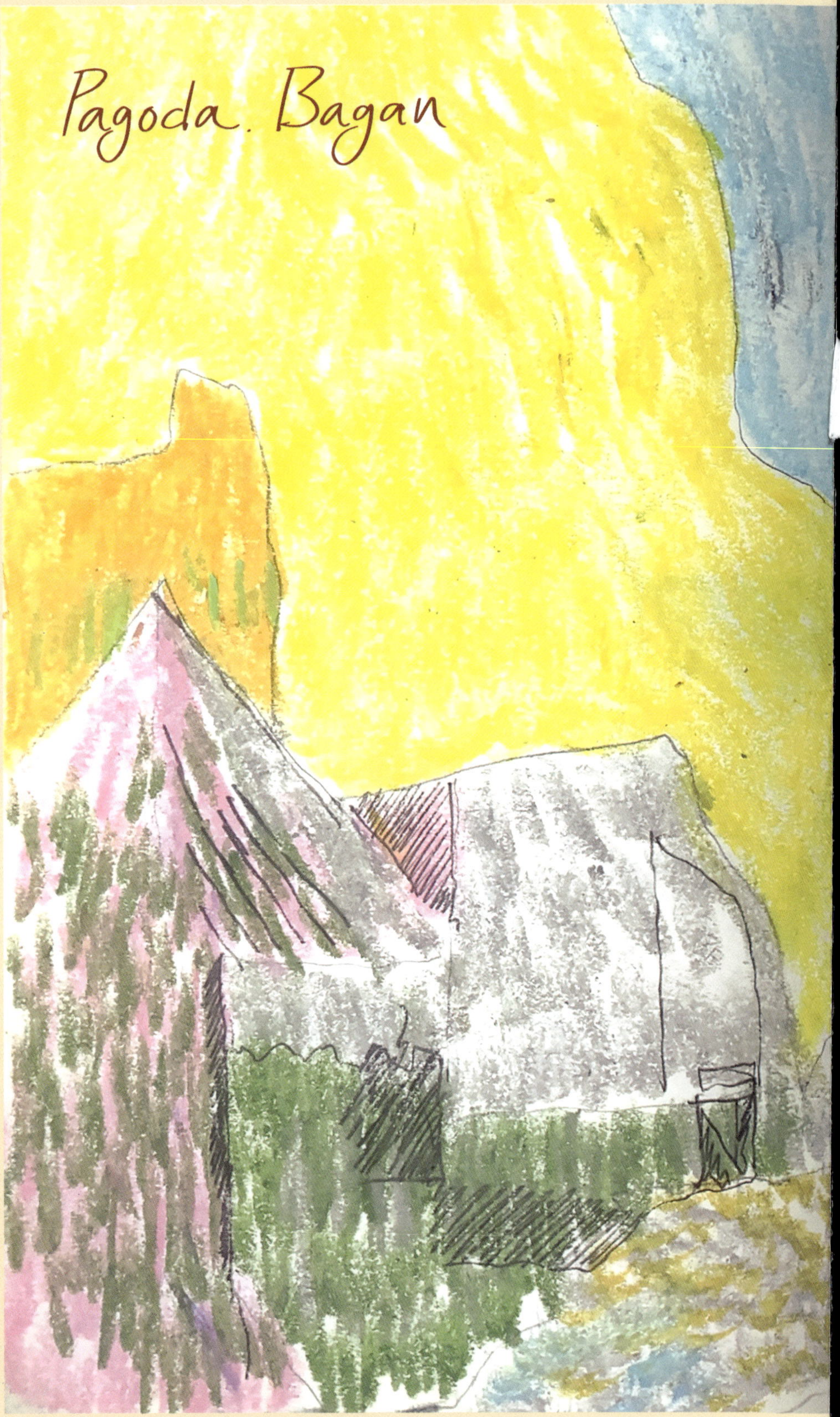
Pagoda. Bagan

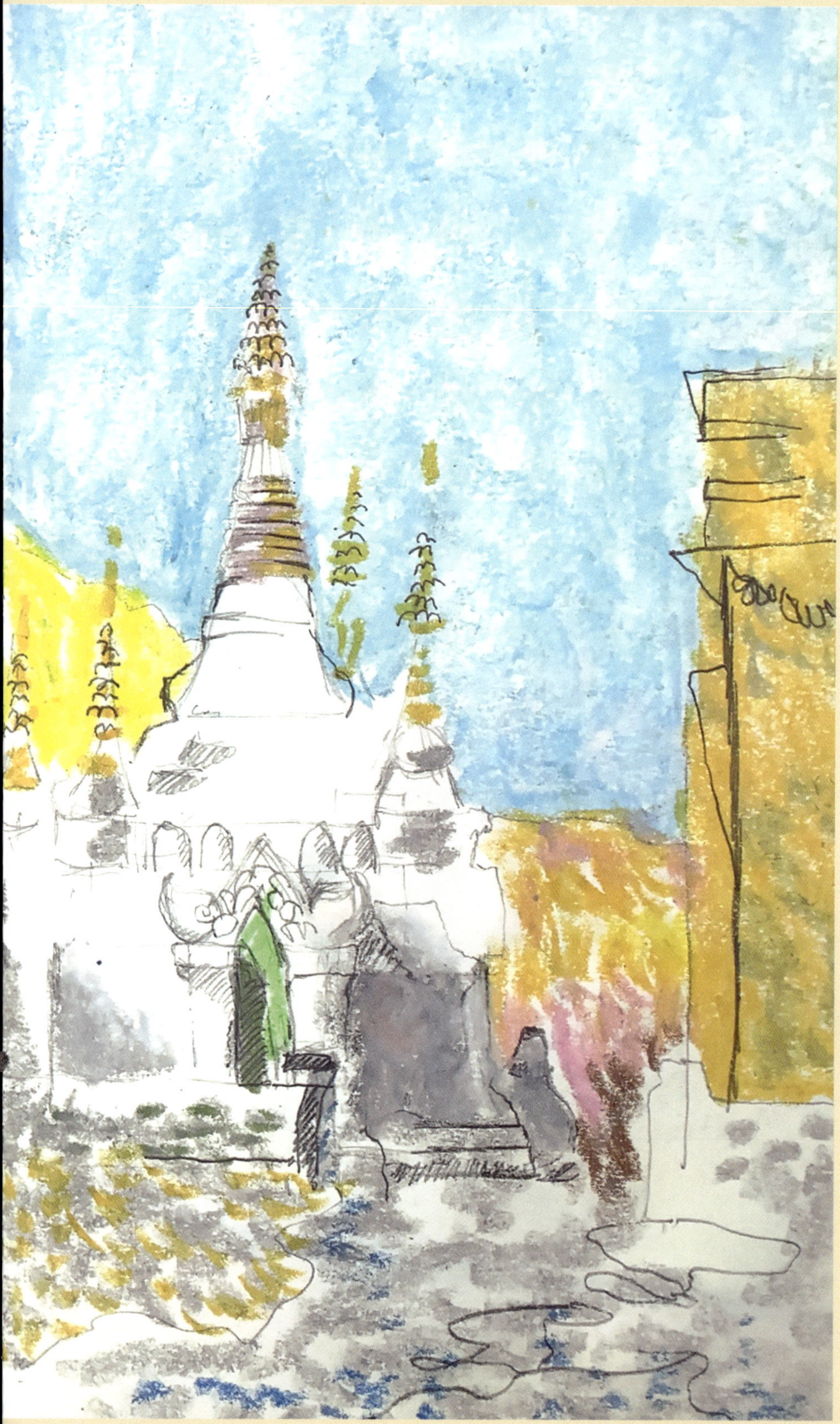

Contents

Beginning with Fairy Tales
Narrator: *Linda Lewin*

My Burmese oath:
I swear that everything I tell you is the truth. I swear by tigers, elephants, buffaloes and poisonous serpents to tell the truth. I swear by fire, water, rulers, thieves and my enemies, may they destroy me if I do not speak the truth.

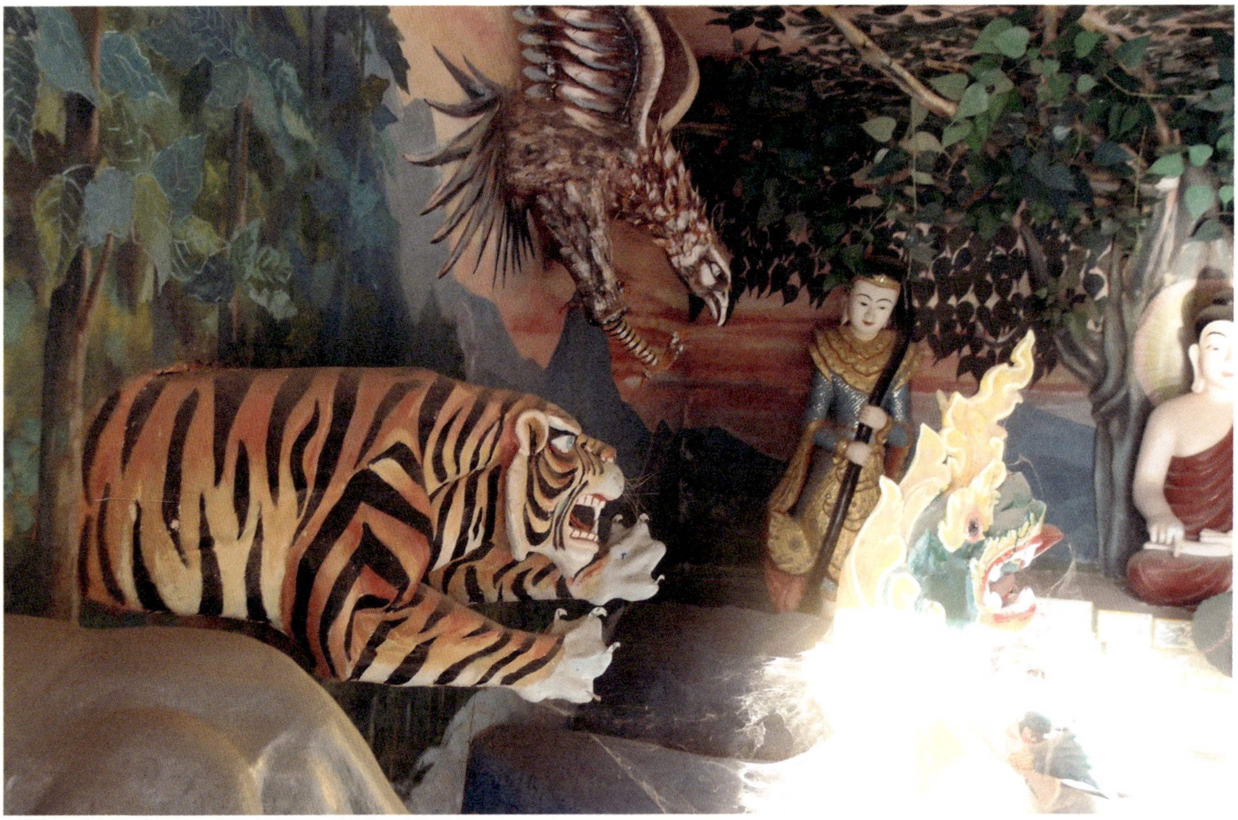

My father could not bear to tell me the truth about his past, instead he told me fairy tales. When I grew up I discovered the truth for myself. I discovered that he was right and I was wrong. I discovered that fairy tales and nightmares are equally true and that truth is hard to live with, but we have no choice.

I have collected my Burmese stories like fancy dress clothes in an old tin trunk. When my father was young and strong he picked it up and carried it on his back over a mud landslide, which was fortunate because otherwise he would have missed his boat to England. He would never have met and married my mother and I would not be here to tell this story. Eventually Father gave me the trunk. The luggage labels are still legible, a 1930 style drawing of a steam ship all done in shades of nautical blue: The Henderson Line, Rangoon to Calcutta, London, Liverpool and Glasgow. Berth 4. Stopping at other ports en route. I like to think they were pasted in place by a clerk wearing a white shirt with rolled up sleeves in an old wood lined shipping office.

When my father arrived in the UK he was a nineteen year old student and all his worldly possessions were contained in the black tin trunk which was standard issue in tropical climates, rat and termite proof, monsoon proof and protected by large padlocks. When I open the lid it still smells of the mothballs my paternal grandmother swore by. We called her Maman, a stick thin, elegant woman with eternal red hair, a cigarette and a husky French accent. She appeared in our house at Christmas time bearing strange foreign gifts, a dolly bag decorated with embroidery and mirrors or a string of misshapen beads. I still have them – my favourite is a bracelet with silver elephants marching along nose to tail. Not all of her presents were well received by her grandchildren – the red and white sailor suits were more 1930 than 1960 and all of her gifts smelt so strongly of camphor mothballs we had to leave them outside for a week before we could get close enough to examine them properly.

We can take out the stories and unfold them one by one but I warn you they are fragile. Some of them are dirty and torn with bits missing. On top is a child's blue bodice and a yellow skirt worn by Snow White at the Bassein commissioner's fancy dress party, so pretty and dainty. Next is a woven shoulder bag and inside that a pair of flat velvet sandals with a thong that slips between your toes. In Burma school children loop this style of bag around their head or neck and wear it in front like a necklace or hanging down their backs. Doctors and teachers hang their bags very neatly over one shoulder. A man on a bicycle will sling his workman's bag across his chest. My father took this bag hill walking in the Himalayas and I have done the same in the Scottish Highlands. But we must keep going,

there is no time for diversions to the Himalayas or anywhere else on this journey. We are on our way to the Irrawaddy Delta. Here are the glorious silk longyi which ladies wrap tight over their hips and tie discreetly at the waist. A man will wear the same thing as a woman but he makes a much bigger, more flamboyant knot in front. There is a strict dress code for all things. You just have to work out what it is. This is my grandfather's best English suit, which happened to have been made by an Indian tailor, and his barrister's wig, my grandmother's string of south sea pearls, and then, the most beautiful of all, an exotic umbrella of painted fabric sewn onto a bamboo frame which opens and closes like butterfly wings and smells of paraffin oil mixed with honey. Hold it up to the light and see how it glows. At the very bottom of the trunk are weapons of war, a Japanese sword, a no.3 dah, and a broken German bayonet. Finally, a Gurkha hat that looks as if it's been dragged through hordes of jungles and a newspaper clipping of a small boy with a serious expression standing beside a white elephant. But that's not quite all – finally, I almost forgot the note from a student folded like a piece of origami because she didn't have an envelope and so neatly written in pencil. 'Teacher, I told my mother, you are my foreigner mother, I will never forget you.' There is something for everyone and you may try on anything you like but please be careful because these are my most precious memories. Hot tropical days stored up against the dark nights of Scottish winters. They will not come again.

Come with me to my faraway country where brave Snow White, who never grew old, lives with the tyrants and the dictators, the liars and the thieves. She is a young woman and she is a young man of astonishing courage. Come with me. Do not worry about the things you do not like or do not understand or just make you feel hot and tired. Above all do not ask: are we there yet? It is a long and difficult journey and the ending is uncertain, but the people we meet along the way are the kindest people you could ever meet: they will share everything with you and ask for nothing. The greatest gift we can offer them is to sit and listen. We will be like relatives living in the same village. Smile a lot, take your shoes off when you enter someone's house, even if it is only a bamboo and matting hut. These gentle people are our willing hosts.

My Darling Gazelles

Your ancestors are waiting.
Where the days and nights are forged hot and equal in length,
where the river floods and rice overflows,
where even the stones in the road could be rubies or sapphires.
There dreams and nightmares have taken root
and grown so intimate with reality
it is impossible to part one from the other.

The pagoda sways its hips
and stretches its golden neck to kiss the blue sky with a desire
which they say has endured more than one thousand years.
Men feed the gods on peanut oil, honey and green bananas.
You might entertain an elephant for breakfast
or a Chinese dragon for tea
and every afternoon the goats process along the road in single file.
Children play and pray
innocent of their own beauty
which is multiplied in a million faceted mirrors.
A vision of heaven on earth.

Be careful, listen, watch and wait.
Wait until your body softens with the heat of the sun,
until your limbs are oiled and supple,
until your northern white skin turns to gold,
wait until your eyes are so accustomed to the light
you can see through the shadows.
When your ears can bear the never-ending din
of boats and men on the dock
and the constant singing and chanting
no longer keep you awake at night
then you will rise at dawn, refreshed.

The stories are only lightly camouflaged
between heaps of rubbish in the market place.
They emerge of their own free will, courageous.

In the warehouses painful memories remain preserved
under bundles of dry tobacco leaves,
glowing embers willing to be ignited by the lightest breath.

Without warning, a crack opens wide between words and fills with tears.
One man will say
'They are changing history.'
Another will say
'You find us in this piteous state because the government took our land.'
A woman will say
'I am afraid for my children.'

A man is following you,
he might be a spy or a thief, either way he knows where you are going.
Orphan girls sing and dance,
they wrap their arms around you
full of soft longing for their mothers
who have left to work in factories and foreign lands.

Invisible to everyone except his men
an insurgent wearing mufti is carried along the street,
his bandaged leg held aloft, raised to salute the sky.
His foot has been amputated by a land mine in the never-ending war.
Next morning an old soldier
with only one onion in his market bag
is grateful for your soiled currency.

A young girl with golden skin and black hair says
'You remind me of my grandmother, my grandmother had blue eyes.'
Your grandmother is lying
under the mangrove roots on the river bank,
surrounded by her children,
the living and the dead.
They are waiting to speak with you.

Your ever loving
Adaw Gyi

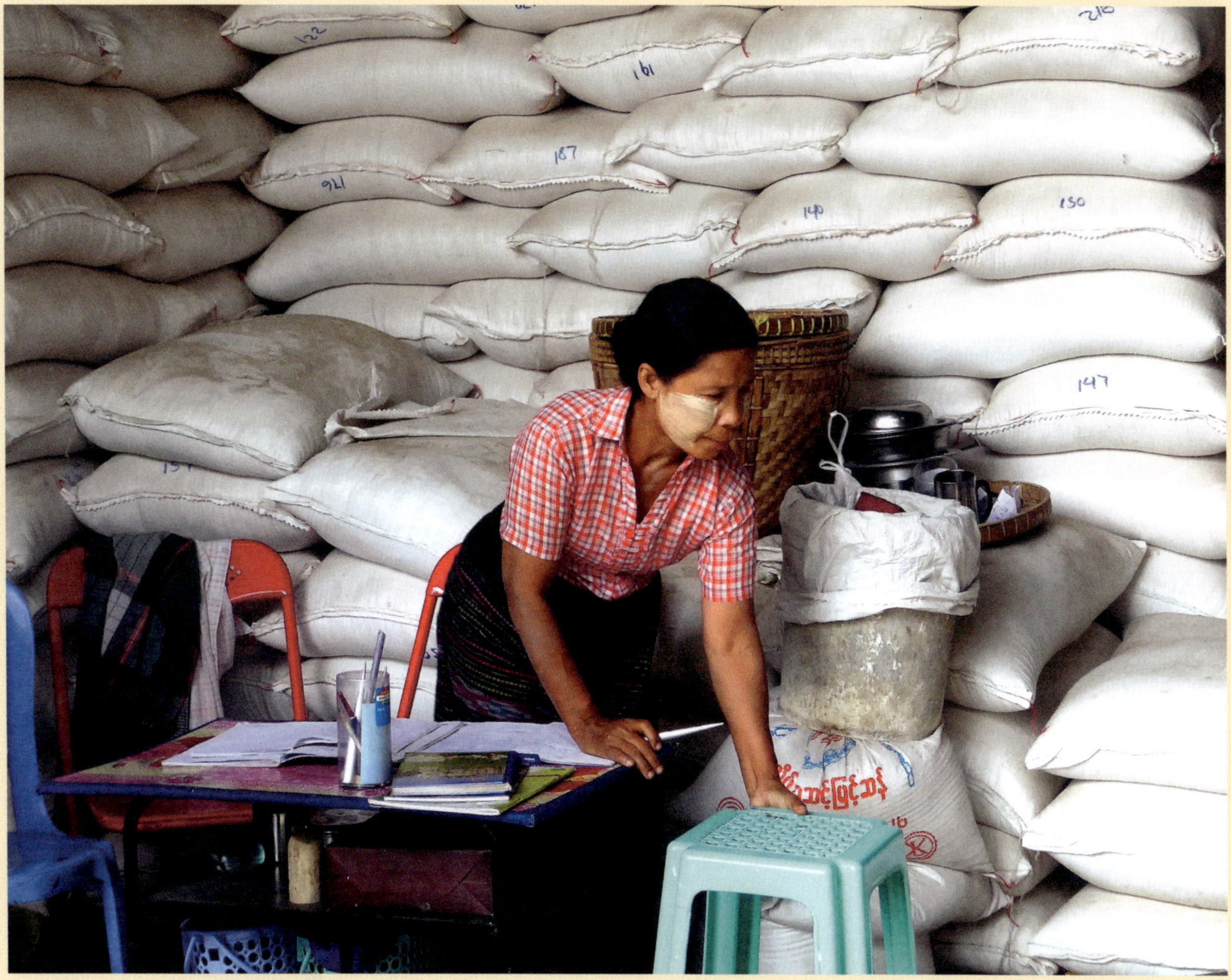

The last family run rice mill in Pathein. 2018

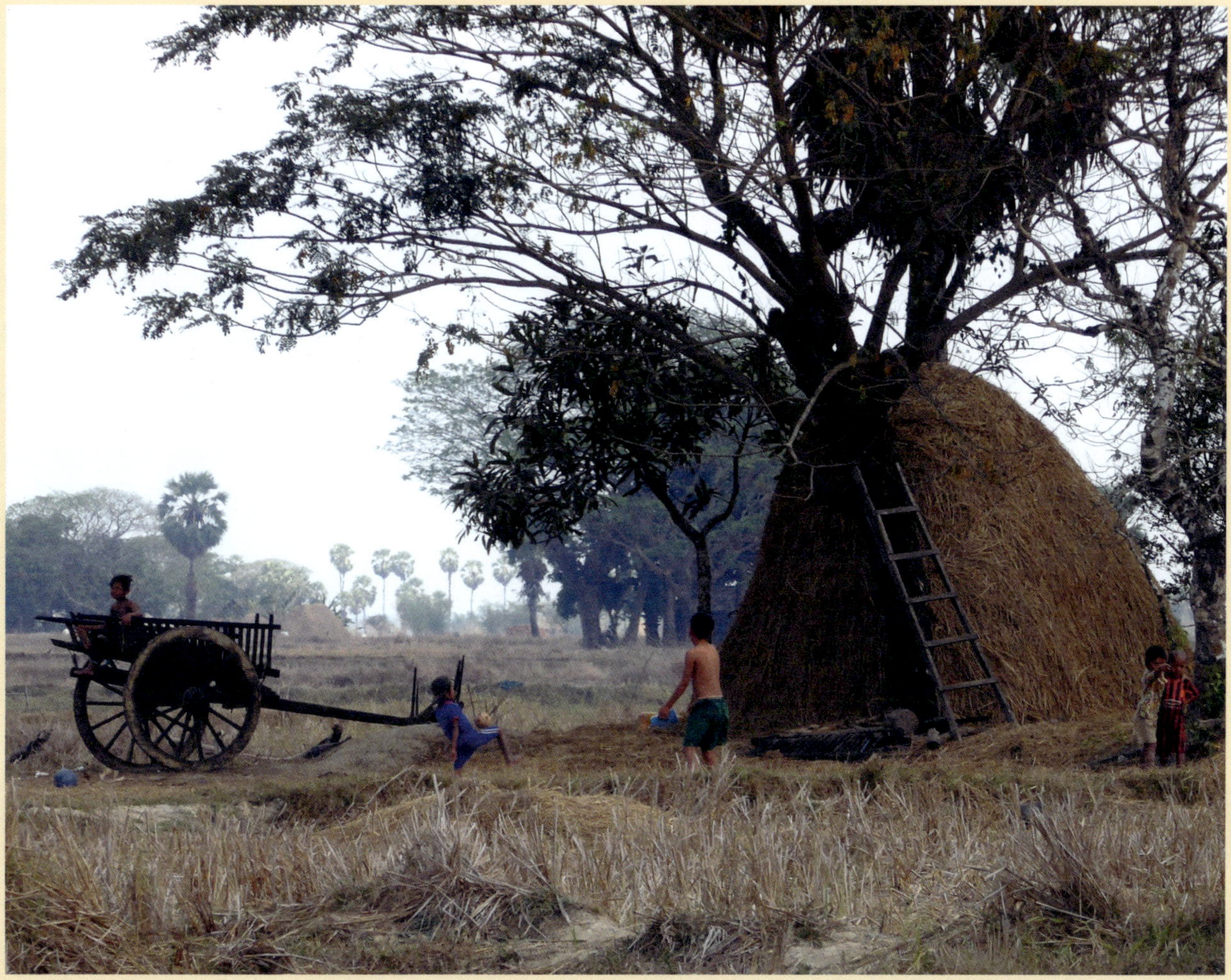

Many family farms have remained unchanged for centuries. Bilou Island 2018

A Terraced House in Glasgow
Narrator: *Linda Lewin*

I grew up in a terraced house in Glasgow, the oldest of six children. It was magic. Our mum was the prettiest mum in the street and our dad was the handsomest, cleverest and strongest dad in the universe. He could throw any one of his children from the oldest to the youngest up in the air and catch them without fear of dropping a single one. He could run races and come home with medals. He could smash a hockey ball from one end of the pitch to the other and was always in the winning team. There was only one thing he could not do and that was, tell us where he came from. We knew where Mum came from, a small town on the east coast of Scotland. We went there for holidays with Granny and played on the beach with our cousins but Dad came from somewhere else and he couldn't or wouldn't say where. If he didn't know where he came from, where did we come from? If people asked us, where are you from, what could we say and why was it so important? They could say 'Here' or 'There,' a west coast village or a Hebridean island. They talked about these places with pride. We knew we came from a mysterious somewhere else, or at least Father did, but if we asked him we got no answers. Just occasionally he would tell us tales of his childhood in a country where he learned to speak French before he spoke English and called his father Sir. He had to walk to school through jungles in the monsoon rain, pitching his wits against leopards and man eating tigers. Apparently, we were, once upon a time, not the richest but the second richest family in this mysterious far away country. A place where 'even the stones in the road could be rubies or sapphires.' Mother said this was nonsense. She knew no more about this faraway place than we did. Father was adamant, there were rubies and sapphires. First hand experience taught us children that the stones in the road were sharp and skint our knees when we fell over. Moreover, we were not a wealthy family, so why had he left behind all the rubies and sapphires which he could so easily have picked up? It made no sense. We had no idea how to tell the difference between fact and fiction where Father was concerned and he had no witnesses, not even a photograph, so we gave up asking. In any case we were fully absorbed in our own small but happy Scottish world and so it remained all through my growing up.

Drawing was my talent. I went to art college, where I learned to observe and record the world in minute practical detail. I specialised in jewellery techniques stretching back thousands of years. At college I met my husband, who told me his father had taken tea with the queen of Burma and he dreamed of marrying a Burmese princess but he was willing to settle for me. I continued to dodge the question, 'Where are you from?' with a slight feeling of embarrassment. It was too complicated to explain.

Looking back at my childhood in Glasgow, we children lived a charmed life. Adult problems were our adventures. Miners' strikes and power cuts meant ice on the inside of the windows and parents eking out lumps of coal one by one, but homework by candle light and sharing a hot bath with younger siblings, three at a time, was nothing but fun. In the Swinging Sixties Scotland was being rebuilt with modern pebble dash houses full of labour saving electric appliances. Grand Victorian and Edwardian mansions built with colonial loot lay empty, waiting to be demolished. These places were our playgrounds. We raced up and down on homemade bogies and played dangerous games with boxes of matches. We risked our lives climbing rotten trees and building wooden huts with hammers and stolen nails. Every house on our street was open to us by right. We had family, friends and neighbours who were the whole world to us.

The future was destined to be bright but evidence of the past remained. An old man wearing a war time trench coat tied up with string shuffled along our street in worn out slippers every evening at four o'clock. His job was lighting the gas lamps. Sometimes the industrial fog was so thick we could hardly find our way home from school. One night when all the cars and buses were stopped in their tracks, a pair of huge Clydesdale horses materialised out of the smog pulling a cart full of coal. The last of their kind.

Every back yard had an air raid shelter furnished with rusty iron bunk beds and dank, stinking mattresses. We children held our noses and dared each other to peer inside, expecting to see ghosts – which we wholeheartedly believed in. The reality was broken bottles, torn stockings and men who drank too much. We were told those places had been built to protect the people from enemy bombs. Huge blocks of concrete littered the east coast beach where we swam in the summer. We used them as a convenient place to sit and rub the sand out from between our toes but their real purpose was to block invading enemy tanks. Listening to these stories we wondered if we might need to be protected from enemies, what would the enemies look like, where would they come from, but luckily the enemies never made it to Scotland. They had all been defeated long since by brave young men in flying machines called Hurricane and Spitfire and we could sleep safely in our beds at night. Mother told us that when she was a child her family had to rush outside in the middle of the night, wearing their nightdresses, because a bomb landed on the house next door. Really quite exciting. A troop of Indian cavalry had been stationed just along the road, at the ready to save their lives, but Granny said all of the men and all of the horses died of cold come winter and we must never run outside in our nightdresses.

Father said nothing about his past.

The advantage of having six brothers and sisters is having six birthday parties every year. Mother made yards of sausage rolls and Father knew how to draw a donkey without a tail. We were not allowed to stay up for the adult supper parties but we sneaked out of bed to spy on them from the upstairs landing. We examined the evidence in the morning, empty glasses and ash trays. I think they played pin the tail on our donkey when we weren't looking. Uncles and Aunties came to visit, the house was always full of noise and laughter but somehow we knew we were different from the neighbours. The children we played with on the street knew it. The answer was not money – pennies had to be counted but that was the same in every house. It was not skin colour. It might have been religion because we were Catholics and everyone else was Protestant. We were obliged to attend after school catechism lessons in a dimly lit convent with nuns who wore squeaky shoes. The catechism lessons varied from tedious to scary descriptions of heaven and hell. Obviously we children had better things to do, if given the choice. At the end of school term everyone marched in crocodile formation to the Scottish Episcopal church, except for one Jewish girl, two Pakistani girls and myself. We were not invited until Mother intervened. I felt no awful discrimination in this – we got the benefit of going home from school early, which made up for the time stolen from us by the catechism lessons.

Religion was not entirely the answer. Children always hear what is not meant to be overheard. Very slowly the clues began to add up. My parents' marriage was considered to be a mixed marriage, on the grounds of religion and of race. My mother had left her family in Dundee and gone to live in London where she met an unsuitable young man from a foreign country and married him. She was a beautiful blonde, he was tall, dark and handsome therefore she had no choice, but she had crossed a line and married against her parents' wishes. My parents were so young my father subsequently grew out of his wedding suit. Mother was warned there would be consequences – at the very least her sister, whose husband made sacks out of jute in India, would not be able to invite her to the Calcutta Club, if she ever visited. None of Mother's family attended the wedding. The photograph is there to prove it but to my father's credit he not only charmed my mother, given time he charmed her parents as well and when I was born the Scottish family were overjoyed.

When we children opened our primary school atlas we felt proud to be British. The oceans were blue and the Empire was pink. There were networks of road and rail and sea lanes marked with dots and dashes showing how to get from one place to another with sheaves of wheat or bags of coal and cotton. I can't remember if rice was mentioned but it should have been. You could reach India by the Suez Canal or round the Cape Of Good Hope. It looked so easy but this was the sixties and our atlas was seriously out of date. Burma had achieved independence in 1947 and India shortly afterwards but waste not want not... why throw the whole book away for a mere detail? My father obligingly added an 'e' to his surname, changing it from *Lwin*, which no one could pronounce, to *Lewin*, which was easier to say and gave the impression we were either Welsh or Jewish, a much easier concept than being Burmese as only a very select few knew where Burma was, and that select few did not include myself.

We did not learn in our history and geography lessons that cities, like people, may have relatives and our city, the great port of Glasgow where stoic men built steel ships which sailed the world, had a beautiful oriental sister. The architects and businessmen of Glasgow got out their grand, imperial rulers and built the sister city in their own image. She had broad tree lined streets and business offices so similar to her Scottish relative it was uncanny. Her name was Rangoon. In her youth she sparkled with

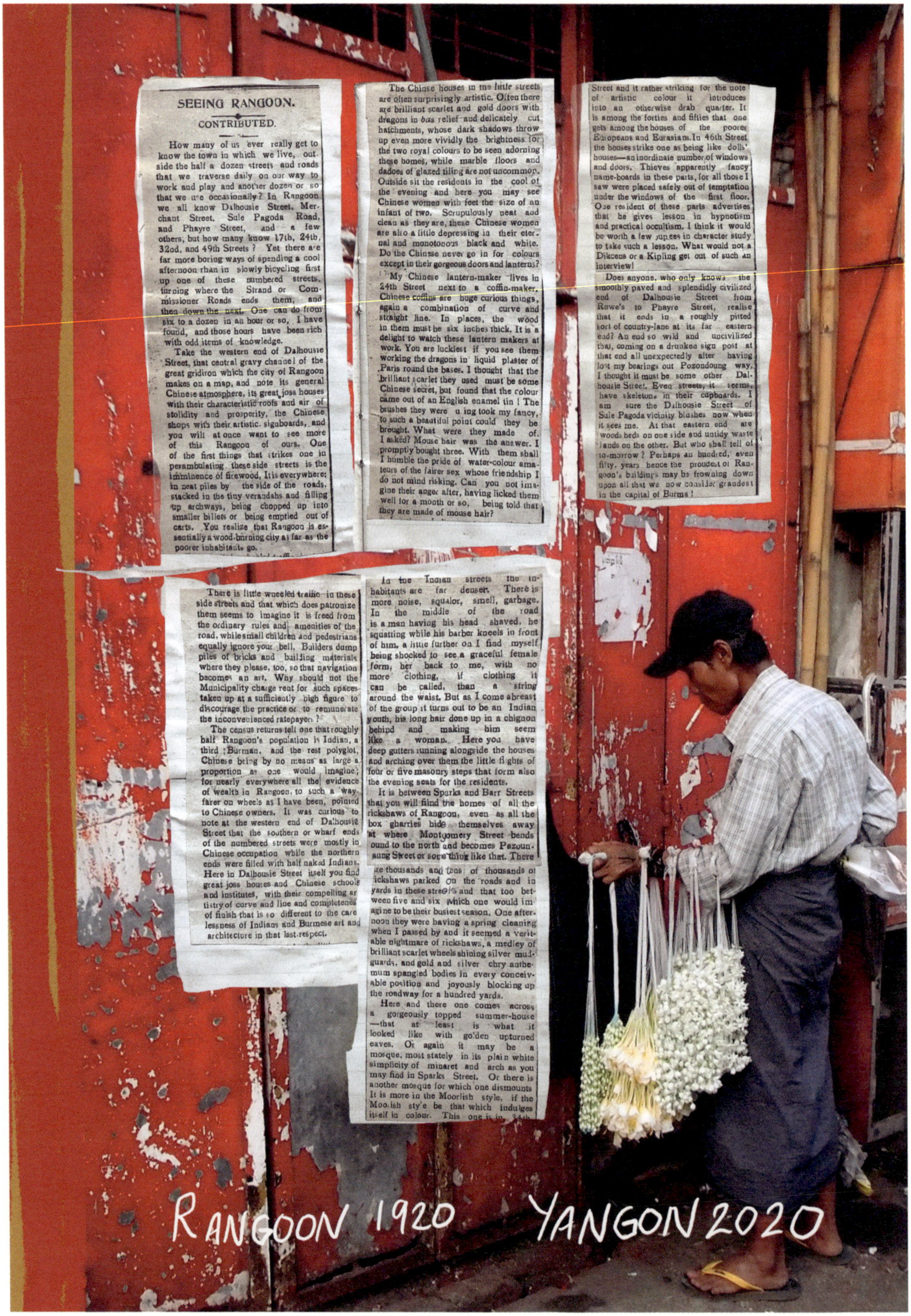
SEEING RANGOON.
CONTRIBUTED.
How many of us ever really get to know the town in which we live, outside the half a dozen streets and roads that we traverse daily on our way to work and play and another dozen or so that we use occasionally? In Rangoon we all know Dalhousie Street, Merchant Street, Sule Pagoda Road, and Phayre Street, and a few others, but how many know 17th, 24th, 32nd, and 49th Streets? Yet there are far more boring ways of spending a cool afternoon than in slowly bicycling first up one of these numbered streets, turning where the Strand or Commissioner Roads ends them, and then down the next. One can do from six to a dozen in an hour or so, I have found, and those hours have been rich with odd items of knowledge.
Take the western end of Dalhousie Street, that central gravy channel of the great gridiron which the city of Rangoon makes on a map, and note its general Chinese atmosphere, its great joss houses with their characteristic roofs and air of stolidity and prosperity, the Chinese shops with their artistic signboards, and you will at once want to see more of this Rangoon of ours. One of the first things that strikes one in perambulating these side streets is the imminence of firewood, It is everywhere: in neat piles by the side of the roads, stacked in the tiny verandahs and filling up archways, being chopped up into smaller billets or being emptied out of carts. You realize that Rangoon is essentially a wood-burning city as far as the poorer inhabitants go.
The Chinse houses in the little streets are often surprisingly artistic. Often there are brilliant scarlet and gold doors with dragons in bas relief and delicately cut hatchments, whose dark shadows throw up even more vividly the brightness for the two royal colours to be seen adorning these homes, while marble floors and dadoes of glazed tiling are not uncommon. Outside sit the residents in the cool of the evening and here you may see Chinese women with feet the size of an infant of two. Scrupulously neat and clean as they are, these Chinese women are also a little depressing in their eternal and monotonous black and white. Do the Chinese never go in for colours except in their gorgeous doors and lanterns?
My Chinese lantern-maker lives in 24th Street next to a coffin-maker. Chinese coffins are huge curious things, again a combination of curve and straight line. In places, the wood in them must be six inches thick. It is a delight to watch these lantern makers at work. You are luckiest if you see them working the dragons in liquid plaster of Paris round the bases. I thought that the brilliant scarlet they used must be some Chinese secret, but found that the colour came out of an English enamel tin! The brushes they were using took my fancy, to such a beautiful point could they be brought. What were they made of, I asked? Mouse hair was the answer. I promptly bought three. With them shall I humble the pride of water-colour amateurs of the fairer sex whose friendship I do not mind risking. Can you not imagine their anger after, having licked them well for a month or so, being told that they are made of mouse hair?
Street and it rather striking for the note of artistic colour it introduces into an otherwise drab quarter. It is among the forties and fifties that one gets among the houses of the poorer Europeans and Eurasians. In 46th Street the houses strike one as being like dolls' houses—an inordinate number of windows and doors. Thieves apparently fancy name-boards in these parts, for all those I saw were placed safely out of temptation under the windows of the first floor. One resident of these parts advertises that he gives lesson in hypnotism and practical occultism. I think it would be worth a few rupees in character study to take such a lesson. What would not a Dikcens or a Kipling get out of such an interview!
Does anyone, who only knows the smoothly paved and splendidly civilized end of Dalhousie Street from Rowe's to Phayre Street, realise that it ends in a roughly pitted sort of country-lane at its far eastern end? An end so wild and uncivilized that, coming on a drunken sign post at that end all unexpectedly after having lost my bearings out Pozondoung way, I thought it must be some other Dalhousie Street. Even streets, it seems, have skeletons in their cupboards. I am sure the Dalhousie Street of Sule Pagoda vicinity blushes now when it sees me. At that eastern end are woods beds on one side and untidy waste lands on the other. But who shall tell of to-morrow? Perhaps an hundred, even fifty, years hence the proudest of Rangoon's buildings may be frowning down upon all that we now consider grandest in the capital of Burma!
There is little wheeled traffic in these side streets and that which does patronize them seems to imagine it is freed from the ordinary rules and amenities of the road, while small children and pedestrians equally ignore your bell. Builders dump piles of bricks and building materials where they please, too, so that navigation becomes an art. Why should not the Municipality charge rent for such spaces taken up at a sufficiently high figure to discourage the practice or to remunerate the inconvenienced ratepayers?
The census returns tell one that roughly half Rangoon's population is Indian, a third Burman, and the rest polyglot, Chinese being by no means as large a proportion as one would imagine; for nearly everywhere all the evidence of wealth in Rangoon, to such a wayfarer on wheels as I have been, pointed to Chinese owners. It was curious to note at the western end of Dalhousie Street that the southern or wharf ends of the numbered streets were mostly in Chinese occupation while the northern ends were filled with half naked Indians. Here in Dalhousie Street itself you find great joss houses and Chinese schools and institutes, with their compelling artistry of curve and line and completeness of finish that is so different to the carelessness of Indians and Burmese art and architecture in that last respect.
In the Indian streets the inhabitants are far denser. There is more noise, squalor, smell, garbage. In the middle of the road is a man having his head shaved, he squatting while his barber kneels in front of him, a little further on I find myself being shocked to see a graceful female form, her back to me, with no more clothing, if clothing it can be called, than a string around the waist. But as I come abreast of the group it turns out to be an Indian youth, his long hair done up in a chignon behind and making him seem like a woman. Here you have deep gutters running alongside the houses and arching over them the little flights of four or five masonry steps that form also the evening seats for the residents.
It is between Sparks and Barr Streets that you will find the homes of all the rickshaws of Rangoon, even as all the box gharries hide themselves away at where Montgomery Street bends round to the north and becomes Pazoundaung Street or something like that. There are thousands and tens of thousands of rickshaws parked on the roads and in yards in these streets and that too between five and six which one would imagine to be their busiest season. One afternoon they were having a spring cleaning when I passed by and it seemed a veritable nightmare of rickshaws, a medley of brilliant scarlet wheels shining silver mudguards, and gold and silver chrysanthemum spangled bodies in every conceivable position and joyously blocking up the roadway for a hundred yards.
Here and there one comes across a gorgeously topped summer-house—that at least is what it looked like with golden upturned eaves. Or again it may be a mosque, most stately in its plain white simplicity of minaret and arch as you may find in Sparks Street. Or there is another mosque for which one dismounts It is more in the Moorlish style, if the Moorish style be that which indulges itself in colour. This one is in 34th
RANGOON 1920 YANGON 2020

golden temples and haunted covetous Western dreams with her oil black eyes. At the end, her colonial masters and mistress abandoned her when she went horribly mad demanding independence and was more trouble than she was worth. They predicted she would come to no good. Over all these years and more years my father's closest cousins, including Aunty Nettie, were growing up, getting married, having babies and ageing in that slowly decomposing city so closely linked to our own. We children never knew.

When asked, Father said it would be foolish to go back, we must look forward. The time was never right. He said we were very lucky to have a father – he had been sent to a boarding school where he had to wash in freezing cold water because he had no father. We were lucky. He said generations of fathers had been shot in two world wars. That was a serious consideration which made us stop to think, especially about the cold water. Mother said that one wet winter night she opened the door to mysterious men asking Father to return. He was the oldest son of the oldest son of an important family and if he went back he would be noticed. If we went back we would be under surveillance. Father had already turned down more than one invitation and he was not inclined to stick his head above the parapet by accepting another. Father claimed nobody would believe him if he had told the truth about his childhood and perhaps he was right. Perhaps nobody was interested. But whatever he said or did not say Father remembered everything. He quietly marked each passing year by sending a Christmas card to Aung San Suu Kyi, the beautiful woman with flowers in her hair, imprisoned in a house beside the lake in Rangoon, not knowing if she ever received them.

Then, the World Wide Web was invented and without warning the door to my father's past, the one which he had long since sealed shut, was wrenched open by my Burmese Aunty Nettie. Her first introducing email, as she called it, came hurtling half way around the world on the wings of modern technology. It was an admirable achievement for a seventy-one-year-old woman living in, to quote her own words, a developing country. When I showed the surreal email to a friend the friend casually tossed it away with two words: 'scam' and 'delete' but I knew better.

The following is an extract from Aunty Nettie's email which she sent from Yangon, Myanmar, and which I received on 22nd November 2009 at 10.13am in the Scottish Borders.

God bless you, my Dearest Linda –
My birthday is May 13th, 1939. My previous name is Snow White, given by my father when he was studying in England 1939. (My mother remained in Burma.) My father requested my mother not to miss that movie on Saturday 13th May. My mother buy the Snow White cinema ticket and she gave birth to me that very morning so she named me after the cinema film name.
My drill master at school address me Snow Black. I felt so embarrassed I changed my name to
Nettie

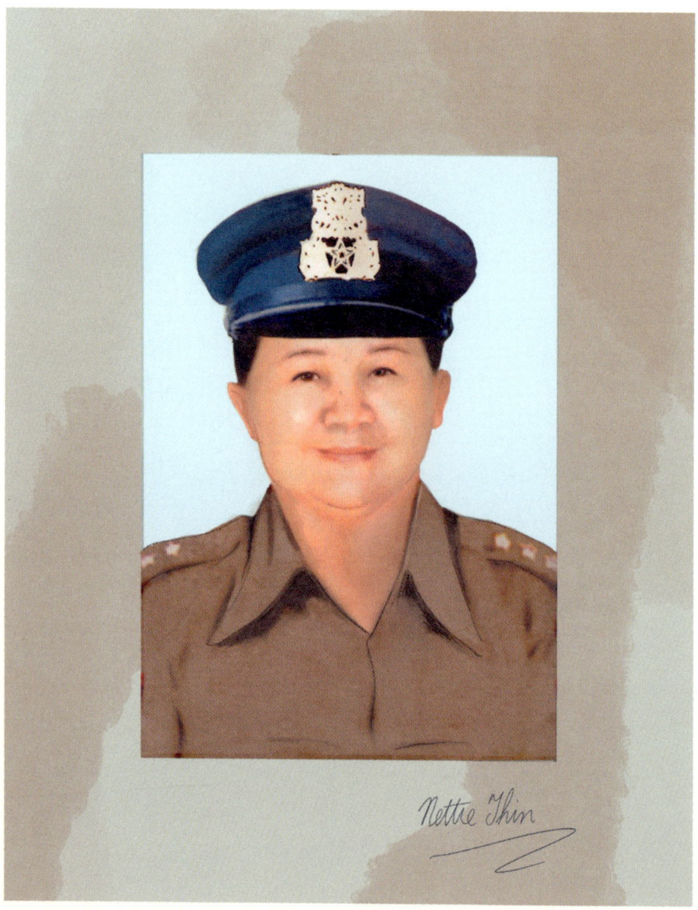

Snow White with three stars on her shoulder

Once she got into her stride Aunty Nettie was a grand story teller. Photographs and lists of unknown relatives appeared in my inbox, including their academic qualifications, which made Aunty Nettie so proud, mixing the past with the present in utter confusion. Nettie's English was almost, but not quite, good and definitely old-fashioned. She seemed to derive some of her vocabulary from an archaic military textbook, where she had learnt words such as squad, latrine and engage, and perhaps other phrases came from the Old Testament. In her letter, she addressed me as 'My Beloved Gazelle of America,' but I suspect if I had shown her a map she would not have been able to locate either Britain or America. Her writing style was dramatic and emotional and her scattergun approach to storytelling was a little unnerving. Because her eyesight was failing she used a scribe, the lovely young A May Sing, which only confused the words even further.

Aunty Nettie's email and news of Suu Kyi's release from house arrest arrived hot on each other's heels. Seventy years since he left his native country Father recognised the moment had come to return. He instructed me to make arrangements and he packed his bags. No more than a man of eighty-two or an evacuee of twelve could carry with one hand. He paid for the tickets and there we were, Father and his daughters, Linda and little sister Hilary peering down from our plane over the dark, electricity-starved city of Yangon. Before we landed he pulled the first surprise out of his inside breast pocket, a modest piece of folded brown paper which I had never seen before. His birth certificate, Desmond Paul Lwin: Place of Birth Bassein. That place was our destination.

Who is Adaw Gyi?

Narrator: *Linda Lewin*

I must introduce you to Adaw Gyi because she is the first person you will meet. Please imagine Adaw Gyi is your aunt, your very Great Aunt. Adaw Gyi is not her name, it is her title. She enjoys an air of authority and she will expect you to address her respectfully. Guided by the expert hands of her great grandmother Daw Bu Ma, Adaw Gyi entered the world feet first and she has maintained a healthy, straightforward, feet first attitude to life ever since. At full stretch she stands no higher than your shoulder but she is tall for a woman of her generation. In her youth she delighted in her beauty but these days she has given all of that up as a waste of time and she wears her plain grey hair in a knot pulled back off her face. Nonetheless, beauty has not deserted her and age has never succeeded in slowing her down. She is animated and loves to tease, but in a gentle way. She belongs to that well intentioned but slightly annoying tribe of Aunts who are inclined to offer old fashioned advice, but be kind and remember you are our family guest and she has your best interests at heart.

Our Adaw Gyi (because she is yours and mine) is a maiden aunt; she never married. Between you and me, I suspect when Adaw Gyi was a young woman she had dozens of suitors. She just couldn't make up her mind which one to choose and rejected them all. Perhaps her first young love was forced to leave the village to find work. He became a seaman and never gave up loving her until he fell into a fight and died on board ship, longing to feel the soft caress of her sweet hands on his brow. Adaw Gyi never knew that he was buried quite alone in foreign soil. She lights a candle each year on the anniversary of the day she kissed him good-bye. Her second lover was a student lawyer and poet, the hero of a people's rebellion who was shot dead defending democracy on the blood stained barricades in Rangoon. She remembers him and his dreams of freedom so fondly and believes they will come true some day.

Sadly, the less romantic but more likely story is, when Adaw Gyi's brothers and sisters married and left home, Adaw Gyi remained to look after her ageing parents because one person in the family must do that job. Adaw Gyi never resented doing her duty. When she was not looking after her parents she looked after her nieces and nephews. She certainly loves children and very often they think they prefer her to their own parents although it is not really true and the children feel sorry for their bad thoughts later on. Adaw Gyi has a pet goose and sits with him on her lap. As she gently strokes his neck she tells the children stories. Adaw Gyi is keeper of the family tree. She has no time for cooking but she is an excellent book keeper and when she opens her exercise book there are all the names of the village children written in pencil alongside their fathers' names, including the children whose families have moved away for work. Every year they get a special present from Adaw Gyi along with some of that very well meant advice to study hard and make their parents proud.

You are now an honorary *Darling Gazelle* and will be addressed as such. You are invited to our village party and storytelling session. If you are a very young gazelle you may sit on a wooden bench in the front row with your new friends. If you are an older female gazelle, you can sit a little further back and help out with a baby or a grandchild on your knee, but if you are a young buck I am afraid we might not have enough chairs. Even the spare red plastic ones are all used up so you will have to stand somewhere on the edge. You will have a good view from there. You will not be allowed to chew betel or sneak out for a cigarette, even if it's a Burmese cheroot. Whichever kind of gazelle you are, I know you are very, very beautiful and you are always warmly welcome in our village. Please do stay for tea. You can have bread with jam or bread with butter, but we can't stretch to both at the same time because there are just too many guests to feed. Please remember, none of Adaw Gyi's stories are written down so you must listen carefully. Books and especially photographs are fragile in tropical climates; they rot and fade, or get eaten by insects in no time at all. Sometimes it is best just to sit and listen.

High Shrimp Mountain Road
Narrator: *Adaw Gyi*

February. The Sweet Year 2021.
Report: *Further loss of life expected.*

My Darling Gazelles

High Shrimp Mountain Road is an average street in a hard working town. It is our perfectly ordinary, everyday place where ordinary people live and die. It is our home and we love it.

On High Shrimp Mountain Road, two rows of corrugated iron, wood and dilapidated, skinny-brick buildings face directly onto the street. From dawn to dusk the front rooms serve as shops. There is a cold water hairdresser, a printer where the floor is perpetually covered in discarded papers, a stationer, a seamstress and a vegetable shop. Here, sacks of rice and there, carpenter-made furniture spill onto the pavements. Everything is covered in dirty plastic because it's better than being covered in dust. If you want to cross the road you need eyes in the back of your head and legs to run like a rabbit. Motorbikes, bicycles and handcarts mingle with herds of lumbering trucks. Every driver uses his horn, just in a friendly conversational way to let the pedestrians know he is there.

We enjoy our daily routines. If you stop to listen a cock is always crowing somewhere. Every morning a middle aged woman in a check shirt walks along the pavement with a tray of vegetables and a soup pan on her head. Breakfast for the early risers. Mothers buy treats for their families in the new bakery. Elegant young women hold parasols over their heads because the sun grows hotter by the minute. After lunch the shop keepers take a short nap. At four o'clock children race home from school in their green and white uniforms, black hair flying and yellow thanaka painted faces. At five o'clock the sound of singing wafts out from the orphanage, Ave

Maria. The shops close at 9pm. The printer is always last. Finally, the dogs, the cats, the children and even the motorbikes are taken inside like cherished family members. The metal security shutters are pulled down and locked up tight. The shop rooms become the family bedrooms. Parents tell their children bed time stories. Someone switches on a TV and sits down to watch a beautiful woman in the capital reading the news, a very encouraging story about bridge building in the delta. Next door a young man sings and plays on his guitar.

In our town we can choose between a pagoda, or a Christian cathedral, or a mosque. We are willing to believe in any Gods for salvation and a better life to come because, although we hate to complain and we often put flowers in our hair to cheer ourselves up, life on this earth can be hard to bear. Years ago we voted for independence and recently we voted for democracy. We believed in our dreams. At the time of voting we were confident that at long last our dreams had come true but dreams are dreams and real life is quite another thing. Life is never ideal and one just has to get used to that. One must never give up. As well as putting flowers in our hair and praying to Gods, we console ourselves with buying a lottery ticket from time to time. We are always hoping for the best and that is the best we can do in these circumstances.

Tonight, the dictator, who lives apart from his people in his purpose built fortress city, is perched like a small, miserable looking frog on his massive golden throne. He has said farewell to his sycophantic advisors and is considering how to maintain his dreams, which are opposed to the people's dreams. He never quite achieved the fairy tale transformation from frog to prince but he has all of the trappings. His personal dreams of great wealth came true years ago but nonetheless he is feeling anxious. My dears, be careful what you wish for. He tries hard to remember a story they taught him at school about a man with a Midas touch but he was never a good scholar and he can't quite remember the ending. He knows he is in a precarious position, balanced on top of a pile of gleaming gems in an expensive but uncomfortable pair of Western shoes which are an important indicator of his status. He is growing older and sometimes when he catches sight of the great emerald stone on his froggy finger, the one his wife gave him because it matches the colour of his uniform, he wishes he could dive deep into its green depths and never reappear. He is afraid that at any moment the whole kit and golden caboodle of his life might come crashing to the ground. He knows it is important to maintain stability. No one could blame him for taking dramatic measures to maintain his balance in such a precarious situation. He knows he must assert his authority, that is what is best, not just for himself but for everyone, and of course, including his heirs and his successors. Hard work, unquestioning discipline and patriotic loyalty will be enforced. That is one thing he learned from the foreigners before they left the country.

He decides to punish the citizens for not agreeing with him and for not loving him quite as much as he thinks he deserves to be loved, after all the hard work and discipline he has maintained. He gave up his youth to fight for his country and he has looked after the people like a father. He has protected the country from overseas invaders and neighbouring dictators who have their own designs on the great golden throne, not forgetting ethnic insurgents who hide in the jungles ready to seize the country's treasures and sell them across the borders. Don't the citizens realise things could have been so much worse but for his magnificent generosity? He has delivered so many benefits to his people. His relatives and advisors understand that very well. They often tell him so.

Somehow the ordinary people fail to understand. They are so lazy. They need to be taught a lesson and he is the man to do it, for their own good. He concludes his deliberations by giving orders to send idiot ex-convicts to the townships, such as High Shrimp Mountain. The ex-cons agree to help him out by setting fire to random buildings and poisoning the water supplies. Even an average brain can tell the difference between what is right and what is wrong, what is murder, what is rape and what is robbery but these guys, the ex-cons, are less than average, perhaps because they never had anything in their lives that came close to average and therefore they are willing to do anything they are asked to do, for a lot less than average. Believe me when I say the price of a downtown cup of coffee is enough to buy a murder on High Shrimp Mountain Road. They are astonishingly cheap labour. The Dictator and his Regime will take advantage of anyone. That is one job the Regime is skilled at, they have the accumulated experience of many years to fall back on.

When the convicts arrive on High Shrimp Mountain Road we joke and call

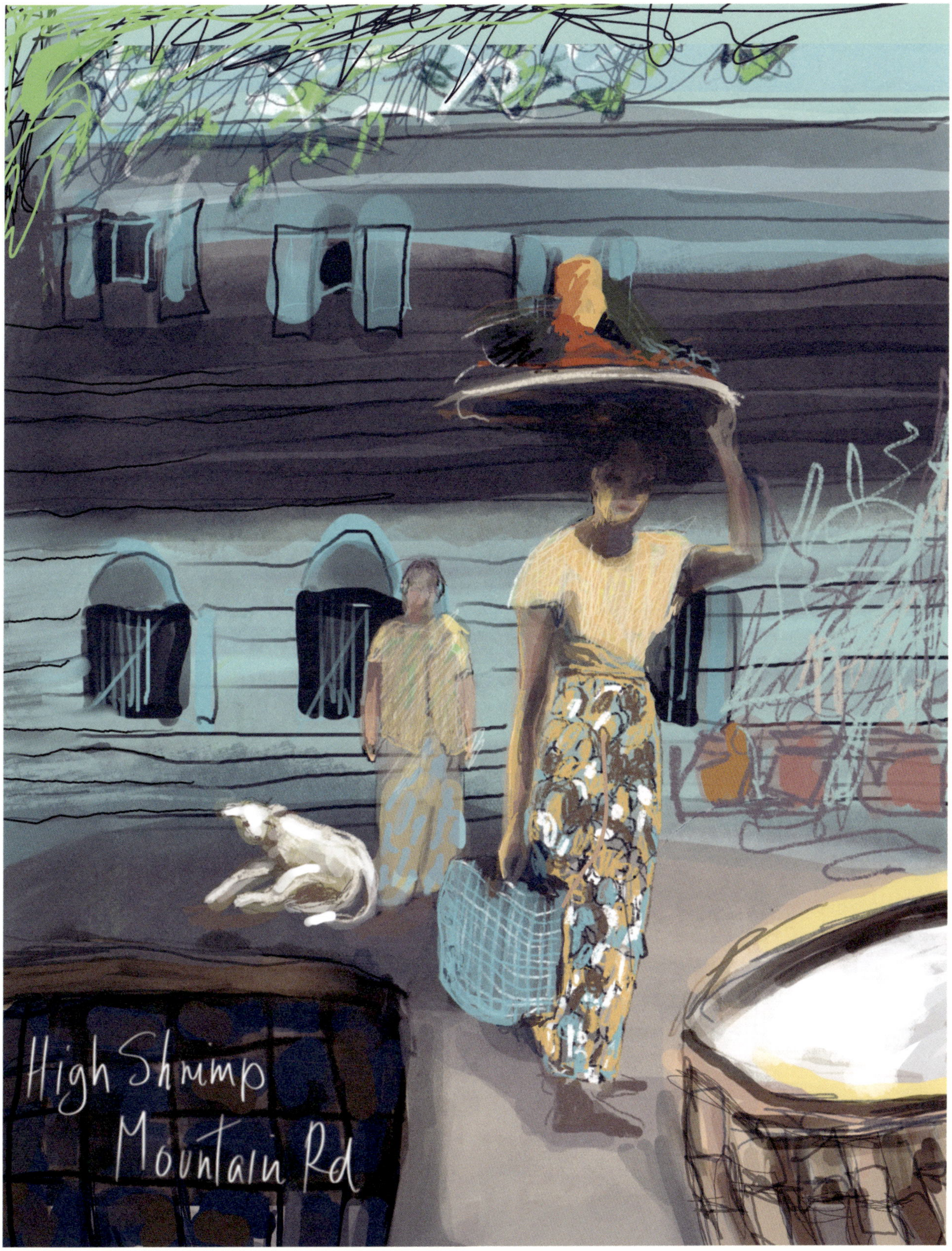
High Shrimp
Mountain Rd

them 5000 Kyat men because that is their rate of pay. We stay awake all night and try our best to catch them. No one gets any sleep. Meanwhile the police turn a blind eye to the murdering arsonist-idiots even though they are in plain sight. Instead the police arrest innocent citizens. It's an easy option. The fathers, mothers and brothers and sisters of idealistic young students-in-hiding are arrested and put in the jails. The empty cells, conveniently vacated by the five thousand Kyat men, must be seen to be filled otherwise the police would look soft and the relatives of anyone who may have, once or twice, admitted to having a political thought, are the profitable, preferred choice. They will make perfect hostages for ransom at a later date.

Very soon soldiers arrive in lorries, ready to join forces with the police, swaggering in their camouflage uniforms and heavy boots. They carry all kinds of weapons, everything from iron bars to automatic rifles and rocket launchers. They have no wish or need to hide their cruelty. In fact they delight in it. Whole families abandon their homes and flee to the jungle, where they hide in holes in the ground, terrified by the sounds of gunshots and shells landing in town, hoping they don't land on High Shrimp Mountain Road. From a distance other people's burning buildings are a beautiful sight but from close up they can only be described as completely terrifying. They crackle and flare in the night sky. The heat is enough to roast a full grown pig in ten minutes at the other end of a football pitch and several squealing pigs are inadvertently roasted but never eaten by their owners. Our citizens' past and their future rise high in clouds of smoke. A storm of broken dreams mixed with ashes return to earth, covering the ground for miles around. Tears burn our eyes and run in furrows down our cheeks.

Dear, sweet Snow White and her father died last week. She was just seven years old, sitting on his lap. A bullet passed through the bamboo wall and stung her behind the ear. It went straight to her brain. That girl was her parents' pure, shining light. All their hopes and dreams evaporated when she died. Less than a silent second is all it took. The neighbours unfolded the girl's fingers from her father's shirt while her mother watched paralysed. Eventually, she took the dead child in her arms, brushed her hair and tied it with a bow. It wasn't difficult to conceal the bullet hole. The family wrapped the girl's body like a doll in a blanket and laid her out on the table where she did her school homework. Her teacher said she had been a good student, full of potential, and her class mates played their guitars all night long to keep her company. The child was too young to leave home, too young to make her way on the long, sorrowful road of the dead but come morning she had company. Her distraught father ran into the road screaming and begged the soldiers to shoot him too. They never hesitated. Poor sweet Snow White's mother, and the dogs were left howling in the dust.

My tears fall with the monsoon rain on High Shrimp Mountain Road. You may well ask what right do I have to disturb the peace by telling these lurid, nightmare tales. What evidence can I offer? On the 1st of February 2021 the military regime in Myanmar staged a coup they claim was not a coup. Our future is the same as our past. In this country dictators do not fall and democracy does not prevail. How much young blood does one old man need to be satiated? Give me wings to fly away. They say all things come to pass and justice will prevail. Pray to your Gods and let them prove merciful because this is our unfortunate life

Your ever loving
Adaw Gyi

Return to the Golden Land
Narrator: *Linda Lewin*

Hilary Lewin's first message home – email to Adrian Hope:
Your wife has passed out face down on her bed and can't even sum up strength to write to you. This morning our lives were taken over by Nettie. We were picked up and driven all over town in an open back truck, went to Shwedagon Pagoda which was unbelievable, then to her son who has four of his own children plus fourteen adopted ones, five pigs, three rooms, no running water or electricity. Then Aunt Marcheta for lunch with the old folk, then an evening service where we sat on the stage with our names in big letters behind us. Children sang and danced and gave us bouquets and traditional clothes which we have to wear to the village tomorrow. Then to some back street money changer with a giant pink school calculator. So surreal. We are a complete spectacle with ladies wanting to have their photos taken with us. xx

Standing in line with my father and sister in the newly carpeted, empty halls of Yangon International Airport, we reduced our conversation to a whisper. It was late night, in an empty building designed to impress vast numbers of foreigners who jostled in during the few years of supposed democracy. We cautiously approached immigration with our jet lagged, pale faces and Tourist Visas at the ready but I didn't feel like a tourist. I wasn't going on a beach holiday. I composed myself, remembering all the warnings I had grown up with, irrationally expecting to be pulled out of the queue and interrogated but there was nothing, not even a smile from the official, who directed me to stand in front of the security camera. One by one, my father, little sister Hilary, and I were permitted to pass without hindrance. We made for the glass exit doors in the most unnecessarily casual way, trying not to be noticed in case somebody changed their mind, still expecting a hand on the shoulder. The glass doors slid open and we entered the Yangon night like characters in Alice Through The Looking Glass. Our first Myanmar breath was hot and damp. The smell of tropical vegetation mixed with city fumes. I could hardly believe it when my feet landed on solid, real life Myanmar soil.

From the taxi windows the street scene appeared to be a vintage silent film played out in flickering lights against a black backdrop. I remember a young boy silhouetted in a window. He was perched on a chair, having his hair cut by a large man who loomed over him with long arms and sharp scissors. Late night shoppers poked at vegetables and sat eating at roadside stalls. I wanted to stop at a workshop where men were heating metal in glowing charcoal braziers and beating it with hammers, orange sparks flying, but I was too late, they were there and gone. We arrived at the hotel where bunches of glittering roses were delivered to our room. Welcome to Myanmar.

Getting started in Myanmar can feel a bit like doing a jigsaw by looking in a mirror. Right becomes left and left becomes right. You think you have all the pieces and you know they fit but it just doesn't work out. You struggle and struggle until unaccountably, for no reason, everything clicks neatly into place and you wonder why you ever bothered to worry.

The following morning, just as we were considering how to proceed, Aunty Nettie and The Amazing Girl, A May Sing, appeared at hotel reception. When we got to know her better we discovered Aunty Nettie had an astonishingly reliable talent for turning up unannounced and we never got to the bottom of how she did it. It was our first face to face meeting and it was extraordinary but at the same time it was perfectly ordinary because Auntie Nettie was family and her family was our family. She explained although we were different colours we were the same blood. Father seemed to know what he was doing. There were beaming round faced smiles from the Myanmar side and handshakes from our side. No one was going to let emotion get the better of them. No sadness spoiled the occasion. There was nothing but pleasure and excitement in the moment.

Nettie was slightly younger than Dad, compact and full of energy, prepared to stand in front of tanks or bulldozers to get her way, but today's business was celebration. Nettie's English flowed, overwhelming all obstacles, mostly but not entirely making sense. After all these long years there was no time to be wasted. Firstly, what was my favourite colour and what was Hilary's? Then, my father reminded her so much of her own father as a young man. It was the great love between the two brothers, her father San Po Thin and my grandfather San Po Lwin which had brought about our reunion. She had looked after her father with her own hands right up to his dying breath and everything she did for us was out of love because he loved his brother and she loved us. San Po Thin dreamed the brothers' families would be reunited. That was the dream Nettie inherited from her father and that was the dream she made come true.

Before we left the hotel Nettie warned me, she didn't like the place – she had called the previous evening to deliver the glittering flowers in person but they didn't believe her story about having Western relatives and wouldn't let her in. In her opinion, the place was full of spies and we should be very careful, they were bound to be listening in on our conversations. I should explain, Nettie and all of our Myanmar family were Karen, not Bamar and not Buddhist. We were Christian Karens, a nation without a country, a persecuted ethnic minority in Myanmar. The Karen ethnic armies' greatest claim to fame is that they have been fighting the longest running guerrilla war on the planet, against the Bamar. My father and Nettie's fear of spies was born from personal experience and common sense, a fear not to be given up lightly. But how could she tell about the spies? I looked around at the very well presented, courteous staff. A young woman in a lurid green outfit stood on guard at the entrance. Her duty was wafting fans over newly arriving guests. Was she a spy? Other staff ran around with cooling drinks on trays. They all looked perfectly peaceful and innocent. We knew Aunty Nettie was a retired police officer. She said she had detective's eyes which could see straight through anyone, directly into their heart, and discern the truth within. Thank goodness she was on our side.

Nettie could walk along the street and pick out the different ethnic people by their appearance – Chin, Kachin, Karen, Mon, Arakanese, Shan. The set of a cheekbone or tone of voice or particular combinations of colours and patterns, a way of wrapping a skirt or a scarf around the head. All these told different stories to Nettie, never mind they looked the same to us. The guide books will truthfully say there are more than 130 languages in Myanmar, each one spoken by a different ethnic group. Sometimes, but less often, the guide books will mention the dozens of ethnic armed forces. All of these peoples walk, talk and think quite differently from each other and most importantly they are not Bamar. However, it seems to me the girl in the unfortunate green outfit at the hotel entrance was not a spy. She was a parody of an ethnic peasant, got up for tourist entertainment, and the boy who startled my father by sneaking into his room to use the hotel telephone when he thought the coast was clear was probably not a spy either, more likely a boy who wanted to make a free call to his girlfriend or his mum. On the other hand, in my opinion, the man taking photographs of us on our hotel balcony without introducing himself, and the monk who knew more about where we were going than I did were both spies. Surely a spy that can be spotted by a fresh from the West amateur is really not very good at his job, unless it's a double bluff? It was all new and so strange and exciting.

Aunty Nettie was well organised. She had a jam packed timetable at the ready – first stop, a visit to the British War Graves Cemetery. Fortunately, my ten years younger little sister Hilary has her own tried and tested, charming methods of getting her own way. She removed the timetable from Nettie's grasp and swiftly replaced War Graves with Shwedagon Pagoda. War graves were not our cup of tea. As far as we sisters were concerned the war, any kind of war, was over. Time to move on please. To her credit, Nettie rescheduled the whole day without a murmur and directed us into the back of a pick up truck, Father and Aunty Nettie shoulder to shoulder in the cab. The driver, Nettie's son, launched his brand new vehicle into downtown Yangon. Since my father had left, the very grand streets had acquired politically correct names but they were the very same streets as laid out by the imperial engineers, now populated by happy Myanmar drivers in their freshly imported cars, symbols of the joyful, new, democratic dawn. It was a wonder anybody remembered how to drive after all the years of socialist austerity. Out of curiosity Dad tested the fledgling banking system with his plastic card. Hallelujah, it worked. Myanmar was connected. Children waved and smiled at the unusual sight of our beautiful white faces rattling around in the back of a truck and yes, we were watched, for entertainment.

If you ever have the opportunity to visit The Golden Land, you will be taken to visit a pagoda, probably hundreds of pagodas. You will find them keeping watch, for better or worse, on the top of each and every hill, large or small. The Shwedagon in Yangon is the grandest and most golden, most famous pagoda in the whole of Myanmar. Nettie agreed to change her plans and take us there but she refused to sully her Christian feet by entering the idolatrous shrine. Perhaps she was frightened of the army of Buddhas or the evil Nats, spirits of the old animist religion who she believed lived there, although she would never admit to such a thing. Perhaps she was worried she might be taken prisoner by the perfidious Bamar. She deputised her

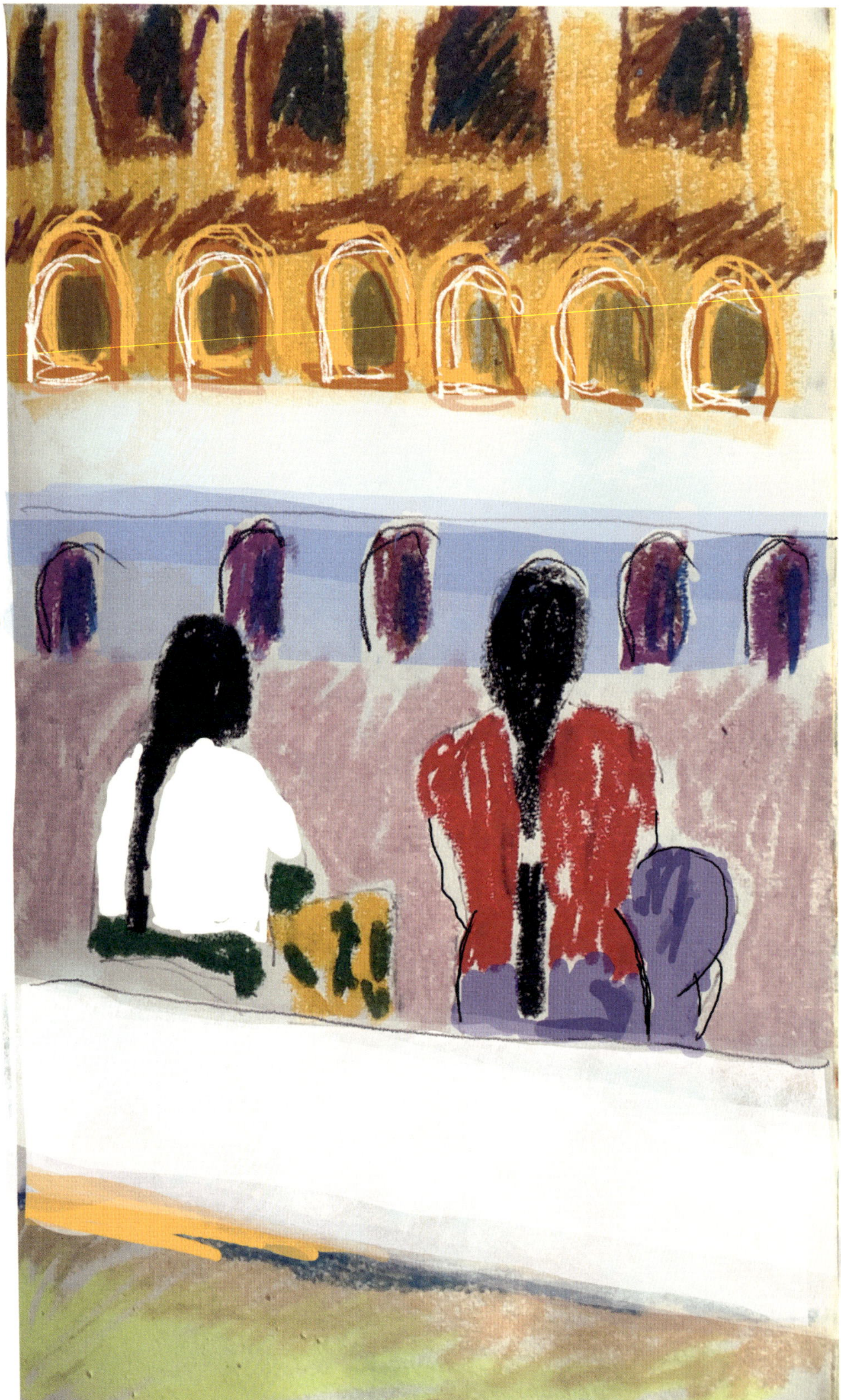

Noon. Bagan. Too hot to move

assistant, A May Sing otherwise known as The Amazing Girl, to escort us. We couldn't be safely trusted out on our own.

I beg you, please, when you visit your pagoda be sure to go barefoot by the proper pilgrim's path. You will recognise the entrance by two giant Chinthe. Not quite lion, not quite dog, they represent a wicked lion king who was murdered by his human son. When the young Prince realised his terrible mistake he set up the Chinthe as temple guardians in honour of his father. You can trust them to guard your shoes and relieve you of your earthly burdens, setting you free to fly up the long dark corridor like a moth towards the glorious golden sunlight. Sometimes, in the late evening, the steps can be empty and mysterious but during the day they are glittering waterfalls overflowing with treasures. Festivals of beads and flowers, embroidered bags, religious relics, children's toys and all kinds of souvenirs. Please shun the glass box lifts installed by dubious business and military benefactors. You will appreciate the heavenly destination so much more if you make the physical effort to get there.

It was midday when we arrived at the Shwedagon. It is not a cathedral, a beautifully engineered casket which you walk inside, it is a glorious golden sandcastle which you walk around, a dazzling spinning top which will make you dizzy, surrounded by tide lines of white elephants, green dragons, drinking fountains and thousands of standing, walking, lying and sitting Buddhas arranged in concentric circles. A May Sing was Christian but she had learned about the great pagoda and the old kings of Burma in her school history lessons. She advised us to process around the pavilions in a lucky clockwise direction which we did, hopping swiftly from one burning hot tile to another on our unaccustomed bare feet.

Lift your gaze higher and higher into the blue sky. When your eyes fail attach them to a convenient telescope and there, at the very top of the stupa, far beyond the reach of ordinary human hands you will find the Htee, a golden umbrella covered in rubies, sapphires, diamonds and tinkling bells. The sound of the clappers sprinkles down to earth in light hearted showers. We were stunned by the vast quantities of gold applied by generations of worshippers, repeatedly pressing layer over layer, leaf upon leaf of gold on the swelling belly of the pagoda. Father beat the great bronze temple bell with a wooden paddle, to let the spirits know he had arrived.

The writer, Kipling, was one visitor who never got as far as entering the Shwedagon Pagoda proper, but his experience on the pagoda steps was so intense he felt just as happy as though he had. The first character he spied was a dacoit descending towards him with a face so frightful he looked as though he could '*crucify on occasion*' but then, '*a brown baby came by in its mother's arms and laughed, wherefore I much desired to shake hands with it, and grinned to that effect. The mother held out the tiny soft pud and laughed, and the baby laughed, and we all laughed together, because that seemed to be the custom of the country, and returned down the now dark corridor where the lamps of the stall-keepers were twinkling and scores of people were helping us to laugh.*'

Kipling was right about the laughter. Once upon a time, struggling to climb the pagoda steps in the ancient city of Mrauk U, beaten down by the fierce afternoon heat and eyes to the ground, I came to a halt in front of two pairs of bare feet tipped with delicate toes, at eye level, on the steps above me. They belonged to a monk and his sister, descending, arm in arm from pagoda heaven. They stopped me in my very sweaty tracks just for the pleasure of telling me I was the most beautiful person they had ever seen. In fact, the most beautiful person in the world, they were convinced. I had to disagree because they were undoubtably the most beautiful people I had ever seen in the entire world. He, with his shaved head and burgundy robes clutched together under his elbow, one bare shoulder, she young and oh so pretty. Brother and sister wearing dazzling smiles. The truth was, in that moment we were the three most beautiful people, not only in the entire world but also in heaven. We laughed and my companion laughed, we all laughed and laughed. Please don't miss out on the magic of the pagoda steps.

But truly, the most lovely thing about golden pagodas is not the countless shrines guarded by white elephants or the white skinned, black haired Buddha statues, not even the ones with flashing neon haloes. The most lovely thing is watching families relaxing, sharing food with their children, laughing and playing, even sleeping in the courtyards. Their workaday homes may be bamboo and matting huts or worn out high rise apartments with damp walls and threadbare electrics, but their pagoda homes from home are their refuge, lit by a million flickering candles and furnished with all the cooling fountains, glitter and grandeur any heart could desire.

I heard later, when A May Sing got home from her visit to the pagoda her mother sent her straight to the family bathroom, instructed to scrub from head to foot with water from the two huge water pots in the basement. Just like Nettie, Amazing Girl's Christian mother lived in fear of the evil Buddhist spells we had inadvertently exposed her daughter to.

The Red Carpet Welcome Party

Narrator: *Adaw Gyi*

My Darling Gazelles,

When Boh Lay Desmond returned I instantly recognised him. He was the spitting image of his father San Po Lwin, the oldest son of the oldest son. He was more than eighty years old but time and Western life had been kind to our Boh Lay, he remained strong and straight. I wondered what he remembered of his life here, if he knew who we were and what happened to us after his mother took him on the foreigner ship to Calcutta. He had been away so long, perhaps he had forgotten our Karen people. When Nettie brought him to her father's church in Yangon, only one person in the room was old enough to remember Boh Lay as he was in childhood and that person was Nettie's older sister Rose Red, but she said it was all such a long time ago, she could hardly say. That may have been the truth but Rose Red was always the diplomat.

We all turned out to welcome Boh Lay and his daughters. There must have been a hundred people from the oldest to the youngest babies, including twin boys wearing their little new born caps. They were Nettie's grandsons but Nettie was so charmed by Boh Lay Desmond she paid them no attention. We dressed in our best, the women who had pearls put them around their necks. If they had rubies and sapphires they wore them. The men got out their red and blue Karen shirts and white jackets with coloured trim. As usual, Nettie had to be different, she refused to dress up, saying she had no need for fine clothes or jewels, but I thought she should have made allowances for Boh Lay's daughters – they would have liked a moment to brush their hair before being rushed on stage in front of such a large, eager audience. I could see the girls were nervous, quite out of their depth really. They understood nothing.

Nettie stood up and made a speech in English. She said God was working his miracles. Praise the Lord. He had blessed her with children and grandchildren. Praise the Lord. Her oldest son was a pastor. Praise the Lord. For her part, she promised God everything in return for his blessings. She was ready to give away all her worldly goods – the houses, the pots and pans, the gold and jewellery, the presents she got from all the people she helped, the ones who owed her favours. She had no need of these things because she had faith in God and God would provide. Aung San Suu Kyi was released from her prison. Nettie had visited her in her home beside the lake and given her two books, a copy of the Bible and a copy of her father San Po Thin's autobiography. Daw Suu Kyi sent kind words, she remembered our family and was pleased to receive both books. At that time we were optimistic and Nettie was proud, even though she denied it and said pride was a sin. The time had come to rejoice with singing and dancing and feasting.

A May Sing made herself busy in the kitchen, she was never the cook but always the manager. Delicious fried rice with chilli and an egg on top for all.

It was my turn on stage. The children know I have the best stories. 'How The Tiger Got His Stripes' and 'Why There Are No More Hares In Myanmar.' I told them, hares are clever animals but success made them silly and arrogant. Once upon a time the hares lived together in their beautiful city but they squabbled and fell out with each other. The tiger persuaded them they could live independently and so they gave up herd protection in favour of individual rights. One by one, they were eaten by the tiger. Brothers and sisters, together we stand, divided we fall.

My Dears, this is our Karen story. We do not know the songs the birds sang in the ancient forests. We do not remember the length of the serpents who sunbathed on the rocks or the colours of the butterflies' wings drying in the sun. We have forgotten the speckled, feline monsters waiting to pounce with sharp teeth and claws and we have forgotten the shy gazelles peering out from behind the trees, but we will never forget the monstrous pig who terrorised our people. A cruel, bristling, black as the night, forever hungry creature, with lethal tusks. He raided the villages, spitting with rage. Rocks shattered beneath his feet and children screamed when they heard his footsteps. He turned our short earthly lives into long years of misery and all our dreams became nightmares.

At last, a wise old man stepped forward. A clever hunter who had fulfilled all his desires except for one last wish, which was to secure the future happiness of his sons and daughters. For this, he was willing to sacrifice himself in a great and final act of courage. He tied his grey hair high on his head and invited the young women to paint yellow sap from the trees on his body. They crowned his head with leaves and berries. He strung his bow tight and ground his arrows sharp because he knew that pig had a thick skin.

He entered the magic forest on his bare feet. Immediately all voices fell silent but all invisible creatures' eyes were on him. He had given up the brute strength of youth because that was the necessary bargain he made to gain the cunning of old age. He continued searching for days and nights, following the faintest of trails, never sleeping, sometimes creeping on all fours, or slithering on his belly like a snake, until at last, deep in the green trees, he found the monstrous pig, resting in a clearing. He slowly pulled himself upright, breathed in and out, releasing his sharpest arrow. His aim was perfect, straight to the heart. He waited. The monster fought for life, roaring and screaming in rage. The hunter watched and waited. When he heard the birds begin to sing he knew he was safe. He crept forward, the pig was warm and ripe with fresh blood, heavy with meat, enough to feed the villages for miles around. The old man knew he could not carry it without help.

He returned to his village and ordered the strongest men to retrieve the carcass, but they could not find their way and returned home empty-handed. They were ashamed of themselves and their failure and claimed the old man had finally lost his senses, laughing with embarrassment.

Once more, the old man entered the forest and led his lost and foolish children to the place where he had been forced to abandon the pig, but the pig was gone, vanished into thin air. One piece of evidence remained lying on the moss beside a flowing stream. A huge ivory tusk. It was a magic gift. The old man took out his knife and carved the tusk into a beautiful comb with delicate teeth. The central tooth was for his wife and he added one tooth each for his children, his grandchildren and his great grandchildren. When it was finished he took the comb and stroked it through his long grey hair, slowly releasing the tangles. All the hard years of toil and injury instantly fell away. He turned towards his children and revealed his face shining gold like the sun. They saw his hair was fresh and black and his neck gleamed pure and white like the moon. His body returned to supple as a young tree. His breath smelled of sweet breezes and flowers bloomed in his every step. His magic comb bestowed the secret of eternal youth on whoever wore it.

The comb was our greatest treasure but it was not enough to protect us from our warlike neighbours. Those were our hungry days. We were forced to leave the forest, to begin our long journey through the wilderness, a fearful, trackless region. The wind blew hard, hot and cold, wet and dry, always in our faces. Waves of sand rolled before us. We walked, men, women and children, with nothing to guide us but bare rocks and the bones of those who had gone before. We owned nothing excepting what we carried on our backs. We sang songs all night long to keep our spirits strong, always searching for a place to rest. We lost our way and we lost the precious book which was given to us by the Lord of The Land and Water. It was taken from us by a dog in the night. Eventually, we built a city to call our own but it was stolen in battle and razed to the ground.

Finally we left the mountains with our empty baskets on our backs. When we reached this place where the wide river opens its cool fingers to the sea we found everything we had imagined our home would be. The promised land. We recognised our birthright. Here, where the river floods and rice overflows we eat and drink as we please. Here, if one man works a family of seven may take their rest. Just one man working can provide grain, fish, fowls and bowls of honey sweet, ripe fruits along with fine clothes for his wife and all his precious children.

We no longer risk our lives hunting in the forest. The river runs in our veins, the blue blood of The Golden Land, the food in our bellies, the road in and out of our happy dreams. This is our home, the place where our golden book was returned to us by our white brothers from across the ocean. That was enough for our Karen people, in the beginning.

Your ever loving
Adaw Gyi

Our Family Village
Narrator: *Linda Lewin*

It was our first proper day. Dad was perfectly composed, Hilary and I were beyond excitement, overwhelmed by lack of sleep and the strangeness of everything. We saw so much and understood so little but we need not have feared because we had family at our backs. Our first expedition party was numerous – Dad, Aunty Nettie, her sister Rose Red and Rose's daughter, Dew Rose, not forgetting The Amazing Girl and goodness only knows how many others.

Myanmar names are confusing to foreigners. Many people possess two or quite possibly three, entirely different names, possibly in different languages, and they will introduce themselves by the name which seems most appropriate at the time. Christians – and of course all our new relatives were Christians – will proudly introduce themselves to foreigners by their Christian name. At first this seems convenient and sensible, because foreigners can't easily pronounce Burmese names but do not be lulled into a false sense of security. When said foreigner goes to search for their new friend they will not find him or her because locally, said friend is known by their Myanmar name. Not so convenient after all. Typically, Myanmar names have three separate parts, but none of these parts are related to the parent's name. In old village Burma everybody knows which child belongs to which parent so naming priorities are not related to property inheritance. My Grandfather and his two brothers were not named after their parents. San Po Lwin, San Po Thin and San Po Thaw were named after Sir San C. Po, a much admired Karen leader in their home town, Bassein.

It is important for younger people to address their elders respectfully by using the appropriate title. Mr or Mrs or Aunty or Uncle or professional qualification. When it comes to filling out Western style administrative forms which require a surname Myanmar people are at a loss and in an effort to be helpful, may resort to making something up just to fill in the gap. This is likely to result in confusion and unwarranted accusations of dishonesty.

Young people in Myanmar are extremely tolerant and forgiving as far as names are concerned but Aunty Nettie seemed to prefer the old colonial versions. Burmese independence was achieved on the 4th January 1948 at exactly 4.20am because that was deemed to be the most auspicious time selected by the best astrologers. Shortly afterwards Burma became Myanmar and Bassein became Pathein. Aunty Nettie and my father were travelling to Bassein as it was in their youth, the younger members of our party were on the road to Pathein. Happy days.

Aunty Nettie arrived at our hotel at an unspeakably early, drab hour in the morning. So early we might as well not have bothered going to bed or paying for the luxury breakfast we never ate. Her mission was to deliver us safely to father's home town and the family village, way down in the Irrawaddy delta, a minimum of five hours drive and a boat ride from Yangon. She had even made a practise run and we certainly couldn't have got there without her. I was surprised to see her looking slightly awkward in a pair of new jeans and a cosy fleece depicting a snow scene, which didn't seem the most appropriate outfit in a tropical climate. When I complimented the jeans she said trousers had always suited her better than skirts. Jeans may have been an unusual choice for an older woman in Myanmar but compared with other women of her age, they gave us the clear message that Nettie was up to date and ready for business. She checked our packing – Dad got full marks for his hand luggage, Hilary and I completely failed the Nettie test. She instructed A May Sing to supervise repacking. She persuaded us to leave almost everything behind, retaining very little beyond the clothes we stood up in and our traditional Karen longyi to wear in the village. We promised not to wear the traditional clothes on the streets of Yangon, for our own safety. We had no plans to be mistaken for insurgents in the longest running civil war on the planet.

Myanmar journeys typically begin in vast and crowded city bus stations. Yangon probably has half a dozen such. Somehow, mistakenly of course, following in Dad's footsteps and surrounded by our new family, Hilary and I were convinced we blended in perfectly with the crowds even without the knitted bobble hats which all locals wear to keep off what they consider chilly and unhealthy early morning mists. Having assimilated so quickly and so successfully, we were surprised to meet two American Foreigners at the Pathein bus stand and took a dim view of their poor attitude. They stood out like petulant sore thumbs, clearly assuming everybody was out to cheat them. Dad will talk to anyone in a reassuring way and Hilary tried to explain that handing your passport to a suspicious-looking man around the corner, not knowing if you would ever see the passport again, regardless of his very sweet smile, was just the normal Burmese bureaucratic procedure required to buy a bus ticket, but they found that hard to accept. In their position I must admit I might have felt the same.

The Yangon-Pathein highway was a rough road, in recovery from Cyclone Nargis, struggling to keep itself above water. We were lucky enough to be travelling in a deluxe motorway bus, imported from Korea after the Koreans had broken it in, but not quite broken it down. The bus steward clearly loved his job. He was wonderfully proud of the worn-out swags and the sagging, upholstered interior. The extraordinarily cheap tickets included bottled water and handy sick bags: it seems that Myanmar bus passengers, particularly the younger ones, are all too often affected by travel sickness. The air conditioning was turned down to freezing, an unusual pleasure to the locals but one the foreigners could have done without. We completed the five hour journey with a couple of rest stops where on board refreshments were provided by old ladies and young children. The smallest and the youngest appeared to be the fastest and the bravest. They pushed forward onto the bus with baskets in hand. The slower entrepreneurs held their baskets up to the open windows, singing out their wares. They offered us tiny roasted birds, no more than a blackened mouthful – no thank you. Tiny blue speckled eggs, samosas and miniature oranges – yes please. So many beautiful little details.

Our bus conductor turned out to be a natural performer who delighted in the extra duties of tour guide. His running commentary was translated by Aunty Nettie. The most interesting story featured a young elephant, escapee from a delta logging camp, and it was very much appreciated by the captive audience. I got the impression this really was a novel, exciting journey and a great adventure for all of the passengers, including ourselves. Despite the fun and games, the conductor was strict about one thing – when we came to a police checkpoint we must keep the flapping

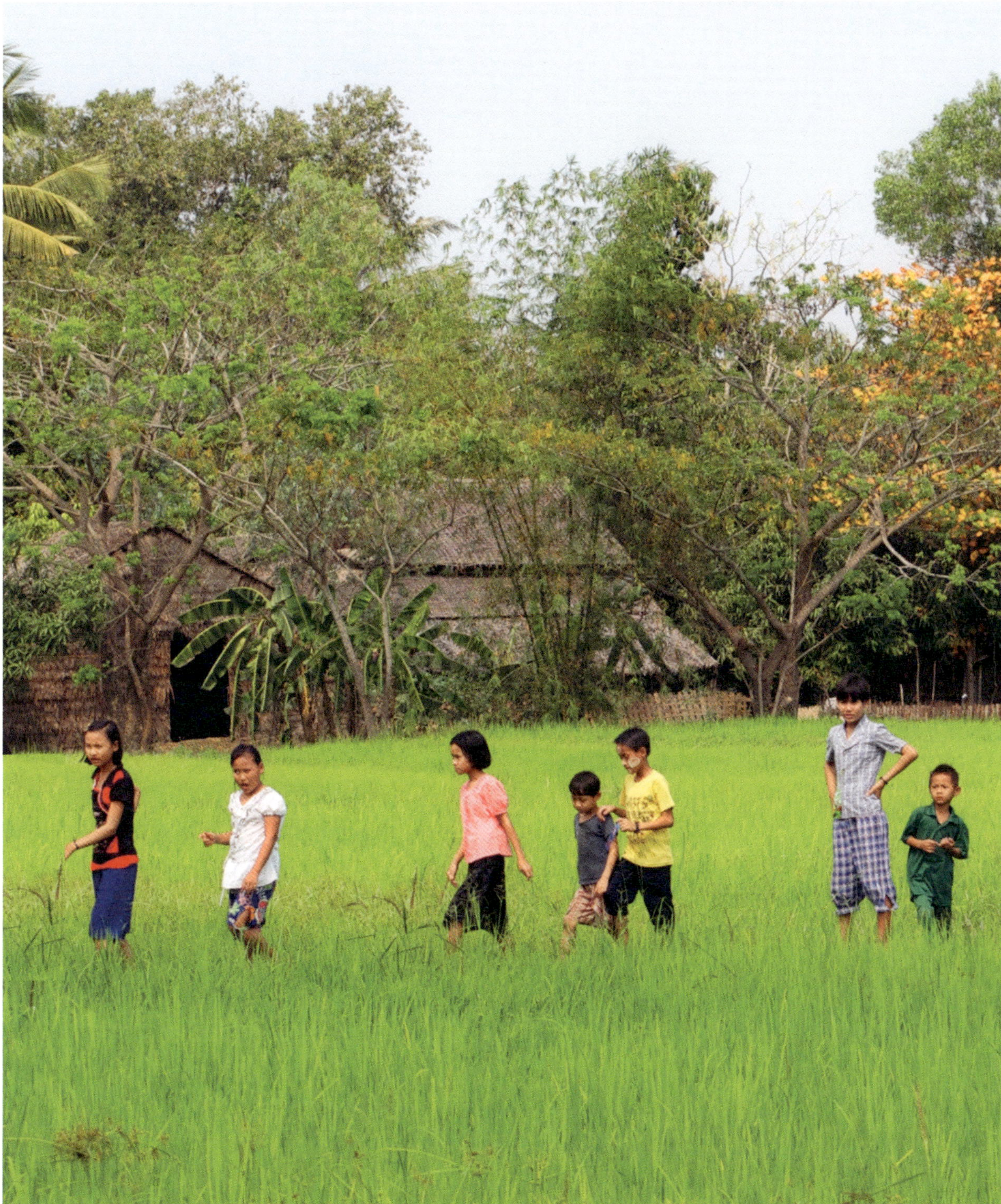

Our family village in the delta

curtains closed to hide the white foreigner passengers from prying eyes. Aunty Nettie explained this was simply to avoid paying the foreigner road tax and all the passengers seemed to agree this was common sense. Who in their right mind would willingly pay taxes? This was despite the fact we had paid a foreigner surcharge, enough to cover the taxes. Whatever happened to that?

The bus journey came to a sudden and ignominious end when the superior Korean bus abandoned us in a half built car park on the outskirts of Pathein. A May Sing gave the bus driver a piece of her mind but the regular passengers had been expecting this. They ejected themselves from their plush bus seats at high speed, landing in a couple of ready and waiting pick-up trucks. The whole thing was very much in the manner of a game of musical chairs – any one left out completed the journey by motorbike, which might have been quite exciting but Aunty Nettie made sure her precious foreigner guests were well and safely placed inside the pick-up truck, where we struggled to find anything solid to hang onto, although we were so tightly wedged by our companions it didn't really matter.

Yet another excited crowd waited to greet us in Pathein. Their willing hands steadied us as we jumped down from the truck in time to see our luggage disappearing into the middle distance on the shoulders of complete strangers, at least to us. Fortunately, a sensible older woman stepped forward to take charge. She turned out to be our 'virgin' cousin, recently retired from her post as financial officer at the local university. No one was even slightly embarrassed by this style of introduction and she graciously treated us to lunch in the best restaurant in town, where the Formica tables were straight out of the sixties and the rice was delicious.

Myanmar people do like to stop for a proper lunch and fully understand the benefit of following it up with an afternoon nap but on this occasion we were not allowed that luxury. When father was a boy he had made the journey to visit his Grandmother in the village by bullock cart but the road had long since washed away so we would travel the final leg of our journey to the village by boat. By now the midday sun was beating down hot enough to fry eggs on the street. Before we left Hilary and I were presented with Pathein umbrellas which turned out to be the prettiest painted satin sun shades and we were glad of them as we made the short walk to the wharf.

I am not a boat person so I can only say our boat was painted green wood with an awning but no deck. It was just big enough for our party plus crew and there appeared to be a six foot drop from the wharf into the bottom of the boat. Was this a sensible leap to take? Of course not, but my eighty year old father never hesitated, extending his hand to the boatmen with complete confidence. I watched him picking his way along the length of the boat, stepping from one precarious plank to another, with Aunty Nettie close behind. They made themselves comfortable on the plastic chairs under the awning, successful beaming smiles on both their faces. The rest of us followed, wedging ourselves between bags full of stout cauliflowers, a keyboard, sacks of rice and bales of blankets. Just as soon as we accomplished all of these acrobatics a boy arrived with a message from the harbour office – the officials needed to see our foreigner passports. We were not behaving in the way that foreigners were expected to behave and I don't think they liked it, or perhaps they were just curious. Once again, A May Sing was annoyed. She took hold of the passports and stamped along to the office, where she made her feelings known. The result was a clear message: we must be back before midnight, no overnight stays permitted. Never think that you, a foreigner, are not noticed in Myanmar.

We happily motored down the broad waters of the Pathein river, cooling wind in our hair, admiring fleets of long tailed canoes, ferries and sand dredgers, with absolutely no idea where we were going or how long it would take to get there. Conversation was limited by the noise of our engine.
All we had was our faith in Aunty Nettie. At last the engine was switched off and I heard Nettie say we were looking for the place where the baby monkey drowned and not even its mother could save it. This was not encouraging.

We drifted downstream, closer to the bank, until the boatmen agreed on an inlet which looked exactly like all the other inlets. They gently nosed the boat into a channel between the mangrove trees. Branches arched overhead, covering the sky leaving nothing on view that was not green and muddy. I had no preconceived ideas of what this journey would be but I would never have guessed anything like this. For all I knew we could have been deep in the Amazon rainforest. Everyone in the boat was full to the brim with anticipation and excitement. The younger Yangon relatives, townies, were on their first visit just as I was. I tried to tell myself I was not nervous, but of course I was, just a little nervous. The boatmen continued paddling, with difficulty, looking for a non-existent deep channel. I could hear the hull scraping along the bottom, and then the absolute relief of ducks cheerfully paddling between shafts of watery sunlight, some farmers' huts made of sticks and leaves on the right hand bank, rough hay stacks and curious, shy faces peering out from between the trees. This was our destination, the family village, deep in the delta. A place far beyond imagination, until now.

Our welcome was biblical. Boh Lay had returned. Aunty Nettie's sister Rose Red, who was easily as fast on her feet as Aunty Nettie, leapt out of the boat and was hauled up the bank by a team of useful children. Baptist hymns blared out from the jungle trees at full volume and we processed to the village church along a narrow dirt path, single file. Father pointed out the fresh water tanks and the corrugated iron church his father had built. All this was just as he remembered, nothing changed. The church was decorated in our honour. A specially commissioned welcome banner printed on top quality vinyl was draped above the open door. Welcome Desmond, Linda, Hilary – family of U Tun Hla and Daw Bu Ma.

We removed our giant Western shoes on the church steps, contributing them to a pile of much smaller worn out sandals belonging to our hosts. Bemused and innocent, once more we found ourselves the focus of curious attention, centre stage on a neatly arranged row of chairs. Father took the centre seat flanked by his daughters. Yet more speeches and I wondered if Aunty Nettie had captured us to perform in a foreigner show? Father made his speech. I can't remember exactly what he said but somehow, in translation from English to Karen, the words multiplied in mysterious ways. They doubled and tripled, singing and dancing in the breeze which filtered through old bricks and sheets of precariously fixed corrugated iron. Centre stage is not my natural habitat but Hilary loves the limelight. She made herself popular by praising the children while I cuddled a remarkably heavy baby who comforted me enormously.

Everyone had an opportunity to tell their story. We settled down to listen to yet another cousin, the village pastor. He was beautifully dressed in a traditional Karen coat with a matching headband but very poor in English, in fact completely devoid of English, so once again Aunty Nettie translated.

From my place of honour on the stage I had a perfect view of the audience. They sat in orderly rows on wooden pews, the children sitting together in the front rows, as lively as anywhere in the world but at the same time, wonderfully well behaved. Their mothers and grandmothers, sitting further behind, looked thin and work worn. There were some men, but not as many men as women. Perhaps they were working in the fields. I listened to the pastor's incomprehensible words, conscious of the old wooden chair and worn floor boards beneath my bare feet. Through the open windows I could see the green and gold paddy fields but after so many years of not knowing and not believing, I could hardly convince myself this was reality.

The Story of U Tun Hla
Narrator: *Adaw Gyi*

My Darling Gazelles,

'As you sow so shall you reap.'

When Great Grandfather U Tun Hla was born the delta lands had barely woken from their long sleeping. The widest road was the river and there were no buildings taller than the tallest trees. U Tun Hla's native village was a tranquil place where everyone knew their neighbours intimately. They shared all the joys and sorrows of life, laughing and crying together just the same as in every other village. There was no need for locked doors because the inhabitants were humble and honest, and even if we must admit life was not a fairy tale and a few were *not* humble and honest, no one was more rich or more poor than his neighbours. They had no means to store their wealth against an uncertain future but instead were forced to rely on each other's goodwill and the fertile paddy fields. That was the secret of their survival, success and happiness.

U Tun Hla was born in a bamboo and matting hut raised up on stilts where his mother delivered him directly into the waiting hands of his grandmother. He thrived on love, quickly growing fat and round. His mother ground sweet yellow thanaka paste from tree bark to paint on his baby cheeks and on her own cheeks to protect them both from the tropical sun. She carried him in a sling wherever she went. Sometimes collecting firewood or water, sometimes collecting wild jungle food. She knew which kinds of mushrooms were good to eat and where to find delicious frogs and crabs, insects and ant larvae, and U Tun Hla's favourite, wild honey. If he fell ill she treated him with herbs just as she had learned from her own mother.

He soon learned to walk, at first stumbling on uncertain legs then confidently clambering up and down ladders, in and out of the hut and

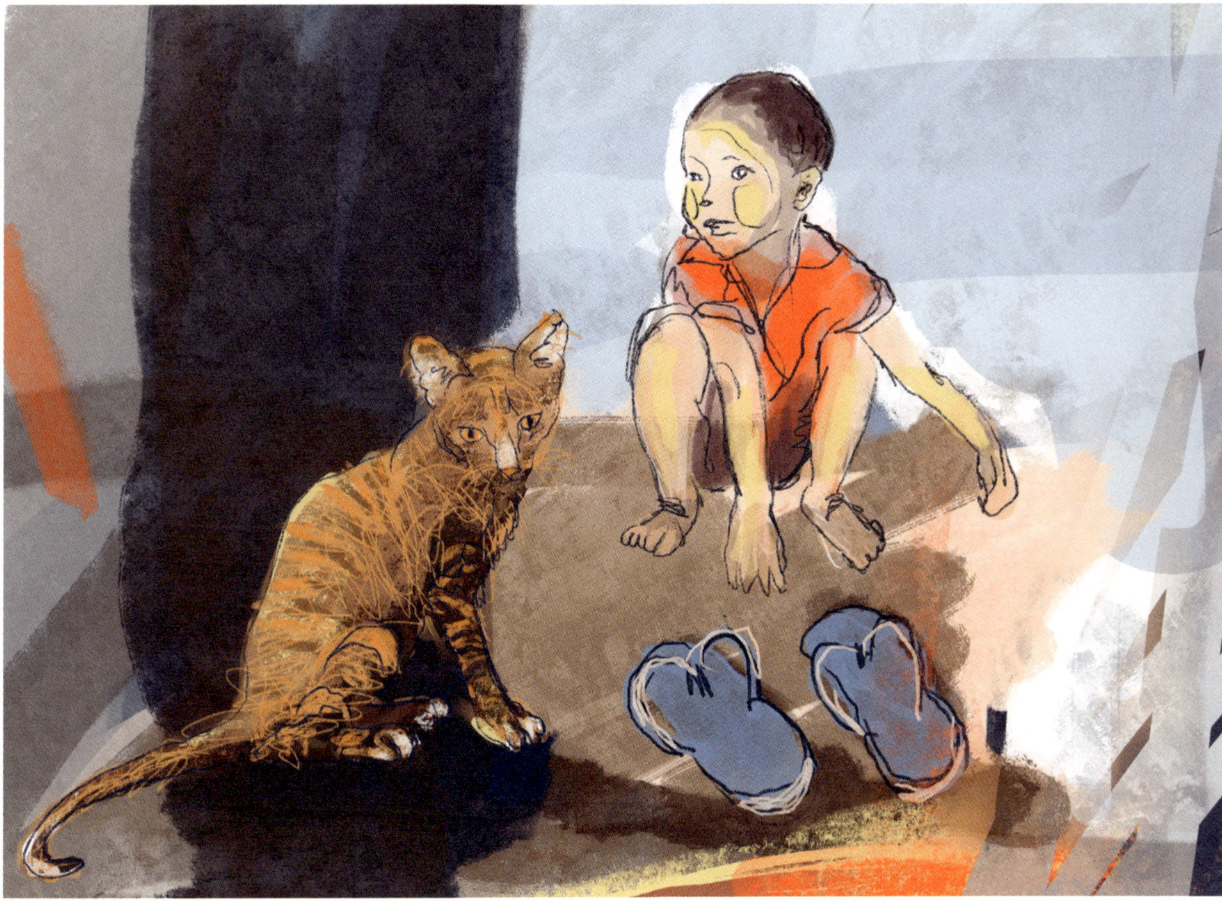

U Tun Hla never kicked his heels under a desk

getting under everyone's feet. His first friend was a golden cat, a tiny stripy tiger who U Tun Hla stretched and pushed and pulled and turned upside down and inside out without ever being scratched. When he was a little older U Tun Hla's father gave him two baby goats whose mother had been eaten by a snake. He stroked their hard heads and fed them by hand every day until they were full grown and could fend for themselves.

All the village elders were his teachers and all the village children were fellow students. His school and his playground consisted of his neighbours' houses, the footpaths, the fields and the river bank. Alongside his young friends U Tun Hla learned the most important lessons of his life: to be gentle and kind, honest, not quarrelsome, respect his elders, love God and support his parents.

U Tun Hla and all the village boys practised hunting from a very young age. Starting close to home with birds and bats and lizards and when they grew old enough they went further afield for bigger game such as wild pigs and deer. They were not allowed to take their fathers' guns, and in any case bullets cost money, which they did not have. Instead they were experts with crossbows and slingshots made with jungle wood. They knew how to train hunting dogs, set snares and build traps. When the paddy fields were flooded with water all the families threw themselves bodily in the mud, catching fish by hand. Nothing could be more fun or more delicious than catching your own food. By the time he reached adolescence U Tun Hla's arms were strong enough to land a net full of fish from the river or haul his body weight twenty feet up into the air, climbing the trunk of a coconut tree. His broad feet and bare toes were familiar with all the jungle paths for miles around. He could wield a machete, build a house and plough a field. His smile stretched from ear to ear and his energy was superfluous to his needs.

When U Tun Hla looked back on his early years it was hard to distinguish one from another because village routine never varied. Survival depended on sowing crops and harvesting. There were two seasons, hot and dry or hot and wet. When the monsoon rains flooded the fields and the birds began to sing with joy, it was time to plant. The farmers rose before dawn, ready for work just as soon as the cool morning mist cleared. The most important crop was paddy but they also grew tobacco, betel nut, mangoes, durian and the sweetest red bananas. In the afternoon, when the sun was too hot for hard labour, the village families rested under the trees. Neighbours gathered to chat and smoke cheroots, their hands were always busy with some useful task such as making bamboo fishing poles or weaving baskets. When the green fields dried out and turned to one hundred shades of forged gold, the paddy was ready to be harvested. The stalks were laid out to dry and the women cleaned and separated the rice from the chaff by throwing it high into the air. Eventually the rice was ready to store in wooden bins and earthenware jars large enough for a child to climb inside. In those days the paddy fields did not belong to any individual, but the village tract was carefully divided between all households according to their needs and reassigned each year so no one worried or complained he had more or less than he deserved.

Each new year, according to the full moon and one more successful harvest, the village celebrated and everyone had a part to play. The women wove new tunics and tied their hair with ribbons and flowers. The men dug a fire pit and cooked a pig which they slaughtered themselves. The young people pounded sticky rice with cane sugar and wrapped it in green leaves, not forgetting to leave some in the Nat shrines. In the evening the young people performed the traditional songs and dances. They sat up late playing guitars and composing love songs, hoping that perhaps the partner of their dreams was listening. The elders were content to let the young people make eyes at each other, as long as they could hear them singing. When the singing stopped the elders wanted to know why. This was the accepted way life continued from one generation to the next.

When the foreigners arrived life began to change. In the few years it took U Tun Hla to mature from child to adult, Thibaw, the last king of Burma, and his family were marched onto a ship and forced into exile across the ocean. The new foreigner queen, Victoria, Empress and Defender of the Faith, took the King's place but she never showed her radiant face to her subject people except by her official portraits. Instead, she gave her most adventurous sons authority to conduct her business and rule in her name, according to her religion and laws.

The foreigners had loud voices and were not afraid to say whatever they wanted. Their strange pale faces made children cry and they were so rude and uneducated they danced on the faces of the pagodas in their leather boots declaring their God, Christ The King, was the most powerful God even to conquering death. They would not bow to any other God. The foreigner God granted mankind dominion over the fish of the sea, the fowl of the air, the cattle and over all the earth and every creeping thing. U Tun Hla had a wonderful voice and he sang his heart out in praise and thanksgiving every Sunday. He never doubted the foreigners or their God and he was always grateful to them for returning the long lost book which they called the Bible, but in his heart one small question remained. Had the foreigner God achieved dominion over the Nats? At night, when U Tun Hla lay in his hut, with his parents and siblings sleeping close by, he could hear the Nats angrily screeching in the jungle. They refused to leave their wild places. Sometimes U Tun Hla lit a candle in the Christian church but sometimes he lit an extra one under the banyan trees and left it there with

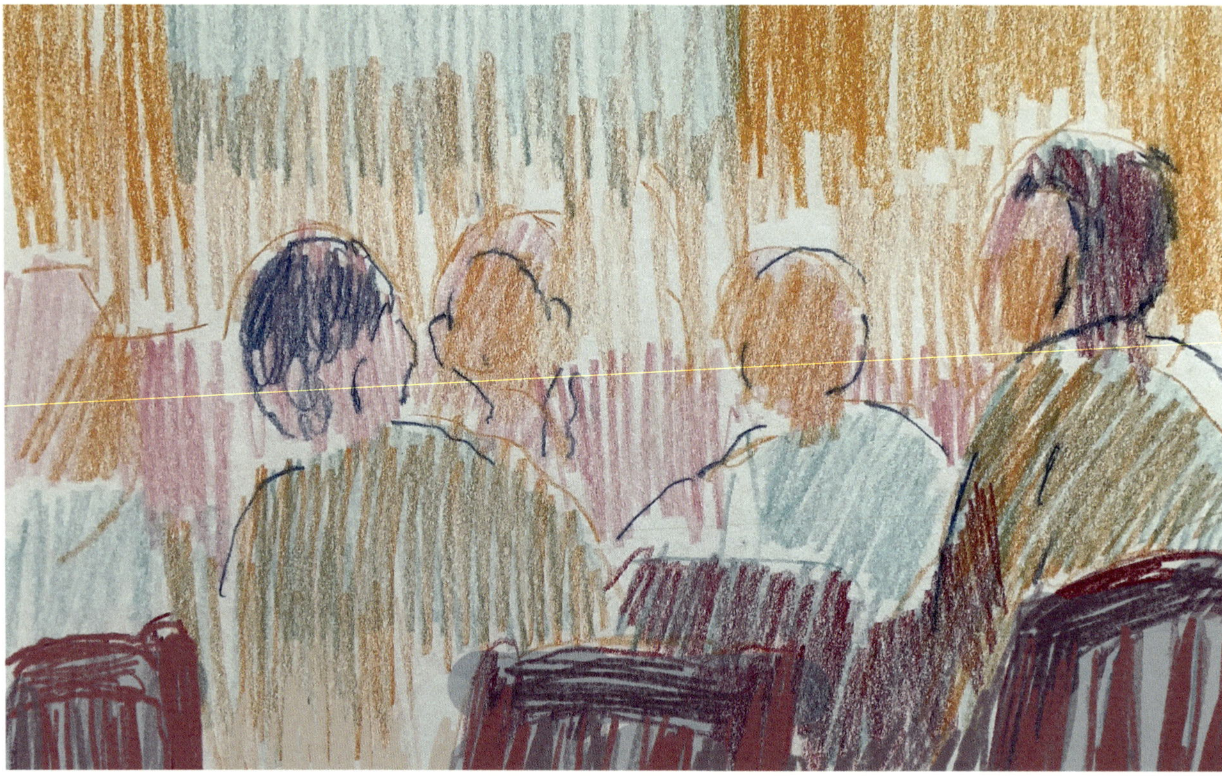

Old men sighed at the pace of change

a little rice and oil for the sake of peace and quiet and good luck. It would be foolish to ignore the Nats and no one need go hungry or be left out in such a bountiful land.

Whatever they needed, the foreigners took it for themselves and because they were devout, God favoured all their endeavours. They said this was progress and if the people loved God and worked hard God and progress would reward them. The foreigners' God would make the people prosperous in the image of the foreign lands but this required many changes. It was time for the people to grow up and stop behaving like children. The foreigners had plans to build roads, railways and chimneys, taller than the tallest tree. Perhaps even taller than the golden pagoda in Bassein with its high umbrella studded with rubies and diamonds. The new chimneys were not crowned with precious jewels, not even a few token trinkets. They were elegant and useful according to science. They were situated at regular intervals all along the river bank and each one marked the sight of a rice factory, powered by modern steam engines which the foreigners transported half way around the world in steel-hulled ships by way of the new Suez canal.

A tribe of itinerant families arrived to work a clay pit beside U Tun Hla's village. They made themselves bashas from rags and sticks and stones and left their babies crawling in the dirt. U Tun Hla had never seen such dreadful poverty, his dog would have refused to live in one of those fly blown places. The men and boys laboured so long and hard in the flooded clay pits no one could tell what colour their skin was, and at night they drowned their sorrows in drink. The foreigners' demand for the pretty little red bricks moulded by women and children was limitless. Perhaps they were a reminder of rose covered cottages in their home towns across the ocean or perhaps it was just old fashioned, unsentimental business.

Clocks were dispatched throughout the land. Some were placed on utilitarian cast iron poles and others were housed in brick towers with coloured tiles and unexpected, oriental curves, all constructed in prominent public places. The fierce little hands never stopped turning, reminding people of their duty not to waste a precious minute that could be used to advance prosperity. Old men squatting on wooden stools in the tea shops sucked in their toothless cheeks as they watched countless sacks of rice floating down river with each passing tide. The foreigners took the most precious treasure of the delta lands, rice, all polished in the steam mills, perfectly curved grains and shining white like the moon, stolen away to foreign cities across the ocean.

When U Tun Hla reached seventeen years old his father gave him a pair of young buffaloes. Nothing could have pleased him more. He pictured himself training them to plough a straight furrow or pull a cart to market or, even better, race in a village tournament. He could already hear the cheering crowds lining the track and see the village girls waving their hankies and cheering when his cart crossed the dusty finish line first, the winner.

That evening U Tun Hla searched out the sweetest forage and softest bedding for his beasts. He left them well fed and safely tethered comforted by a sweet scented fire to keep the flies away. Then he went to celebrate his birthday with the village boys. They gathered under a banyan tree on the river bank, playing their guitars and singing plaintive love songs which they hoped the girls would hear but, unfortunately for the boys, if any girls did hear they had been well taught by their parents to turn a deaf ear. Eventually U Tun Hla returned home and settled to the comfort of his sleeping mat surrounded by his family. His not always ever-vigilant hunting dog lay snoring under the hut, oblivious to the world.

But the bullocks had not consented to these new arrangements. Exchange of gold coins meant nothing to them. Not even the sweetest hand cut hay was compensation for the loss they felt at being removed from their familiar place. They slept fitfully, stamping their feet with frustration. Eventually, when the sound of the boys' guitars fell silent, they slipped loose from their tethers. Lifting their heads to the night air, they could smell home and they remembered every step of the way. In the morning they were gone and the only witness to their departure were the naughty Nats.

When the family woke up they discovered two broken ropes hanging from the tree where the bullocks had been tethered. They were distraught. Their entire fortune had been invested in those precious animals. U Tun Hla swore he would brave all dangers to find them. He was prepared to swim across rivers in full flood, fight crocodiles and wrestle serpents in the jungle or run through fields of grass blades, sharp as knives, in his bare feet. Anything to get the ungrateful beasts back. Fortunately very few, if any, of these things were required but at the very least he had a long hot walk ahead of him without any breakfast.

Following his father's instructions he walked all day. Starting in the cool morning mist, skirting past village duck ponds, sweating through swamps under the white heat of the midday sun, always wary of stepping on poisonous snakes, leaping across bamboo bridges, jumping ditches until at last, late in the afternoon when the blue sky faded and the glorious red and yellow light of evening flooded the horizon, he came to rest under a tree on the river bank. He sat there in misery, wondering just what he would say to his father when he returned home empty handed but then, as they do in fairy tales, his fortunes changed. He spied the young bullocks frolicking in a washing pool close to their favourite old haunts. With a great sigh of relief and thanks be to God he jumped in beside them, slipped two ropes around their necks and gently persuaded them to follow him out of the water.

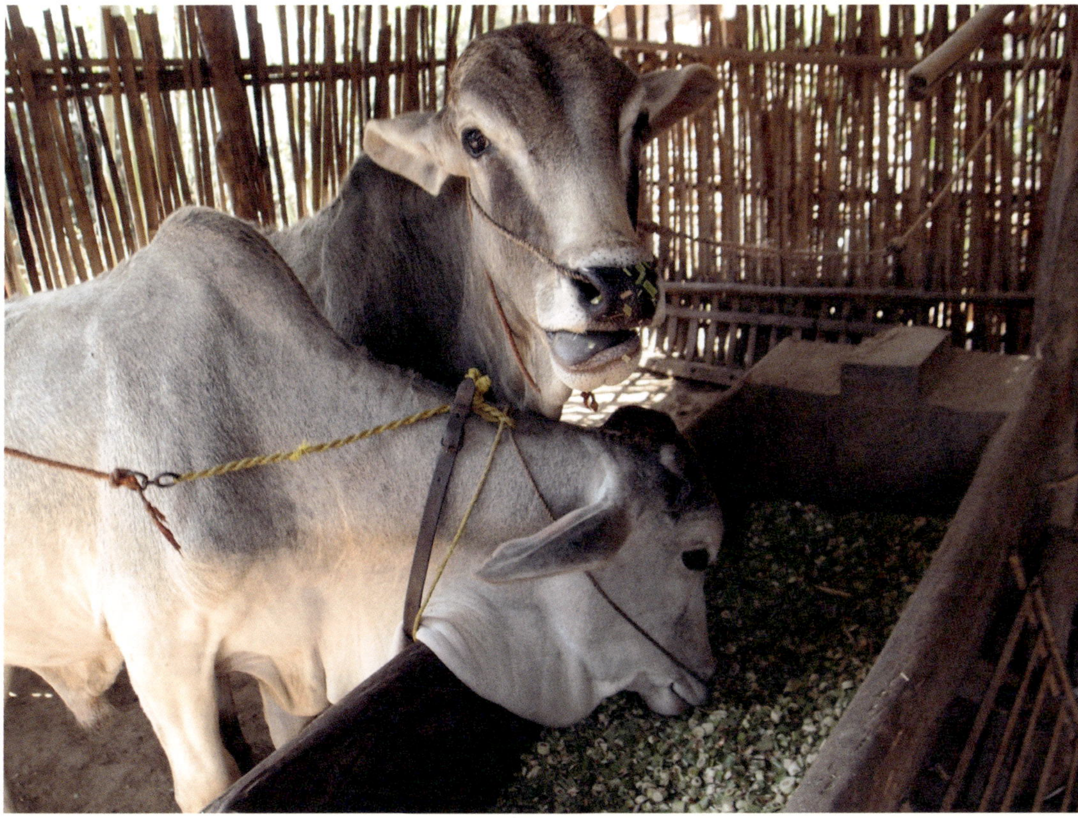

Those long ago days when life was so simple

By this time it was late in the day, so he was delighted to accept an invitation to spend the night in the local village. The village was famous for its beautiful women who were all considered to have very fine noses, perhaps even as pretty as the foreigners' noses, and U Tun Hla was keen to know if rumour was true. His host sat him down at a table laden with delicious meat, rice and curry. The food was served by a young woman who entered the room in her bare feet, wearing a traditional white Karen tunic. One might have thought he had never have seen a woman before. The light of her beauty shone so brightly he was blinded. The glance of her melting eyes was powerful enough to tame a savage beast. He heard birds singing and imagined them folding their wings over her head to shade her pale skin from the powerful sun. All nature fell silent when she slept in fear of disturbing her slumbers. Our brave young hero was not one to hesitate. By the time the meal was finished he was determined to ask the beautiful young woman with the perfect nose and the perfect eyes and every other perfect part of her body to marry him.

It sometimes occurs to me that perhaps U Tun Hla's father's hand had more of an influence in this story than I have given him credit for and perhaps the bullocks were not clever enough to free themselves by undoing their own ropes. What I can truthfully say is that the bullocks were never sorry for causing so much trouble and neither was U Tun Hla, who discovered the true love of his life. As I am sure you have already guessed, the young woman in the white tunic was great grandmother Daw Bu Ma and she was as wise as she was beautiful and practical. In particular, she knew the fastest way to a man's heart lies through his stomach. Of course Daw Bu Ma's father said no when U Tun Hla asked for her hand in marriage because, as he said, his daughter was far too young, a beautiful chicken but not one ready for the pot. At that time, poor U Tun Hla was sent home alone and Daw Bu Ma was banished to her loom while practical enquires were made.

By the end of the year Daw Bu Ma had woven a beautiful wedding longyi. For those of you who are interested in fashion it was black with brightly coloured intricate patterns running crossways and she wore it with a figure hugging blouse. I know this because it is a great treasure preserved by Daw Bu Ma's granddaughters in Yangon, where I have seen it with my own eyes. U Tun Hla made excellent use of his time, building an elegant wooden cart with rosewood spokes and expensive iron-rimmed wheels. No loving parent could find fault with any aspect of their behaviour. 'As you sow, so shall you reap the rewards' was a lesson well learnt. U Tun Hla was given permission to decorate his cart with ribbons and his village brothers leapt in, singing brave young men songs. They drove to Daw Bu Ma's home where the marriage of U Tun Hla and Daw Bu Ma was celebrated by slaughtering a fat pig and just about one hundred different kinds of sticky rice sweetmeats and cold drinks were served to the happy guests.

And this is the story of how great grandfather came to leave his village and set up home with great grandmother in Chaung Zauk village.

Your ever loving
Adaw Gyi

Escape from Death by Drowning

Narrator: *Linda Lewin*

May the thunderbolts and lightning, the Nat of the waters and all sea animals love me that I may be safe from them. A Burmese oath.

After the church service and after we had shaken hands with the entire congregation Father retired to the pastor's house which was the remains of his grandparents,' Daw Bu Ma and U Tun Hla's house. Someone had thoughtfully laid a fresh blanket and pillow on a hard plank bed in front of the upstairs window. It could very easily have been the bed his grandmother slept on. It would have been churlish and out of character for him to refuse to take a refreshing nap.

The village children conducted Hilary and me on a tour. They surrounded us, skipping and dancing with shy excitement. We were herded across the paddy fields, bare golden stubble after harvest. We learned how to tightrope over a single pole bamboo bridge and splashed through puddles with the assistance of a local Walter Raleigh who laid fresh straw beneath our visiting feet. The children knew where to take us, to Daw Bu Ma's grave on the river bank where she lay interred next to her husband and her son, San Po Thin. The graves were marked by slabs of concrete. I asked a small girl her name. Nine Blessings, she said. All the children were blessings. Their gift to us was this unexpected moment of peace and tranquility at our ancestors' graves. Time stood still. I turned to Hilary and caught sight of our cousin A May Sing, in floods of tears. We three women could not have looked more different, a pair of tall, white skinned, blue eyed Westerners and one minute Asian beauty, our golden skinned cousin. We had barely any words in common but our Great Grandmother welcomed all three equally, returned to her, in this smallest of villages, in the paddy fields of the great Irrawaddy delta.

The fatted calf was killed. We discovered father holding court at table in his grandmother's house. The food was delicious and his appetite was good. A joke was made about the neighbours eating rats – apparently rats are a Karen delicacy. They are sweet to eat because they help themselves to the best of everything. It makes sense if you don't think about it too hard. Father said when he was young he could eat bare bones and chair legs. Nettie said Karens eat dogs and cats and bats. They are famous for it. They can live off anything at a cost of nothing. Nettie offered me a bowl of what looked like chopped snakes with a warning there would be a lot of bones. She wasn't surprised when I declined in favour of hard boiled eggs and cauliflowers. By the time our bellies were full we could have been forgiven for forgetting we had any other homes to return to. More to the point, we had completely forgotten that like Cinderella, our permission to attend the party expired at midnight.

All this happy time, unnoticed by anyone, the tide had sneakily slipped away and abandoned us. We had left our boat nicely tethered by the bank. Now, they said, it was well beyond reach, out of sight in the river. We would need a canoe to get to it. This was a worrying situation, for us and for Nettie. She asked if we wanted to return to Pathein, or spend the night in the village? A difficult choice and why did she assume we were qualified to make the decision? I would like to say I opted to return to Pathein because I did not want to compromise my hosts by breaking the law but the less generous truth is, I was out of my comfort zone. I looked around at the bare floorboards – no evidence of any convenient plumbing, no mattress and the insects were beginning to bite. Without a second thought I said no, thank you very much and generously offered to leave my insect repellent as a gift to those family guests who were busy unrolling their blankets.

We had to move fast. We were directed to slip into a canoe, first Hilary, then Father, then myself. We quite literally slipped in, one behind the other. As Hilary said, looking at her oily hand, we appreciated them taking the trouble to grease the outside in our honour but was it really necessary to grease the inside as well? I had no answer. It had been a long, jet lagged day and quite possibly I was hallucinating. We had left the solid ground of reality and were caught in a tangle of heat and water and mud, suspended in one of father's stories, exploring uncharted jungles in a dug out canoe. It was not the first time he had sailed down the river in the dark but it was all new to me. I thought of Mother, who had died the year before. Was she watching? What would she say if we arrived knocking on heaven's

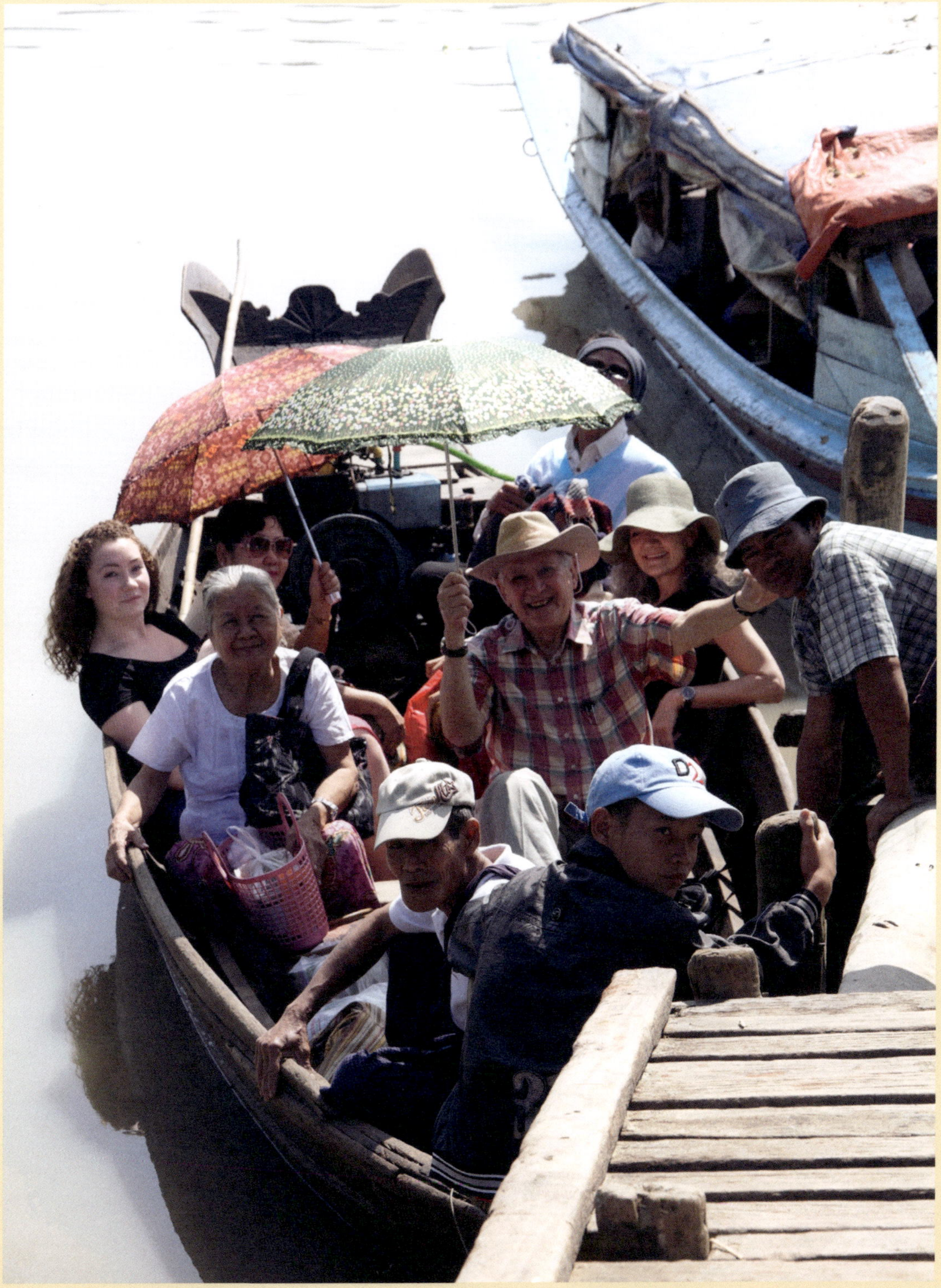

Dad and Aunty Nettie Family boating party

door looking like drowned rats? The canoe rocked slightly from side to side, increasing my sense of dislocation. Moonlight drained all colour from everything so I could not distinguish between land and sky and water. It was all the same. A team of young men took hold of the sides of the canoe, wading through the mud, pushing and pulling us down the creek. We could barely make out their faces in the dark. They continued till the water reached their shoulders. Karen men may be handsome and brave but they are generally not very tall. One of the boys started laughing so it must be a game, not a dream.

The big boat was waiting in the river, a reassuring shadow, just slightly blacker than the water which supported it. More disembodied hands appeared in the dark, lifting us into the boat. Our bags followed. Nothing forgotten. Nothing left behind. In fact we had gained a bag of hard boiled eggs and a live chicken trussed up in a green plastic basket. The chicken was a present for A May Sing to take back to town and the eggs were for me because I had appreciated them so much at dinner. We found our places, the engine rattled into action and there we were, heading towards our hotel in Pathein, back to reality. Two boys, with their arms wrapped around each other for security, perched on the front of the boat, lighting our way with a handy little battery torch. Someone steering at the back, out of sight and that should have been the end of the adventure, except it wasn't.

We hit......... something which stopped us dead in our tracks, in the middle of the deep and wide Irrawaddy river.

The prow of the boat lifted out of the water. We rocked ninety degrees to one side, ninety degrees to the other side, then returned to the centre. Three times. Are you counting? All in terrifying slow motion. My life did not flash before my eyes. It took advantage of an eternity to amble before my eyes. Father and I looked at each other in silence, wondering whether to jump or wait to be capsized. I had a vision of myself trapped, gasping for air underneath the overturned boat. I wondered if it would be better to take the initiative and leap overboard with or without my shoes. Obviously I could swim better without shoes, but then how would I manage to walk back to the hotel through the jungle, in my bare feet? I assumed of course, I would reach the bank. Hilary prepared to say farewell to her new laptop and then, Nettie jumped up with a loud voice crying, 'Devil be gone' and it was so. For miraculous reasons, having completed three full one hundred and eighty degree swings, the boat returned to normal, vertical, floating position.

Nettie and her son Christopher burst into a duet, 'Sweet Honey in the Rock,' surely the sweetest song I ever heard. If you have ever had a near death experience you will understand our enormous appreciation of life resuming its normal course, stretching out into the happy and distant future. We were filled with a combination of joy and relief beyond comparison. The village boat returned us to the wharf in Pathein where I watched my father make one last intrepid walk over the long and narrow plank which connected our boat to safe and dry land. I followed, supported by the helping hands which always seemed to appear out of nowhere.

We were saved, but why and by who? By our Christian God or by the Nats of the river? I would swear it was the Nats and I think Nettie, the greatest evangelical Christian I ever met, agreed. I have to admit, even though I am fairly confident of being able to swim, especially if my life depended on it, I was shocked by the thought we had been in such close proximity to those imaginary creatures known as devils. Later, I discovered that Nettie was well known for casting out devils because I was presented with a video of her banishing a devil from a sick baby held in the arms of a poor and desperate looking mother. I would obviously have preferred the mother to take her baby to a doctor but perhaps that wasn't a locally available option. Hilary confessed she had personally cast out a devil on more than one occasion and she had clients who were grateful for her services! Well I never, it must be a talent which ran in the family. I knew my fearless little sister was a doula, accustomed to accompanying souls on their perilous way into this world and sometimes, sadly, on the way out. Very important work no doubt, but even so, I could have fallen out with my very own sibling there and then. If you want to know more of this story, interesting no doubt, you will have to ask her because I was too cross.

In one day we had experienced a remarkable number of different types of Myanmar transport, a Yangon taxi, the deluxe bus, an open back truck, the village boat and a fish tail canoe. We had started at four o'clock in the morning and just before midnight we squeezed in one last vehicle which is unique to Myanmar. The Sidecar. A Myanmar sidecar is a dainty, dilapidated version of a rickshaw with two back to back seats attached to the side of the bicycle. Unfortunately the seats are always just a tiny bit too small for a normal Western backside to be properly accommodated. Even if I lost a lot of weight my Western hips would never fit. I always have to sit sideways in a sidecar and it is always slightly uncomfortable but this was not a moment to complain. We engaged a swarm of sidecars, one for each member of the family. Pathein is perfectly flat so the job of sidecar driver is not one of the worst jobs in Myanmar. Our sidecar drivers had absolutely no idea where we were going and neither did I. I didn't care, my dilapidated sidecar was as good as a golden chariot, just as long as it was on dry land. We spent twenty minutes spinning around the deserted night streets of Pathein, hollering at each other for directions. There are very few street lights in Pathein, or indeed anywhere in Myanmar but I could swear I saw Nettie's sister, Rose Red, heading up and down the same street three times while I was being conveyed in the opposite direction.

Eventually, we rendezvoused at the hotel which had been selected by Aunty Nettie because it was the best value for money available in Pathein. Much to Auntie's disapproval Father insisted on paying the sidecar drivers twice the going rate, quite possibly upsetting the entire balance of the local economy with his generosity, but it was well worth the money for our entertainment and the astonished smiles on the drivers' faces.

The hotel turned out to be the scariest hotel I have ever had the misfortune not to sleep a wink in. In retrospect we would have been better off avoiding the near death experience by sleeping in the village. Every wall of every room and corridor in the hotel was painted a sickly shade of Myanmar green. I would be surprised to find that particular shade of green in any other country but it seems to be the only colour available in Myanmar and it looks even worse in the light of a naked electric light bulb. All the corners of our room, the small window located too high in the wall to see out of, the air conditioner, the mattress, and the bathroom fittings were mouldy and draped with dust and cobwebs which looked as if they had lain undisturbed for a hundred haunted years. I know that was not the case. Compared to our temperate seasons the monsoon climate is a powerful beast, capable of eating through solid concrete in a very short time. A little bit of interior paintwork is nothing more than a light lunch for a hungry monsoon. I had to force myself to touch anything in the room. On the bright side, a Myanmar longyi is an ideal travelling accessory because it can easily double up as a towel or a bed sheet, therefore providing one clean thing in the room.

I was not planning to mention spitting but now have started I will say it is a common and bad habit in Myanmar. I have not forgotten our fellow guest who, presumably, was so uncomfortable in his room he spent the whole night in the corridor, just outside our door, clearing his throat. Poor man!

The practical motto of this story is, never travel on the Irrawaddy river in the dark with nothing but two boys with one hand torch to guide you. No one who was there will ever forget that night and we all learnt a valuable lesson because however many times I have travelled to or from the village by boat it has never again been in the dark. Strictly speaking the river at Pathein is only a tributary amongst many in the mighty Irrawaddy delta but it is more than wide and deep enough to drown in. I doubt any of us would have made it out alive if we had to swim unaided. I did mention to Aunty Nettie, who was not a swimmer, that she might consider wearing a life jacket next time around but she said she had faith in God to protect her, her conscience was clear, she was ready, indeed eager to meet her maker, whenever he decided to call her.

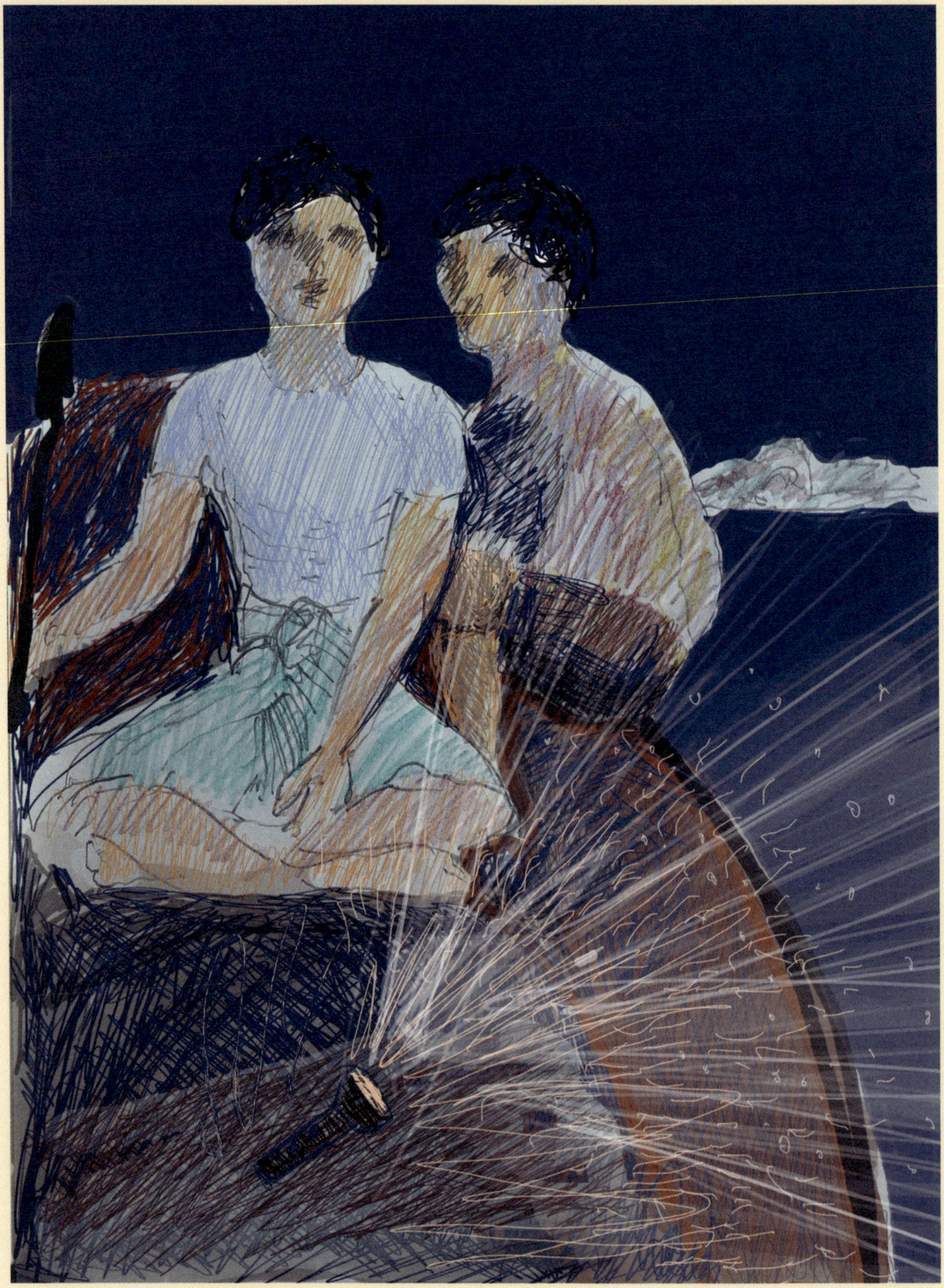

Two boys and a hand torch

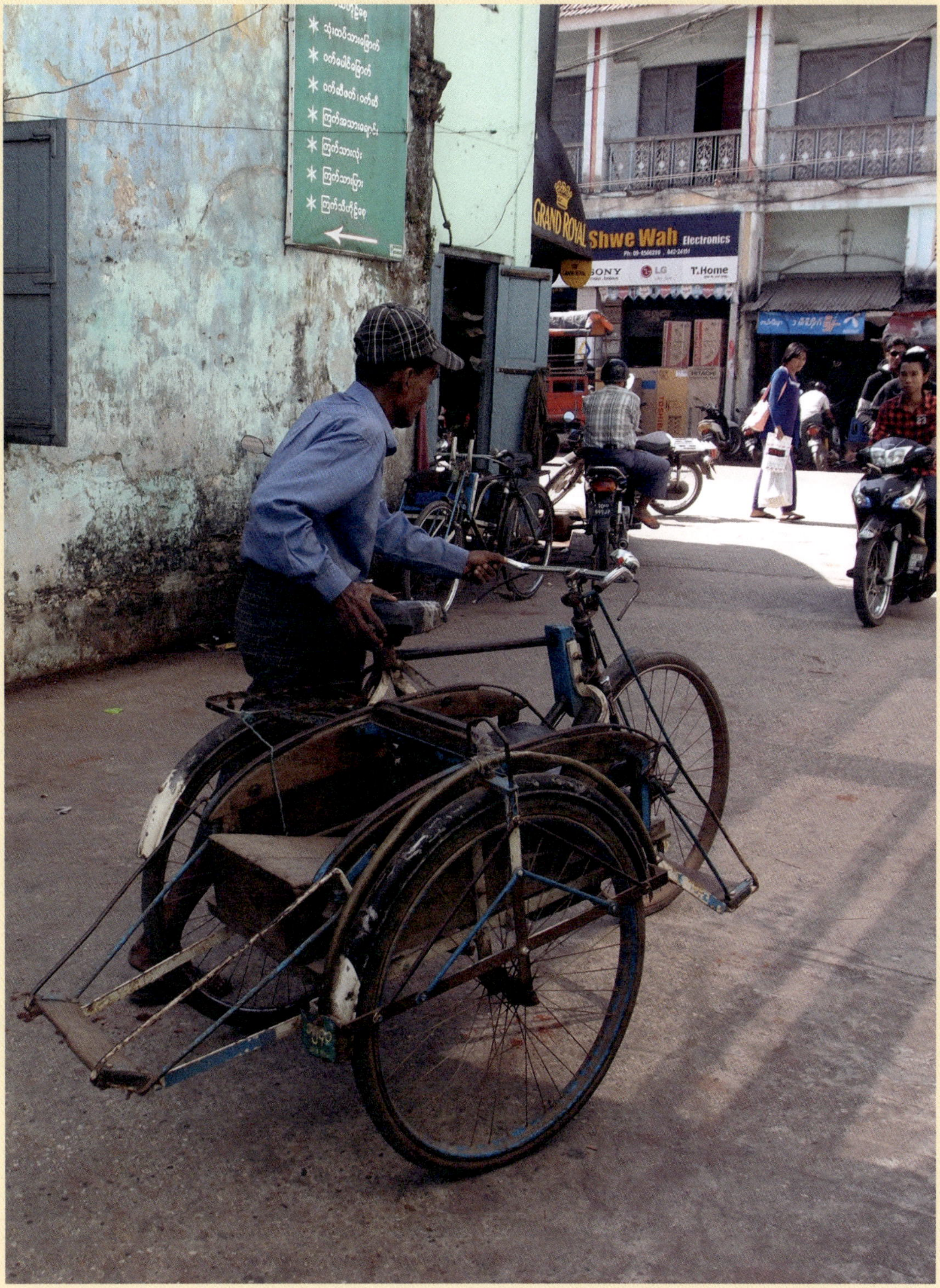

Pathein sidecar

The Story of Daw Bu Ma
Narrator: *Adaw Gyi*

My Dearest Darling Gazelles,

'Western thought is that marriage is a partnership. Well and good. Of course it is a partnership. Wife helps husband, husband helps wife. Myanmar elders say that marriage is like tongue and teeth: like husband and wife tongue and teeth cannot be apart, but accidentally the tongue gets bitten sometimes. What? Sometimes it's quite a bite and hurts like blazes.' U Thein Pe Myint.

Daw Bu Ma's pet name was 'peacock,' the most beautiful bird and royal emblem of our country. I have told you how U Tun Hla fell in love with Daw Bu Ma but there is more than one version of every story. A peacock is a bird with countless eyes including the ones in its beautiful, turquoise tail. Daw Bu Ma saw U Tun Hla first, before ever he saw her, and she made up her mind to marry him immediately, he had no choice in the matter but I don't believe she ever told him so.

You must remember, My Dears, there were no bathrooms, no swimsuits and no underwear in those old-fashioned village days when you were not even a golden twinkle in your grandmother's sweet almond eyes. On those long ago afternoons when the tropical heat pressed deep and suffocating across the land, all sensible animals lay dozing in the shade except for Daw Bu Ma and her lovely sisters. While the rest of the world slept they ran to the river and jumped in fully clothed. Their longyies billowed upwards through the cool water transforming each young woman into a beautiful, floating lotus blossom. They washed their hair with bark and berry shampoo from the wild jungle trees and when they finished playing, emerged sparkling clean, figures perfectly draped in their clinging, wet garments. Then, they dressed in the fresh clothes they had left hanging in the trees and sat on the bank, combing each other's long hair which never felt the sharp blades of the scissors, until it flowed gleaming down their backs, falling even below their knees. It was on one such sultry afternoon that fate brought Daw Bu Ma to the river and she set her romantic eyes on U Tun Hla. When she saw him bathed in water and sunlight, with his longyi pulled up short, apparently absorbed in the task of washing his father's cows, her heart was fatally pierced by Cupid's arrow of love and desire. She knew U Tun Hla was her shining prince and she never regretted her instant decision to marry him.

So you see my Dearest Gazelles, Daw Bu Ma was not surprised and she had her answer ready when U Tun Hla asked her the most important question, 'Will you marry me,' and I would have no stories to tell you and you would not be here to listen if lost cows did not need to be washed in the river or if Daw Bu Ma had possessed a bathroom with a tap of her own so that is what I like to call a blessing in disguise.

Daw Bu Ma was an observant child and clever from the start. Her parents were not educated but they sent her to the foreigner school where she learned to read and write in three languages: Karen which was her mother tongue, Bamar, and the foreigners' English but her greatest skill was in numbers. Her sharp mind quickly grasped the important facts of life. The first was that her family security depended on growing and selling rice, the second that compound interest was a double-edged sword expertly wielded by the hands of Indian and Chinese money lenders, and the third that her family must pay the foreigners' taxes on time. My Dear Gazelles, Daw Bu Ma loved to read from the foreigner bible on Sunday mornings in church and she could quote the most important passages by heart. Jesus instructed man to render unto Caesar what is Caesar's, and that was the lesson which meant the foreigner taxes must be paid or there would be grave consequences.

People liked to gossip and say that she had married beneath her station in life and U Tun Hla was nothing more than an uneducated cowherd but her marriage was an ideal partnership. She made plans and U Tun Hla willingly carried them out. All her decisions were well informed. Somehow news arrived in her farm compound fresh and regular as the new-laid eggs from her own ducks and hens. She knew when to plant, when to harvest, when to buy, when to sell and who she in her turn could afford to lend money to at a good profit. Daw Bu Ma was ambitious but she never wanted anything for herself. Her motivation was to do what was best for her family: not just to survive but to be successful and respected.

Daw Bu Ma was busy every minute of the day and often into the night. Her favourite motto was, 'Fetch water when it rains and spin when the moon shines.' In the evenings, she spent hours at her loom weaving wedding blankets for each of her children in turn. Keeping her hands busy set her mind free to roam. Events never took her by surprise. Everything she touched turned to success. Daw Bu Ma and U Tun Hla thrived while other farmers struggled to pay their seed debts to the money lenders. Daw Bu Ma acquired fertile land, field by field. She sowed the best paddy seed and reaped good harvests, season by season. She secured the financial security of her family for generations to come. If any of her neighbours had a new baby they laughed and said they would take it to Daw Bu Ma for her to suckle, in the hopes it too might grow up handsome, clever, rich. Many years later, in a cold foreigner country, Daw Bu Ma's grandson, Bo Lay would say, 'Everything good in my life came from my grandmother in the village.'

In time, Daw Bu Ma built a two storey farmhouse tucked in between her paddy fields and the mangrove trees bedside the river. It was greatly admired by her less astute neighbours whose own houses were flimsy bashas, darned together with matting and jungle bamboo which easily washed away in the monsoon floods. Their huts had to be rebuilt every year. Daw Bu Ma's house was different. The teak posts from the forests were floated down river and landed in the creek at high tide. Even this far inland, the tide rises and falls, recording its highs and lows with trails of oozing mud between the mangrove trees. The boatmen were forced to navigate slowly through the swamps, sometimes wading barefoot, pushing and pulling by hand until they found a place to haul the beams up onto the shore. The house Daw Bu Ma built remains firmly rooted to this day. The massive wooden pillars lift it so high off the ground a person can walk beneath without bowing their head. The walls are solid overlapping planks with small shuttered windows and the roof is traditional, intricately-woven palm thatch where every leaf is folded by a woman's hand and stitched in place with a needle broken from its own rib.

Daw Bu Ma rejoiced in six strong and healthy children, three handsome boys and three pretty girls. God asked for one sweet boy to be returned to him and she cried on the day she buried him but she accepted that God's will must be done and rejoiced in her six remaining blessings. Her family thrived. Each morning she sent the children to the village school in smart green and white uniforms and in the evening she dutifully listened to them chanting their homework. No one drowned in the river or got eaten by a tiger when they went to wash their clothes. No one was trampled by a wild elephant, no one died from a snake bite although, later in life, Daw Bu Ma came close – she was bitten by a cobra, the only creature that ever caught her unawares. Poor terrified U Tun Hla beat her over the head to stop her losing consciousness. She was not entirely grateful for his intervention and accused him of making the cure worse than the bite. She sang out loud, 'If I die it is because of you.'

All her children, boys and girls, remembered every day of their village childhood as a happy one. A single footpath ran between the houses; they visited their Christian friends at one end and their Buddhist friends at the other and played football in the middle. The place was full of life and completely without privacy. Ducks, cows, pigs and chickens were born under the houses and children were born inside the houses. They grew up together, chasing each other along the narrow ways raised up between the paddy fields, until the former were eaten by the latter and the latter were sent away to school. That is, provided they passed their exams, but that was never a problem for Daw Bu Ma's children who matriculated with flying colours and graduated to the high school as a matter of course. Daw Bu Ma sent them to the school boarding house by boat or in a wooden bullock cart, well supplied with home-grown sacks of rice and money to pay for text books. Of course there was always a present for the teacher.

Daw Bu Ma loved all of her children with good sense and tried her best to prepare them for the future. San Po Lwin was her first son and he carried her expectations so lightly she never worried about him. He was an excellent student who took life in his long, easy stride. Her second son, San Po Thin, was every bit as clever as his older brother but if Daw Bu Ma had a sleepless night it was because of him. Thin was a little monkey who found school more entertaining than educating and was always ready for an out of bounds adventure. She never forgot the day she sat at his bedside in the missionary hospital, waiting for him to open his eyes and recognise her, because he had captured a runaway horse and jumped on its back, only to be thrown off and land on the ground unconscious.

Somehow, Thin always turned disaster into good fortune. The accident brought him to the attention of his American teacher who said it was lucky he had a thick skull but if he learned to use his head more wisely he might do great things. The teacher's wife smiled kindly and said he was a brave boy and Daw Bu Ma should be proud of him. Daw Bu Ma's third and youngest son was her great comfort, a daydreamer and a musician. And what of the pretty girls? Daw Bu Ma made sure they could pull their weight just as hard as any of the boys.

Eventually, when her youngest son was old enough to attend high school, Daw Bu Ma noticed the carved wooden bed she had commissioned to be made in town was growing a little harder at night and when she looked at U Tun Hla she was concerned. He could not carry on working in the fields for ever. His skin was burned thin and brown by the seasons and stretched so tight over his broad cheek bones it exposed the work worn hollows below. He spent more and more of his time smoking cheroots and playing cards with his friends upstairs in the two-storey wooden house while she continued to conduct her business affairs on the ground floor. Then Daw Bu Ma's thoughts turned to her chosen successor, San Po Lwin, who was ready to graduate from university in Calcutta. On the day he left home she set aside her best piglet and fed it until it was fat and succulent, ready to slaughter just as soon as he returned and she collected him from the ferry boat.

When the homecoming feast was over and the dishes were removed for washing Daw Bu Ma invited Lwin to join her upstairs. He climbed the stairs, curling his toes on the warm wooden boards saturated with all the collected heat of the day. Daw Bu Ma opened the bedroom shutters and instantly the room filled with the light of the setting sun reflecting off the stubble fields. Lwin could see his parents' bed in one corner of the room with a mosquito net let down for the night and his father's hunting rifles propped against the wall in the other corner. Nothing had changed since he left home. This room had been his childhood refuge when the paddy fields were flooded with monsoon waters deep enough to drown a man. He had grown taller than his mother but he paused deferentially, waiting for her to speak.

She began, 'Everything you can see from this window belongs to our family, the fat pigs tethered under the house, the cows, the ducks and chickens, the vegetable gardens, the fishing boats and most important of all, the paddy fields. By God's grace our land is fertile, the people who work for us are honest and the harvest is good. I know how to trade well. Every day the English foreigners who are our fathers sail the rice we grow down the river and sell it to their far away countries who depend on us to put the food in their mouths. The American foreigners who love us like mothers bring us teachers and doctors. We Karen are blessed to be the foreigners' favourite children, but the people of this country are divided because neither the mothers nor the fathers treat their children equally. You must be vigilant. You know the foreigners' Indian servants are treacherous dogs who grow fat on scraps from the masters' table. They smile at the masters on one side of their black face and smile at our women on the other but those Kala are full of false promises. Be careful or the Kala money lenders will take our land and grow rich off our backs and still the English fathers will not let us say one bad word to their Kala servants. In this village our Karen people are protected by God and the foreigners' great love for us, otherwise we would be defenceless as crabs without shells on the river bank but Lwin, when we leave the village we must keep our eyes open and our wits about us, because even here in the delta lands where we grow enough food to feed the whole of the glorious Empire upon which the sun never sets, there are men who have lost everything and have nothing to feed their children. They have turned their ploughshares into angry swords and spears. I tell you honestly, if you meet those dacoits on the road they will take everything you have. You will be lucky to be left with your life. Lwin, I have done my best for you, you are grown up and graduated and it is time to begin work. I have three sons but you are the son born to secure the future of our family.'

Lwin's reply was not what his mother wanted to hear. He had returned from university with letters inviting him to study law in the great capital city of the empire upon which the sun never sets. For a moment Daw Bu Ma was torn between fear of losing her son and pride in his achievement. 'Lwin, I have waited patiently, two long years, and now you want to sail across the ocean to a land where you will always be the foreigner in The Temple. In that country they do not understand our ways or know our family. In that place you will hear all the languages of the earth, even the dead language Latin, but you will not hear your mother tongue. Your story will never be written in those languages.' Lwin had studied too many long, lamplit nights to give up his ambitions. He had heard so many wonderful things about the foreigner lands, he must discover the truth for himself. He said his family would remain in the village waiting for him and God would protect him. He would study well and when he returned he would be laden with presents and he would provide for the family's future. Lwin knelt at his mother's feet, asking for her blessing.

Then, U Tun Hla stepped into the room. He smiled at his wife and said in his youth a young man could journey by foot or canoe from one village to another village on the riverbank but even if the women were wonderfully beautiful with very fine noses life in one village was no different from life in the next. In these miraculous new days a man could travel across the vast ocean without any trouble because the foreigners ruled the waves with their great steam ships and God commanded the monsters in the deep places to be calm and peaceful. The very same guardian angels who protected the foreigners' sons would protect Lwin. By now, the night stars had replaced the sunset. Lwin felt the trembling of the wooden building, breathing in and out with relief in the cool evening air. U Tun Hla turned away and picked up his hunting rifle, checking it for the next day. Daw Bu Ma rested her hand on Lwin's head and gave her blessing with grace. She was the source of all the charm and confidence he carried with him from his first to his last days.

Your ever loving
Adaw Gyi

Thanaka
Narrator: *Linda Lewin*

There are details of Myanmar daily life which are delightful, astonishing surprises such as the sight of everyday people, mostly children but including adults, going about the streets wearing yellow face paint, as if that might be a perfectly normal thing to do, which it is in Myanmar. Their yellow cheeks are coloured by thanaka paste which can be worn by anyone from the coolest Western sophisticate to school children and babies in their mother's arms. There are a few killjoys who condemn it for being an old-fashioned bad habit but 'as for me,' one of Aunty Nettie's favourite English phrases, it is a daily visual pleasure unique to Myanmar.

The paste is made by grinding small branches of wood, Limonia Acdissima, on a stone mortar. The raw material can be bought everywhere from supermarkets to pavement stalls. These days there are some ready-made pastes but either way it is a cooling, antiseptic beauty product. Farmers paint it on in thick layers for super sun protection and office ladies powder their faces so delicately that it is barely noticeable but has the effect of lightening their complexions by several sophisticated shades.

Boys love it just as much as girls. Mothers paint their children's faces with leaves and flowers or spots and stripes before sending them out in the morning, fingerprinted with loving care. While eating dinner one night, I watched a young lad, supposed to be helping in his father's noodle shop, so absorbed in painting his nose and cheeks with kitten whiskers that he was oblivious to his surroundings. I took him completely by surprise with a mew of appreciation. We both fell about laughing.

Unfortunately, thanaka is not so much appreciated in other Asian countries, whose inhabitants look down on it as a low, dirty habit, and the stoic Myanmar girls employed as maids are scolded by their madams and forced to wash away this little vestige of home comfort.

If I thought the pale yellow colour suited my complexion just a little better, I would certainly cheer up my friends by wearing it myself.

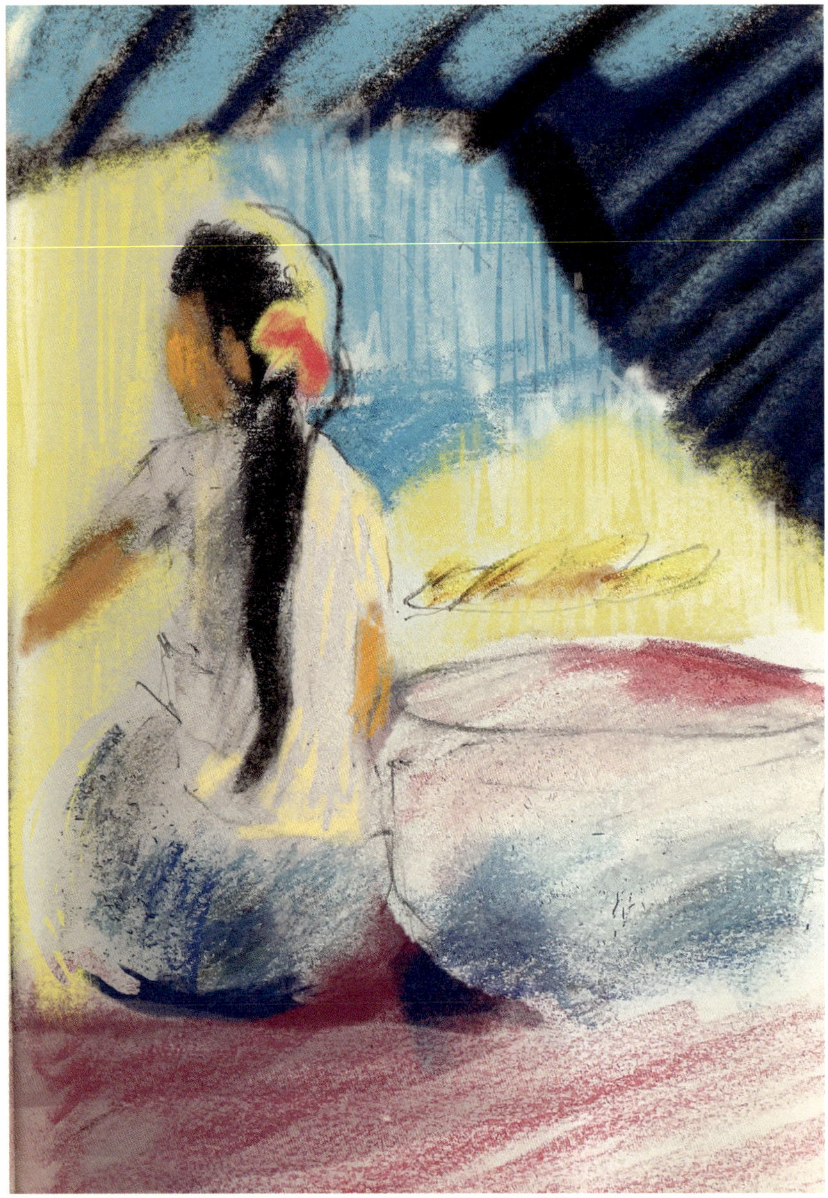

Mohinga – Soup. traditional breakfast

Modern Kit
Narrator: *Adaw Gyi*

My Dearest Darling Gazelles,

'All things considered there are only two kinds of men in the world: those that stay at home and those that do not.' Rudyard Kipling.

When it was time for Lwin to depart for the West there was so much business and pleasure to attend to the entire family traveled to Rangoon for a week. They took the overnight ferry and disembarked in the early hours of the morning. Daw Bu Ma was immediately confronted with a vision of her son's future world. An official masculine world of business facts and figures laid out in columns, all transposed into the wide paved streets and imposing architecture of the colonial capital. Buildings with square cut corners and polished glass on the outside, opening into commercial banking halls and vast warehouses supported by steel pillars on the inside. This was the foreigners' land of law and order. She was impressed, but not intimidated as the architects intended. Even as she raised her eyes to admire the future she could smell the past. She took a deep breath, in and out, wrinkling the very fine nose which her husband was so fond of, savouring the wood smoke curling out from a back street and rotten fish paste in the drains. A trace of salt on the hot air. Rust and peeling paint. A coolie walked past with a bamboo pole and two baskets balanced on his shoulders. Men and boys harnessed themselves like animals between the shafts of carts, hauling richer men from one lucrative appointment to the next. Daw Bu Ma sensed the wet fingers of the monsoon probing between the iron ribs of these imposing buildings, vegetable capillaries silently prising apart the bricks and mortar.

Setting thoughts of the past aside she engaged two horse-drawn gharries which delivered her party to the biggest, most modern, most well-appointed department store in the city. Now her son was invited to live and study amongst the foreigners she would make sure he had everything he required

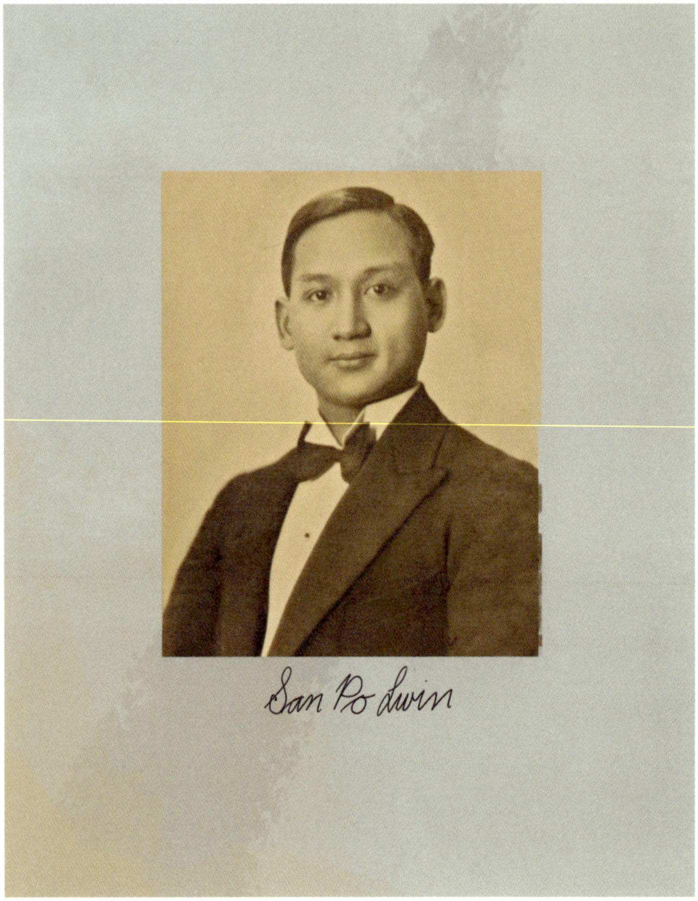

San Po Lwin made his mother proud

to hold his head high. He would need modern kit, a comfortable travelling suit to wear on deck, sports wear, day wear, evening wear, indoor wear, outdoor wear, underwear, and most importantly a pair of stout leather shoes, not forgetting a black umbrella and a rattan walking cane. All of these desirable things, advertised in the shop windows, were carefully inspected by the sisters. Every inch of San Po Lwin was measured by the superior Indian tailor who prepared the garments in a very short time. His sisters poked and prodded and when the work was finished they declared their brother fit to meet King George.

Having purchased everything a young man about town could possibly want, anywhere in the world, including a set of ruby shirt studs, the girls turned their gaze on their own reflections in the shop mirrors and said they would die if they didn't have see through nylon blouses and lacy corsets. U Tun Hla refused his daughters nothing but as for him, he kept one old fashioned silk paso for best and one pair of comfortable velvet sandals – they were all he needed to attend weddings and funerals for all the years he had left. Daw Bu Ma said if her daughters wanted to look like modern miss they would have to behave like modern miss and earn their keep. She ordered a new typewriter to keep them busy but even she could not resist something special for herself – the most elegant pair of bright blue leather shoes with a bar and button. When she wore them to church on Sundays her friends would know she was a modern woman and she would proudly tell them her son was in a high place given to him by the foreigners. The final purchase was chosen by Lwin. An exquisite pen with a black and green striped body which reminded him of the beetles he collected when he was a boy in the village. All of San Po Lwin's fine things were laced with camphor balls and packed into termite-proof black tin trucks with his name and the instructions, 'HOLD' or 'CABIN' and 'BERTH' written across the top in white painted capital letters.

The grand shopping excursion finished in a barber shop where the chairs reclined and revolved in remarkable ways. The barber gave the boys English cuts and the girls wanted to have their hair cut short as illustrated in the magazines but Daw Bu Ma draw the line and said no, at least for the time being.

Finally, there was a visit to a fashionable studio photographer in the Chinese quarter. U Tun Hla and Daw Bu Ma were seated on imposing carved wooden chairs; Lwin and his two brothers stood respectfully behind their parents wearing matching suits with bow ties, their English cuts parted on one side. Lwin wore his leather shoes, although he knew they would not be seen in the photograph. The three girls sat at their parents' feet on a deep red carpet. On that occasion U Tun Hla and Daw Bu Ma forsook their traditional Karen dresses and wore smart Bamar costumes excepting for one detail. Daw Bu Ma wore her still gloriously long black hair neatly wrapped with a headband and a flower at the side in traditional Karen style. When the photographer pulled the black cloth over his head and called out 'Smile, one, two, three,' his subjects composed their faces with solemn expressions befitting the seriousness of the occasion.

The young people had no difficulty adjusting to the novelties of city life. They slept late as if they had all the time in the world and took breakfast in downtown tea shops, lingering over the morning papers. Pawah, the famous white elephant and his owner, a fellow Karen named Dr. Saw Durmay Po Min were headline news. Po Min had first come to public attention, at least in his native village, when a chicken miraculously laid an egg in his pocket from a seated position on his shoulder. He was undoubtedly a clever man. He had captured Pawah in the jungle when Pawah was a baby, one and a half years old and less than four feet high. Contrary to village opinion, popular journalists in Rangoon painted Po Min to be an outright villain. They claimed the wealth of the country, including the noble white elephant Pawah, was being stolen away to foreign lands and why was nothing done about it? White elephants were sacred animals. When Lord Buddha returned to earth he would be seated on a white elephant, but Po Min was planning to export Pawah and make a lot of money for himself by entertaining the colonial masters at The Empire Exhibition in London. When the inevitable bad luck, famines, floods and plagues rained down on the land, the Bamar people would know who was to blame. It was a very bad omen. The foreigner dogs were treated with more respect than the rightful owners of the country. It was an insult. Anyone with eyes could see that Burma was a prostitute to the English foreigners. Po Min had been offered vast amounts of money for his elephant but he refused to change his mind.

In Lwin's opinion it was about time the backward people of his country caught up with science. Pawah was nothing more than a distraction. While Buddha was meditating on his mythical white elephant God's engineers had invented aeroplanes and pretty soon people would be queuing up to buy tickets to fly around the world at high speed. White elephants were an expensive thing of the past. The most interesting fact about Pawah was that he was not a painted white elephant like the American version but had been proved to be a true and rare albino with white skin all over and pink eyes. It was noticed that Thin, the family entertainer, was unusually quiet. The girls teased him, saying he was jealous of Lwin because he would be returning home to feed the village pigs while his brother strolled along the streets of London Town and took tea with Pawah at The Empire Exhibition in Wembley.

On the appointed day of Lwin's departure Daw Bu Ma and her girls made sure they had clean hankies ready to mop up the inevitable tears and the family made their way down Strand Road to the pier, where the black and dripping hull of the liner soared over shoals of smaller boats that clustered around it. There were people, thousands of people, all colours, all religions and all classes. Export of rice and teak, gold, rubies and sapphires. And more people. White babies taken home for the good of their health and education. Babies wrapped in shawls stitched by nuns and maiden aunts. Golden babies and their mothers abandoned in the dust. Western women wearing precious gems, carrying pet dogs in their arms. Privileged female voices commanding beautiful native boys and girls to run their errands. Cars and engines for rice mills and timber mills arriving. The railway tracks. The sea lanes. Tugs. Fishtail ferries with school children and workers from the far side of the river. Oars, sails and steam. Ropes and chains. Christians, Buddhists, Armenians, Arabians, commanding Scottish voices. So many tears were shed on the pontoon bridges. Daw Bu Ma saw a young woman with a swelling belly and a young child in hand fall on the ground in front of a turbaned man. He turned on his well-polished heel and boarded the ship with disregard. Daw Bu Ma pushed a silver coin into the uncomprehending child's hand.

All of this was perfectly normal except for one extraordinary thing. Surrounded by a crowd of Karen boys one small elephant and one large elephant were preparing to board the ship. It was Pawah the albino, gleaming white in contrast to his black skinned companion, Moora Aung, and the director of operations was none other than Thin. He appeared to be waving his arms around, brandishing a bull hook. Both elephants successfully flew through the air. One supposed they were suspended on ropes but looked as if they were supernatural. They disappeared down the hatch, into the hold with delightful precision. The family were stunned. Not one of them could find a thing to say, not even the girls. Thin had a lot of explaining to do. Without consulting anyone he had secured himself a job, not pig keeper but elephant keeper. Apparently Po Min had greeted him with inexpressible happiness and immediately offered him the position of volunteer elephant tamer in the school holidays, with possible promotion if he did well. He told his parents he would be travelling to London and America with Pawah and the best band of young Karens a fellow could ever expect to meet. It was a fait accompli. U Tun Hla and Daw Bu Ma were not sending one son West, they were sending two.

Of course, at heart, both boys felt a little emotional when they said goodbye to their family. For a fraction of a second they felt apprehensive, but the final parting was brief and they were distracted by directing Lwin's luggage on board. Thin had none. Having said their farewells the family did not linger. That evening Daw Bu Ma sat alone, noting all of her city purchases in pencil on the pages of her spotless account book. Mr Rudyard Kipling might say there are two kinds of men in the world, those that remain at home and those that leave but from a mother's point of view there are three. Those that remain, those that leave and those that return. When Daw Bu Ma bravely waved her sons goodbye she had no way to tell which kind they were. Before retiring to bed she prayed for God to protect her boys on their long ocean voyage. At the same time she beseeched him to protect her daughters from black-hearted foreigners wearing turbans.

Family Values
Narrator: *Linda Lewin*

Email letter received from Aunty Nettie:
Linda, Dearest English niece. 17th February, 2011.
Thank you for your compliments. While I have life left in me I will spend it on my Western relatives. I have a patient who is your third cousin, Marcheta, her brother and I took her to the Baptist clinic, the place where you bought Karen shirt and longyi, we paid her expenses.
The girl is very weak and she is expecting a baby boy in two weeks' time. Her condition is so poor, only when she got drip she got better. She remains in the clinic. We have all the health checks done, the doctor said she might have TB.

This email is typical of Aunty Nettie and the family elders caring for less well off relations. They never question their duty although they might get a little judgemental at times. My Karen extended family could best be described as an interdependent tribe in which all members, rich or poor, play their parts in supporting each other. The system depends on knowing your family history and in our case that history is rooted in the village, Chaung Zauk. Whenever I visited the family compound in Yangon they would say this boy or that girl is from the village. These young people may have been Cinderella servants but they were cheerful. I hope they were paid for their service. I'm sure they benefited from seniors' advice and education. Working for a rich relative in town can be a step towards getting a better job in Myanmar or overseas.

Not only Karens, but Myanmar people in general are fantastically generous and never seem to begrudge their charitable obligations. Every morning the entire country receives a lesson in giving and receiving from the Buddhist monks who process the streets with their begging bowls. This ease of giving is fortunate because in Myanmar the state does not provide much in the way of social services and very often appears hostile to the people it professes to serve. The idea of a health service, by right and free at the point of delivery, is beyond public imagination. Family and community are the Myanmar solution. It was noticed and approved that the two sisters, Hilary and I, shared our money from a single purse.

Aunty Nettie always had a young person in tow. One afternoon she arrived at my hotel with a girl of about fourteen years old, not a relation but a child who needed rescuing. We sat at a table with cold drinks and I tried to explain I was powerless to do anything. Nettie didn't understand why I had to say no. The girl's father had died and she had been employed as maid of all work by a family in town. At the end of one year she took her wages home and gave everything to her mother, who felt obliged to spend it on a feast for her neighbours. I was shocked at the mother's profligate behaviour.

The girl returned to work. Unfortunately she dropped her employer's baby on the floor in the middle of the night and got the sack. Her employer was demanding money from her. Nettie suggested I take the girl to England and give her to my father because he was an old man who should have help. The girl's qualifications were: she could speak a few words of English – not many, I thought. She would work hard and could sleep anywhere, and she knew how to cook rice because Nettie had been training her. Nettie apparently knew the right people and she would have the girl listed as a refugee. No problem with the paper work. My father might have been quite at home with this idea and I would love him to have a beautiful little Karen girl to take care of him. I know he would be kind to her and she would do all his housework. I tried to explain, we don't do this sort of thing in the UK – it's against the law. Father would be put in jail for people smuggling or employing underage girls who should be in school. I could tell none of that washed with Aunty Nettie. On that day I must have been a disappointment.

Of course the Karens appreciate worldly wealth just as much as any other people. In the west we say, remember you can't take your money with you, it's no use when you're dead, but most of us assume we can cling onto our money until the day of judgement. We are taught to be prudent and save for our old age. Money secures our independence and we say there is nothing more valuable than that.

History has taught the Karens very different economic lessons and it taught them the hard way. They have a delightful way of laughing at themselves and calling themselves lazy but in their hearts they must know the rewards of hard work in Myanmar are at very best, uncertain. They are living proof that saving money and planning for the future is pointless because natural and political disasters have a bad habit of taking everything away.

There are no banks in the villages. A person cannot save his or her money in a non existent bank account. They could try putting it under the bed or they might think a hole in the ground would be safer but if you attempt to save your paper money in a hole in the ground in a monsoon climate it will rot and stink to high heaven. I know this because I was made responsible for a bag of honest but truly filthy lucre, which had been faithfully saved in a hole in the ground, awaiting my arrival to distribute to the village children, and I had to store it a long way from my nose. Conclusion: money may not be worth the paper it's printed on, especially in a monsoon climate.

In a village if you have food you share it because you cannot store it. If you have money, spend it on your family and friends today because it can easily be devalued tomorrow. If you have gold and gems, enjoy wearing them. You can take them with you when you have to run. This brings me back to the young girl's profligate mother. Give your neighbours a feast and they will remember their social obligation to pay you back in due season. Investing in a complex network of community relationships, a you scratch my back and I'll scratch yours system, pays far better dividends than any other kind of bank account in Myanmar.

There is only is one thing the Karens say can never be stolen away or devalued and that is education. More valuable than silver or gold. Spend your money on education, study hard and reap the benefits. But this begs a question. Just where are the beneficial jobs in Myanmar?

According to Aunty Nettie, my father, Hilary and I were welcome in any Karen home and every Karen home was our home. Although we looked like foreigners, talked and thought like foreigners we were not – we were Karens. We were never visitors in the delta. From the beginning we were known to be family. That was quite simply a fact.

I was entertained and shepherded around by all of my father's cousins, my senior family members in Myanmar, but Aunty Nettie was the chief organiser who took responsibility for every aspect of our foreigner well-being. If she sometimes seemed a little slow in replying to my emails from Scotland it was probably because she was out of town on a 'case.' Exactly what kind of a 'case' was hard to tell. It ranged from murders to evictions to work place injustice. I believed her when she said she stood in front of the bulldozers. A lot of people depended on Aunty Nettie riding to the rescue but whenever I needed her she appeared, as if by telepathy.

In Myanmar, there are foreigner prices and local prices for goods and services. When we were with Nettie, she made sure we were part of the local economy. She was thrifty and her budgeting skills were something any of our Scottish Aunties would have approved of. Nothing escaped her notice and no task was too big or too small. For instance – engaging a taxi by stealth. We were instructed to keep our foreigner faces out of sight while she went ahead, pretending to be a little old grandmother from the village. Once she had hooked an unsuspecting driver at a rock bottom rate, she commanded him to double back and pick us up. Too late he realised his mistake. He was not part of our family.

Centre stage is not my preferred position but every year I would set aside my Western embarrassment for what I hoped was the greater good and go on stage in the village, the foreign celebrity, star of a public ceremony donating blankets and mosquito nets. It was important to do this in public, to be seen to be fair and even handed but useful as these goods were, the acknowledgement of family caring went way beyond monetary price. My cousin made this very clear when she explained she would accept a love gift from her foreign 'uncle.' She meant my father, but I could see she was embarrassed to accept Western charity, even on behalf of others. She had no desire to explain her actions or make herself accountable to anyone outside the family. I wanted to give, I thought there were some simple and easy things which could be done to improve prospects for the village children and I was blessed by generous friends willing to support me but I wanted a documented trail of Western style accountability. Why was that such a problem?

Come the latest military coup I realised just how dangerous traceable documentary evidence of accountability can be. Anyone, including charity workers, who comes to the attention of the hostile administration, is putting themselves at risk. Anyone in possession of goods which the bullies can appropriate for themselves is at risk. Foreign aid can be and is turned into weapons against the very people it is intended to benefit. I hung my head in shame. My Western assumptions of right and wrong ways of doing things were just not applicable here, and they never had been. I asked my elderly Karen uncle, a retired university chancellor and survivor of two coups in his lifetime, for advice. His attitude was straightforward, 'When they ask me for money I give. You must teach them,' and he followed through by saying, if I ever needed money I only had to ask him. I would be treated like any other family member.

Aunty Nettie had an impressive network of people she had helped and who were apparently delighted to help her in return. She was an operator in the exchange and barter economy but when she added Christianity to the mix it could lead to extreme behaviour. If a well-meaning relative gave Nettie a coat, she would immediately give it away to someone who needed it more, and there was never any shortage of people who needed more. Relatives grumbled she was letting the well dressed side of the family down but Nettie set no store on her personal appearance. She was a master of disguise who could perfectly well adjust her looks to act any part she chose. She was amazing and kind and generous. She knew God would reward her good deeds but she also required generous amounts of acknowledgement here on earth, thanks and respect for her good deeds. She was human after all.

From East to West: A First Class Passenger

Narrator: *Adaw Gyi*

My Dearest Darling Gazelles,

'It's so easy to love a little, flirt a little on a big ship even if a husband or a bridegroom or duty with a big 'D' is waiting at the other end'. Amy J Baker, 'Six Merry Mummers'.

One hundred industrious years ago, in the roaring years of the nineteen twenties, the foreigner ship left the muddy waters of the Irrawaddy delta and squared up to the ocean waves. Life on board was a perfect miracle of organisation ruled over by the ship's captain. It took a mere three weeks to travel five and a half thousand miles around the world from east to west, from the Indian Ocean to the English Channel, by way of the Suez Canal, and finally arriving at Tilbury docks. The pistons hammered day and night according to the timetable, without faltering, from beginning to end of the voyage.

Lwin and Saw Durmay Po Min were first class passengers. Although he had heard sailors' tales of furniture being hurled around the cabins and broken crockery flying overhead Lwin could not conceive of any storms fierce enough to cause the ship's steel hull to deviate its measured course. He settled down to enjoy the journey and he had a small library of law text books to read along the way, but it turned out life on board was rather busier than he planned. Po Min made his well fed, well tailored presence felt immediately. He had too much energy to be contained by the ship's elegant indoor saloons; he needed open space around him. His name, which he had chosen himself, translated as 'black biting ant' but the way he paced the decks gave Lwin the impression of a black buffalo endlessly circling, nose to tail, in a too small pen.

In the elephant world Po Min was well known but his grand ambitions were not satisfied. He intended to be an international success. He was a great admirer of the British Nation and the Prince of Wales and had sent two of his elephants to the British Empire Exhibition in Wembley, where all nations who owed allegiance to the red, white and blue flag met on common ground and came to know each other. He was a fervent believer in his own version of Christianity and considered Pawah to be a gift from God, confirming his status and ambition because after all, white elephants were the sacred property of kings. His present plan was to take Pawah to London Zoo and then to New York for a season with Barnum and Bailey's Circus. In this way he would demonstrate the sterling character and talents of the Karen people to the world, or at least to the one quarter of its peoples who belonged to the Great British Empire and the Americas. He would use the profits to found a school and promote the education of Karen boys. Po Min had five such boys in his entourage. There was only one impediment – his English was poor and it was Thin's responsibility to act as translator. Thin was destined to fill the bill perfectly and Pawah had no choice in the matter. Po Min would make the white elephant a star of stage and screen, like it or not.

Within one day on board, Lwin and Thin had a multitude of new friends inviting them to join tennis and card games. They slicked back their hair, laced up their deck shoes and set out to enjoy nautical social life. Their striking looks and charming manners were noticed by the young ladies, especially at the fancy dress parties, and no one could find a bad word to say about them.

The brothers were allocated seats in the dining saloon alongside two Bamar students making their way to Oxford University. The young men eyed each other suspiciously over the polished cutlery and stiff peaked napkins. After several excellent courses, one of the Bamar students, round glasses perched on the end of his nose, dared to whisper, he intended to work for independence. He was ready to spill his own red blood for his country's freedom. Damnation to the colonisers, the missionaries, the chief commissioner this and the chief secretary that along with all their insults and their land taxes, although he would make an exception for the whisky. He raised his glass in toast. To Lwin's irritation his younger brother was immediately engaged, intrigued, and seconded the toast, but Lwin had heard all of these arguments in Calcutta and thankfully his fellow students had been persuaded to follow the path of peaceful non-cooperation, so far. Lwin was distracted for a moment by the man's stained shirtfront. How could a man who hadn't mastered the use of a knife and fork, who couldn't construct a decent English sentence, expect to be taken seriously. It wasn't worth engaging in argument. He agreed the country was in a dreadful state and left the table.

On deck in the cool air, encircled by the vast black sky, full to the brim with shining stars, he stood for a moment at the centre of the universe, remembering the men of past times who had nothing but the stars to guide them. Times had changed. With each turn of the ship's propeller the distance travelled increased, as the distance to be covered correspondingly decreased, manifest by the endlessly trailing sea foam from the stern of the boat. It was a comforting certainty. He remembered his father, so strong and fearless – he could make anything with his bare hands – and his mother, who turned her accounts to a profit every year. He would make them proud and he would find his place in the law courts in London, the centre of the civilised world. His equanimity was restored.

Thin made friends with and found out everything there was to know about everyone on the boat. It was his way. People confided in him and he couldn't help himself. He spent a lot of time with a Karen boy very close to his own age. The boy, named San Dwe, was one of Po Min's protégés, who had previously never left home and was shy to speak. In between bouts of sea sickness San Dwe and Thin discussed the A to Z of elephants. A is for ankus, the awful spear thing some drivers use to prick their animals. B is for big – most elephants are. C is for curse, which is what happens when a white elephant is removed from its native country. D is for drunk and also for disorderly, which is something you never want for your elephant or his driver. E is obviously for elephant and for ear. Elephants have very big ears. F is for fright, which is what you would get if an elephant entered your dining room looking for his dinner. G is for God, who gave Po Min his white elephant to be used for great and noble purposes, and so on.

San Dwe's English improved enormously under Thin's tuition. San Dwe had endless stories of his own about the superior qualities of elephants, how clever and gentle they are, how to take a thorn out of an elephant's foot and how an elephant never forgets a service, good or bad. Once upon a

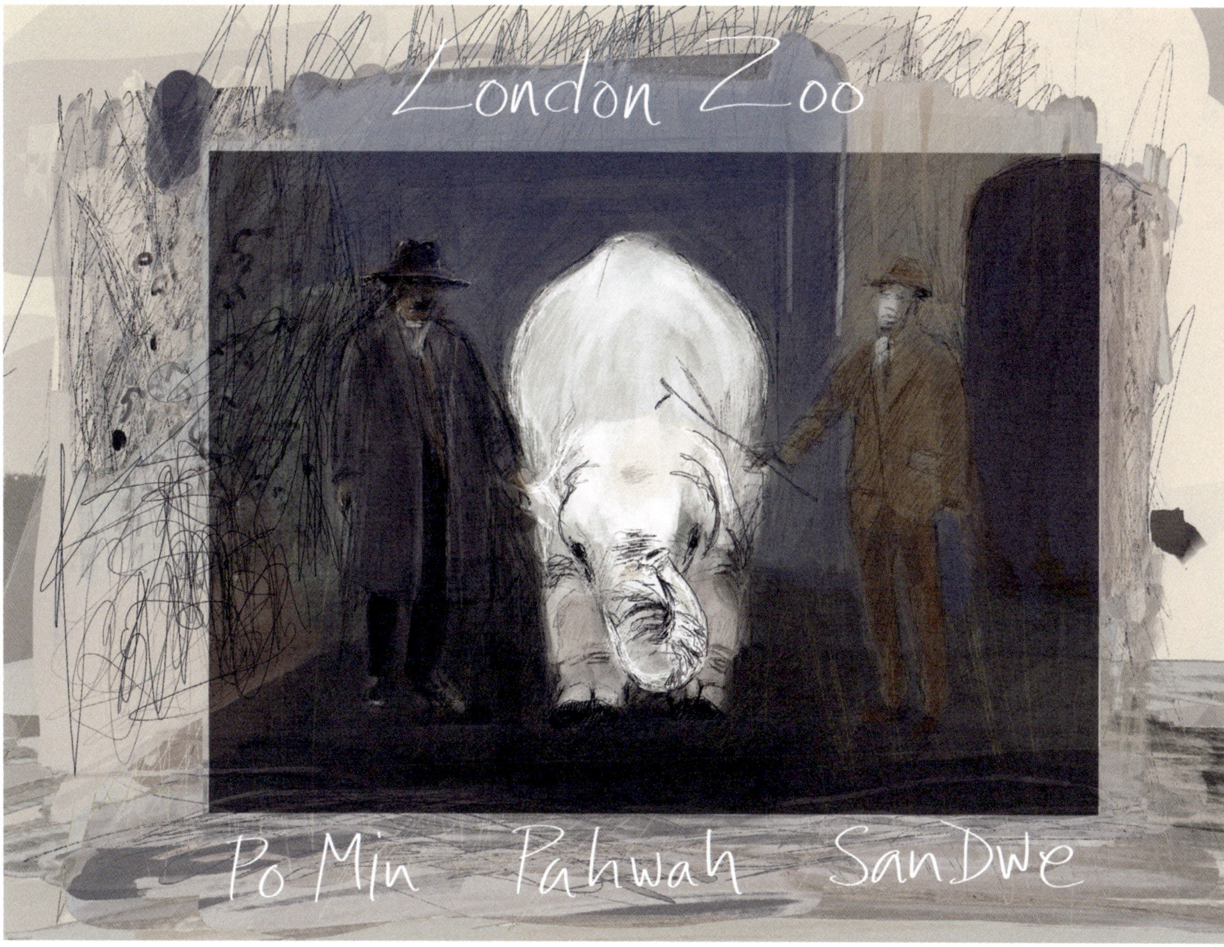

time the old king of Burma had stables full of elephants, for himself and his wives and his children and his servants. Thin relayed all this information in his most entertaining way to the children and their mothers who ventured into the hold with their left over breakfast buns to feed Moora Aung and Pawah. The elephants stretched out their trunks cautiously and so politely, accepting the small gifts.

My Dears, if you had seen Daw Bu Ma's sons disembark at Tilbury docks, at the head of an oriental procession, with Pawah and Moora Aung, complete with golden umbrellas, you would have thought, and they would have agreed, they were young princes. Pawah made a brief appearance at London Zoo where he starred in a news film. San Dwe wore a Western suit with a felt brimmed hat for the occasion. The film shows Pawah the albino, and his black companion Moora Aung. Pawah was too young to be ridden but he was well trained. He paid close attention to instructions and made a brave attempt to roll over and play dead on the rather uncomfortable concrete floor of the zoo compound, and the pair became quite famous.

On the strength of his excellent performance San Dwe was engaged to look after the zoo elephants until the regular Mahout, Said Ali, returned from his winter break in India. San Dwe had full responsibility to care for the zoo's elephants but he was not entrusted to be a driver. That was Said Ali's job and he was famous for it. The remaining members of Po Min's troop, including Thin, continued on the second leg of their journey to New York. Po Min left San Dwe strict instructions to say his prayers every day and not to let him down. When he returned he expected a good report.

Batchelor in Town
Narrator: *Adaw Gyi*

My Darling Gazelles,

'*This song of two humans is of no place and every place. You might hear it anywhere, at any time.*' Quote from the spectacular Hollywood 1927 black and white film, 'Sunrise', which San Po Lwin and Lucienne may well have seen. A young married man is seduced by a sophisticated city temptress and falls in love with city life but eventually realises the error of his ways and returns to his wife and family in the village.

There had been a great deal of money talk on the boat. One glorious blond hero, known to his friends as Piglet P, who happened to be very good at deck sports and didn't care if the natives were listening because he knew they couldn't rub two decent words of English together, proclaimed he intended to invest all of his family fortune in a frontier goldmine, a bargain and an absolute fortune winning certainty. From his pocket, he pulled a fragment of glittering rock, given to him by a tribal chief who promised to manage everything for Burmese peanuts. An excellent chap who had no idea what kind of a fortune he was sitting on. At night Mr Piglet P removed the rock from his cotton shorts and placed it under his pillow. What happy recurring dreams he had of his old man welcoming him home with open arms and high praise. He couldn't wait to set the wheels in motion. Mr Piglet P was prepared to bet his grandmother's inheritance, with or without approval. He would evict his parents and sell the family home if necessary. Lwin had heard enough about frontier affairs and primitive hill tribes – Wild Red Karenni with golden rings around their necks, and mountain men, armed to the teeth with ancient rifles, quite possibly head hunters with tattooed arms and legs, who owed allegiance to no one. He concluded that his future investments would be better placed in peaceful London bricks and mortar occupied by law abiding, hard working Great British civil servants.

With her permission, he spent his mother's money on a new house in Acton Town and only five minutes walk from Acton station, one hour commute to The Temple. The journey was simple, all one had to do was arrive on the platform on time, at the same time, every day, remembering that shortcuts on foot across the railway track were strictly prohibited by a man with nothing more frightening than an embarrassingly loud whistle. On his homeward journey he was greeted by the local children playing their games on the street. He always had a smile for them and a few sweets to distribute from his overcoat pockets, just the same as he did at home.

Lwin was not short of familiar company in London. His mother and his college professors had provided him with a well-connected address book. His first social call was to Daw Phar Hmee. He knew she was one of the very first women called to the Bar, and certainly the first Bamar woman. In addition, according to his mother, she came from a very good family. Daw Phar Hmee advised him never to stand on the kerb waiting for the traffic to stop as it did at home, because here in this city it never would. If he hadn't got a raincoat he would need to purchase one immediately because already, the leaves were falling from the trees and it rained nearly every day, especially in the winter. If he ever wanted to catch a bus he had better develop an ear for the local accent, which was quite different from any English they had learned at home. Once he had attended to these things, he might like to take some exercise in the parks or rowing on the river because Daw Phar Hmee was convinced that the good health of Western people, especially the girls, was directly linked to their love of exercise and long refreshing walks in the countryside. With that good advice she was sorry to leave him so abruptly, but it was time for her to return to the home country. Her family were very impatient to see her and there was so much work to do for the girls at home.

Lwin took her advice seriously and bought a raincoat but weather was never a problem to him. He wrote to his sisters and told them Londoners had no need for rubies and sapphires because God supplied them with glittering frosty diamonds every winter morning and when it snowed he was entranced. He ran out into the street to play with the children. He was fascinated by London life. Everything was so efficient compared to Rangoon or even Calcutta, where the traffic could be brought to a standstill by a cow in the middle of the grandest street. There was none of that sort of silliness here.

Lwin was especially fascinated by the girls, so modern, so advanced. In his opinion they took their exercise running for trains and jumping on and off the London Underground escalators on their way to and from work, as nimble as circus acrobats. They seemed to have business in every part of town and let nothing stand in their way. Surely they didn't have any free time left over for walking in the parks? Their elbows and their tongues were equally sharp and when pressed in a crowd, they used both extremely effectively. With their short hair and bright red lipstick they all looked like film stars and Lwin was a fan.

Although he considered himself to be a modern young fellow, Lwin felt that in matters of courtship an old-fashioned formal approach would be best. Two fascinating young women happened to live next door. Both of them went to work dressed in the very latest, short-skirted Chanel suits and they had captivating French accents. Either one would make a delightful companion and it might be hard to choose which one he preferred. One of the girls worked in a millinery studio. If Daw Bu Ma and his sisters had been there they would have ordered a hat for every day of the week and in the process, discovered everything necessary to know. In their absence, Lwin formally invited the whole family, the mother, Mrs Auberhoffer, the two daughters and the younger brother to join him in a private box at the theatre. The evening was a huge success. Lwin's guests were tremendously excited and amused by the old-fashioned style of the invitation but Mrs Auberhoffer was encouraged to think it was an indication of Lwin's serious and good intentions. Her daughters' good looks attracted attention but Lucienne would be thirty years old before she knew it and she had already turned away too many of the men so carefully selected by her mother.

Lwin soon decided commuting was not quite the thing and he must have a new car. One Sunday afternoon he appeared in the street and made all his admirers laugh by tooting the horn of a sweet little two seater. He had an eye for the young Auberhoffer girl but it was the older one, Lucienne, who eagerly stepped forward, saying she would love to go for a spin and perhaps he could teach her to drive? For both Lucienne and Lwin English was a second language but language is no barrier to love. Lwin was not disadvantaged by any lack of vocabulary. Lucienne could teach him French, a language so well suited to romance. He entertained her enormously by shouting out a few words above the noise of the engine.

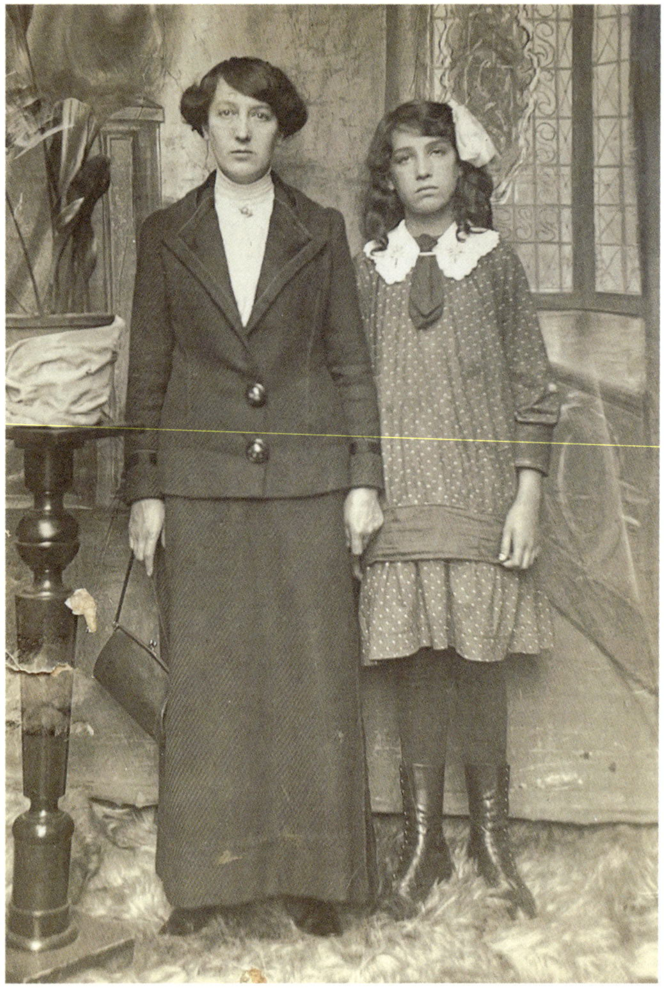

The life she left behind

Lwin soon discovered Lucienne was beautiful, quick-witted and amusing, a spirited and determined young spinster who earned her living in a millinery workshop. Her father had brought his young family to London from the south of France but when war came he was afraid of being mistaken for a quisling, what with his German name. He wanted to be seen to do his duty so, I have been informed, he quite unnecessarily volunteered for the front line trenches, the sad result being he died defending his adopted king and country. Lucienne was her father's favourite and missed him dreadfully. Since his death she had been the main family bread winner, modelling hats and delivering millinery to clients in their grand houses. The only fault Lwin could find in her was that she was a hopeless learner driver but nonetheless he swiftly fell head over heels in love and presented her with a beautiful driving coat complete with a fur collar. She was so dazzled by Lwin's confident good looks, his ruby shirt studs and the excitement of sitting beside him in the new car wearing a fur collar she forgot all about her daily toils and troubles. She was so distracted she discovered very little in the way of factual information but Mother soon discovered Lwin was the oldest son of an important, wealthy family in a fabulously wealthy country where he had excellent career prospects. As far as Lucienne was concerned his colourful stories of colonial life and trips to the horse races in Rangoon were all she needed to know.

When he showed her the photograph of his family and his three sisters wearing pretty tiaras and fashionable blouses she knew she could be friends with such elegant girls. In comparison the photograph her mother kept on the piano at home was a sad thing. Her father had commissioned it when he left for the war, before Lucienne was quite grown up and before she had her long curls cut into a short, fashionable bob. She had insisted on wearing her best satin dress with the hem let down and ribbons she had sewn on herself. Her mother stood by her side, weighed down in a heavy wool suit which dragged at her shoulders and made her look years older than she was. Neither of them was smiling, at each other or the camera.

Lucienne warned her mother not to introduce her to any more pot bellied British businessmen or pasty-faced local politicians. If her mother found them so attractive, well, she was young enough to marry one herself. All in all, Lucienne was tired of running around after wealthy women whose looks never improved, however much money they spent on their hats. She was tired of keeping her younger brothers and sisters in order and she had no decent romantic prospects in London, so many young men had died in the trenches along with her father. She would put on her red shoes and her red dress and go dancing with her foreign prince, the best looking man in the town. Lucienne had fallen head over high heels in love. It was a story book romance.

Your ever loving
Adaw Gyi

The Rice Bowl
Narrator: *Linda Lewin*

'*A pleasant damp country where rice grew of itself and fish came up to be caught, putrified and pickled.*' Rudyard Kipling.

San Po Thin told his daughter Snow White, '*Everything in life is political, even a bowl of rice.*' He was absolutely correct then and now.

My first impression of The Golden Land, composed of rivers and rice and villages, was glorious but in my uninformed state I struggled to understand what I was looking at. On the surface everything appeared to be just as my father and my grandfather would have known it but every kind of wealth had drained away long since. The economy was broken. Everyone looked poor. I watched men and beasts, as docile as each other, labouring side by side in the fields, women winnowing the golden grain like figures from my Ladybird Old Testament illustrations. What had been modern eighty or even one hundred years before was still in use but out of date and broken. I could not set eyes on so much as one modest farm tractor.

Aunty Nettie had scheduled a trip to the beach, which meant an hour and a half drive from Pathein, up and over the Yoma mountains on the local bus. The local bus was a very different animal from its intercity Korean relative. It was a dented blue and white workaday beast of modest build, which looked as if it might have been new around about Burmese independence in 1947. Hilary and I were escorted to the bus station at a civilised after lunch hour. We had time to watch the bus being loaded, a delightful performance. Inside, long wooden planks filled the passageway and sacks of rice were stacked between the bench seats, which meant one had to sit cross legged on top of the rice, at least to start. On the roof, sugar cane and drums of cooking oil, passenger bags piled high. The finishing touch was brightly coloured plastic stools and chairs attached like Christmas decorations to the roof bars. Strictly no passenger luggage allowed inside.

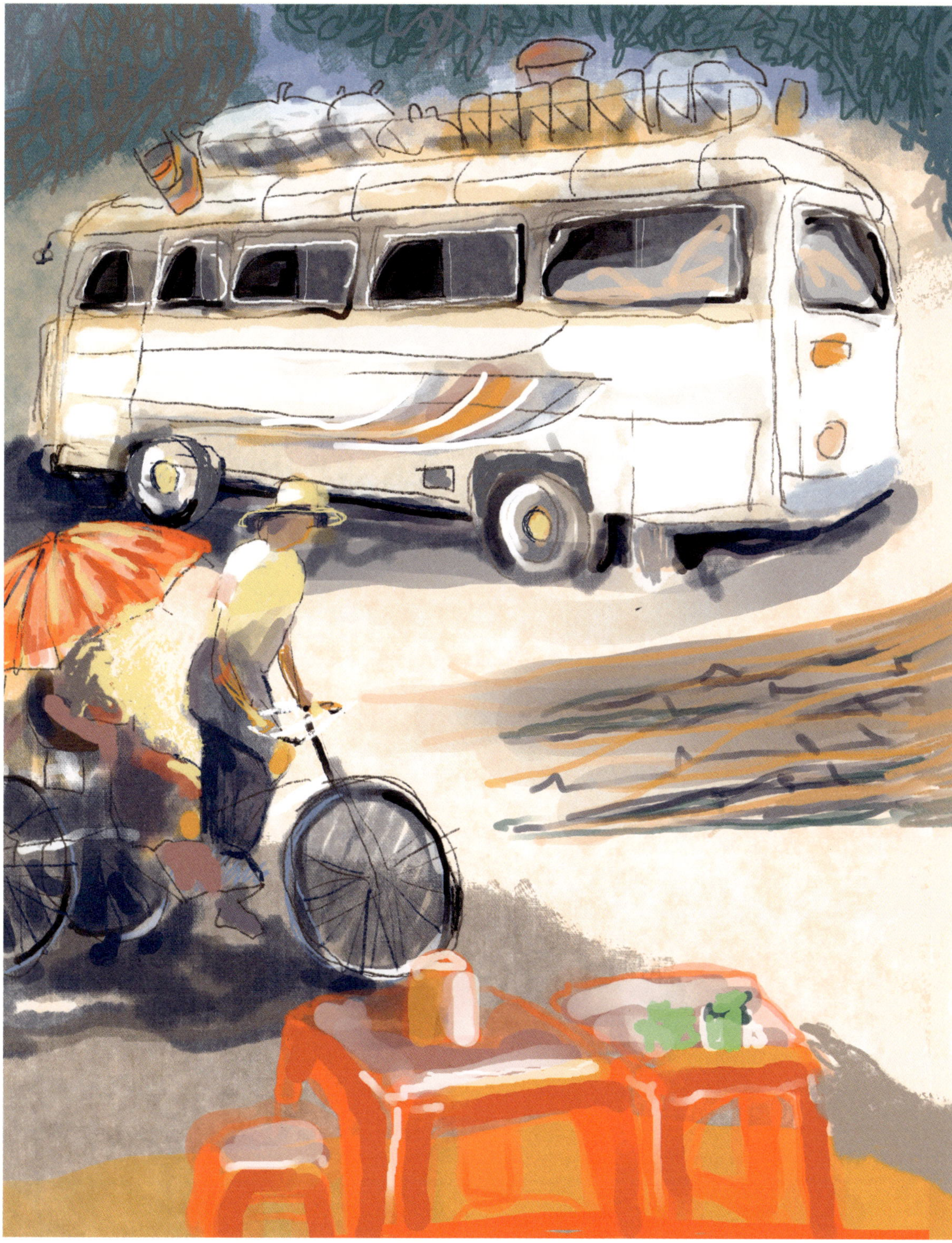

The local bus

Nettie was not frightened to face uncomfortable facts. It was obvious Western backsides were bigger than eastern backsides and the tickets on the local bus cost almost nothing even by Aunty Nettie standards, so she booked two for one seats for visitors and singles for locals. A practical plan which I appreciated and subsequently used myself. Now we realised why Aunty Nettie had suggested we leave most of our luggage behind in Yangon. There was no room for it. As for herself, Aunty Nettie simply wore everything she needed for the trip, three separate outfits one on top of the other, and she carried a plastic shopping bag for the leftovers. Again, a very practical travelling tip and good insulation against early morning mists, which in Myanmar are at least as cold as a hot summer day in Scotland. Hilary and I were directed to the second-best, front seats in the bus, immediately behind the driver. Hilary, who is very astute about things which I never notice, observed the first best seats were reserved for a monk, no doubt out of respect, and a pretty girl to give the driver something nice to look at when he was not fully occupied with looking at the road, thus ensuring he was in a good mood. We climbed into our allotted places from where we had the pleasure of observing a strapping young German traveller who refused to be separated from his extra large rucksack. Despite his best attempts at negotiations he was obliged to crawl on his hands and knees, over the planks and rice sacks all the way to the back of the bus, dragging his oversize bag along behind. Of course we smirked, but only a little. He was very cross.

There was one other person in the front of the bus who did not have a seat of his own, because he was too busy to sit on it. In 1970, for no known sensible reason, General Ne Win decided to make the change from vehicles driving on the left to vehicles driving on the right hand side of the road. It might have been on the advice of astrologers or it might have been because he had a dream, but it happened and the gentle, obliging public obeyed. At that time, all Myanmar cars were right-hand-drive vehicles so jobs on the buses were multiplied by two – a driver and an additional lookout who takes his place on the left side of the vehicle. The job of lookout is stressful because it carries the responsibility for the safety of everyone on the bus, so lookouts generally resort to chewing a calming narcotic known as betel. You can always spot a betel chewer by his dark red-stained teeth and his fascinating but off-putting habit of regularly spitting saliva into bottles and plastic bags which he carries

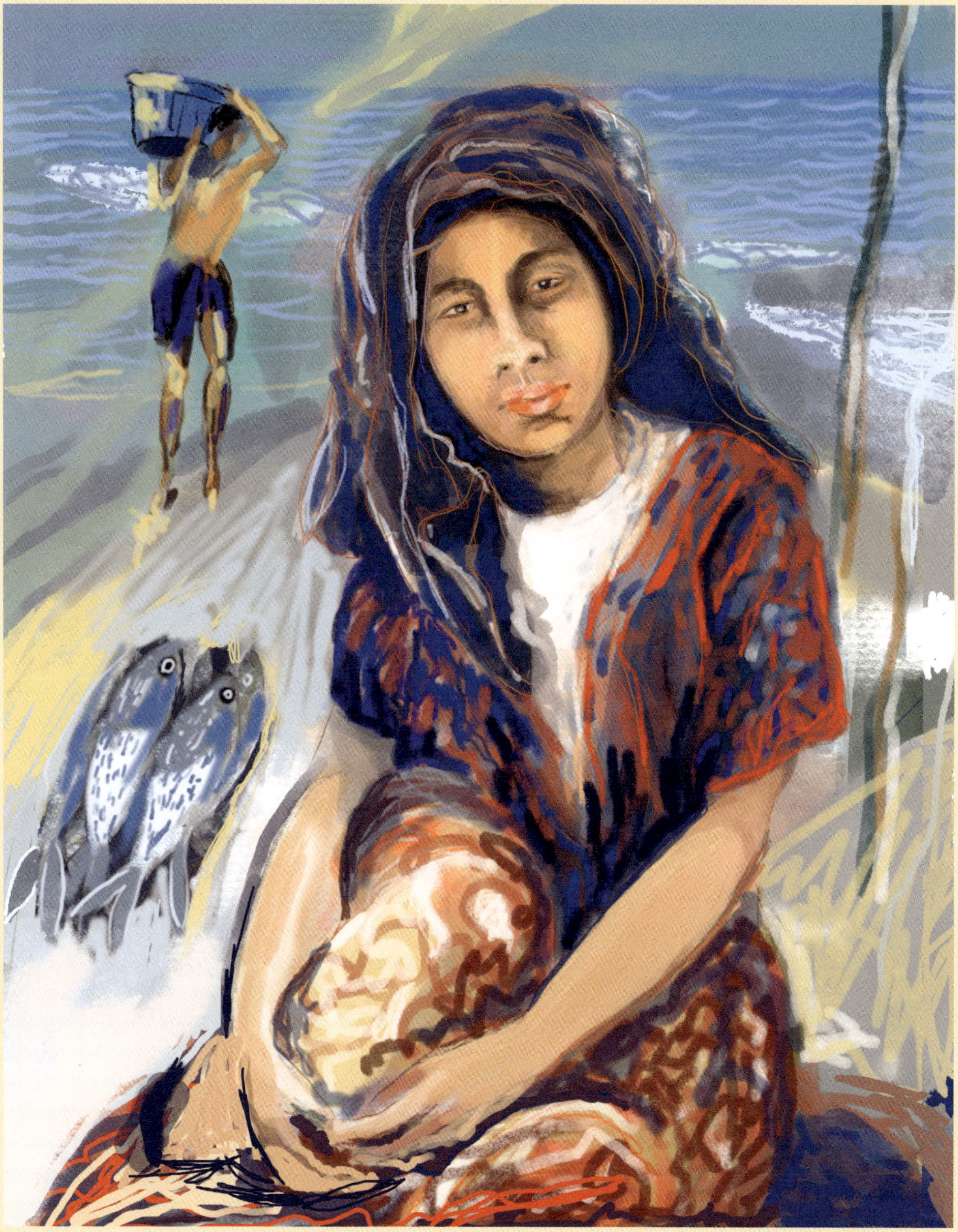

Figures in a biblical landscape

around with him, or simply on the pavement. Obviously the lookout has to be young and fit, but that is not a problem in Myanmar where statistically speaking, most men are young, less than thirty years old and as far as I can see, they are all fit. I had been wondering why the market places were full of triangular rolling pins. It turned out they were not rolling pins but chocks to put behind the wheels of buses and lorries attempting to climb hills slightly beyond their engine's capacity. Every few yards, as our bus crawled onwards and upwards, the betel-chewing lookout leapt on and off, replacing the chocks behind the wheels as necessary, thereby saving us all from careering backwards into a ditch.

Perched on top of my rice sack, looking out from the bus windows, I thought about my Grandfather, San Po Lwin, and wondered where he could possibly have found the vast quantity of money needed to travel overseas and study for admittance to The Bar in London.

The family had one answer: 'Rice. We are born with rice in our mouths and we die with rice in our mouths.' When I looked around it was there, rice or rather paddy, hidden in plain sight. January is harvest time and I could see the bountiful paddy spread out to dry on tarpaulins beside the road, all the way from Yangon to Pathein and back. I had not recognised it at first because paddy is unprocessed brown rice and so plentiful it looked like common dirt beside the road.

The difficulties of communicating in English, well learned but unpractised for so many years, did not prevent Aunty Nettie and Rose Red from making themselves absolutely clear: they were not 'from' the village, they 'owned' the village and of course I could see they understood the difference between the past glories and present day poverty of our family and of their country and felt the shame of their fallen fortunes as if somehow, it was their fault. My father said that in his childhood his family were the second-biggest land owners in Bassein. They must have had rice coming out of their ears and that meant they had money to spend. The two brothers, San Po Lwin and Nettie's father, San Po Thin, were close in age but San Po Lwin was the older and perhaps more conservative son. Aunty Nettie constantly referred to the love held between the two brothers but a little whiff of old family rivalries floated like a distracting feather through the conversation. On more than one occasion, Aunty Nettie said that my grandfather had the benefit of all the family money whereas her father had done everything for himself.

My second wondering was – how could a boy from a thatched village hut, even one with two storeys and teak pillars, possibly have found the strength of character he needed to survive life in London, the greatest city on earth, the hub of the Great British Empire, and we might think, culturally so far removed from his native home and family in the delta?

But young men are fearless by nature. San Po Lwin would have been around twenty when he left home to study in Calcutta and twenty-five when he arrived in London to qualify for the English Bar. At the same time other young men, white of course, sometimes even younger than San Po Lwin, were making the journey in the opposite direction, entrusted with managing vast territories and important affairs of the British overseas colonies and they thought nothing of it. Please do not imagine my grandfather, San Po Lwin, to be an untutored village boy, a type of Dick Whittington with nothing but dreams in his pockets. From the first day he set foot in his village school he was precision educated, machine tooled to be a fit for purpose product of the Great British Empire, moulded by an educational culture that was not much different in Bassein, Calcutta or London. The schoolmasters and mistresses of all the far flung corners of the British Empire, including American missionaries and Scottish professors, all sang from the same hymn sheet in Baptist churches, Anglican cathedrals and the dining halls of colleges designed by colonial architects. San Po Lwin may have been born in a palm thatched village farmhouse, but he was the clever son of a wealthy family whose land lay at the heart of the steam-powered delta, the great colonial rice-growing machine, where fortunes were being made and lost with every harvest. His quick-witted mother was one of the winners, willing to invest a great deal of money in the future of her family, which she equated with the education of her first son. Lwin was a promising student, one of the elite, fast-tracked by his family, the Karen community, the American Baptists and the British administrative system. Regardless of any individual's best altruistic intentions these powerful colonial forces combined with one overarching ambition, which was to make the foreigners wealthy. The Great British Empire needed San Po Lwin and others like him, local men conveniently educated to administer colonial justice and collect colonial taxes. It was all a grand adventure.

In 2014, I sat beside the upper window in what remained of Daw Bu Ma's two-storey house. My guide books said people in Myanmar sit on the floor and although it is true that local tea shops provide infant-size plastic stools for their customers so you might as well be sitting on the floor, my family and almost everyone I met sensibly preferred full size tables and chairs. My cousin Douglas sat opposite me wearing his habitual costume, a pair of children's blue Wellington boots, a torn green jumper and a bobble hat, but he was not a clown. He was a retired health care administrator. He had charm, more feminine than masculine, and he spoke English with a gentle elegance which suggested fallen aristocracy. I had observed him walking amongst the people, extending both hands in greeting and pausing to give each person due respect and attention. Always smiling.

On this occasion he waved his hand at the dilapidated, corrugated iron church which my grandfather, Lwin, had built in the 1930's heydays, the old water tanks fringed with palm trees, their decayed edges softening into the landscape, and the barefoot children playing around the bamboo and matting huts. He apologised for the general state of things in his old-fashioned English voice. I struggled to understand the history of degradation which was part of his everyday life. I could see he longed for the bygone days of the British Empire when the family had money and the children had education. 'We are ashamed,' he said. 'You find us in this pitiful state because the government took our land.'

By government, he meant the Generals and their cronies, sometimes known as The Regime or The Tatmadaw or the Junta. Between themselves they have created the country's most successful business but that is not to say they are great businessmen. They are a closed shop and they have succeeded by closing every opposing shop. General Ne Win consolidated the military position with his coup in 1962, which he followed up by setting the country on 'The Burmese Way to Socialism.' The military government assumed ownership of all land, conveniently adopting the old colonial laws for their own purposes. It didn't go well. I soon became familiar with the phrase, 'We are ashamed,' not only from my family members, but from anyone and everyone. The shame of citizens who know they and their country deserve better and don't quite understand how or where they went wrong. Not only did the government take the land, they took everything else as well. The jade and copper mines, the teak forests, the rivers, bananas and coffee, fabulous

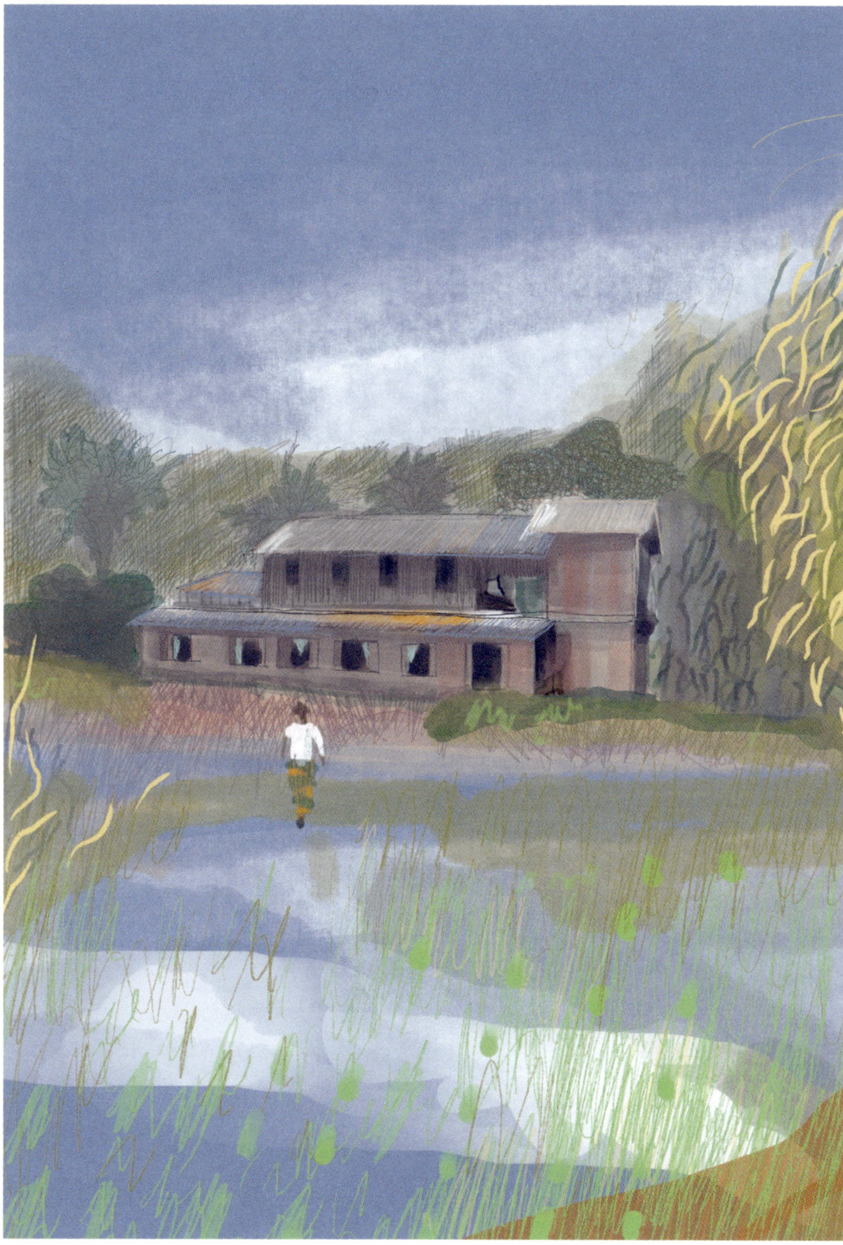

Grandfather's church and paddy fields

Inlay lake. The tourist industry. Transport and precious stones. Anything you care to think of. They took the assets of the country and put the money in their military bank accounts. So many of the citizens are damaged goods who have lost everything, including their self-respect.

Everyone in Myanmar has a village home but they don't all live there. When I became more familiar with my family village I realised two generations were missing, the older adolescents and the young parents. The paddy fields are still fabulously green but the harvest does not pay well enough to support the people who break their backs growing it. Some travel no further than the city factories for a better wage but many use employment agencies to get work overseas. Village students soon discover the school and college certificates they value so highly, the education they worked so hard to achieve and their parents sold land to pay for, are worth no more than the paper they are printed on. They accept low paid jobs, in caring, labouring and service industries, but somehow they survive and send money home. Older siblings willingly sacrifice themselves to send a brother or sister to school, build a brick house for the family or just pay for food on the table. Even a low wage in a foreign country is enough to make a difference at home. Sadly, whatever the reason for leaving, many never return to the chaotic, insecure country and the people they left behind. It just doesn't make practical economic sense.

Looking around the village I could see the place was scraped bare. One would have supposed there was nothing much left worth taking, but that was not true. What I did not know at the time was that a supersize big business with a contact address in China was surveying the land. Aunty Nettie believed they were looking for clay but she was deceived. It turned out my family village, Chaung Zauk, was destined to be the site of Pathein Industrial City and Port. A couple of years later, all the paddy fields would be parcelled into industrial plots divided by roads that resembled motorways. The village houses remain on a narrow strip of land between the industrial zone and the river. As a goodwill gift from the company the villagers have received a bare, three-room concrete school which they are expected to share with several other villages – and presumably some cash. It is impossible to know exactly what has been agreed because no one who lives in the village seems to fully understand the situation. The industrial plots are guarded by watchmen who demand to see visitors' identity cards in exchange for access to the village, but they take no responsibility for village property. The new road has become a highway for thieves. The village pigs, generators and school books – all gone with the wind.

San Po Thin Joins the Circus
Narrator: *Adaw Gyi*

My Dearest Darling Gazelles,

The circus leaves a sweet memory. Fernando Botero.

When Uncle Thin joined Barnum and Bailey-Ringling Brothers' Combined Circus in America they desired to be The Greatest Show On Earth and that became the truth. They employed famous actors and actresses, painted clowns, flying acrobats, animal keepers and all kinds of men and beasts including the human curiosities Uncle Thin refers to as 'strange' people. They owned hotels. They travelled the length and breadth of the USA in purpose built railroad cars and paraded in front of cheering crowds in a different town every week. In one of their publicity stunts they used elephants to plough a field. The list of their sensational attractions was endless. The audience appetite to pay for novelty never diminished. By all of this the circus became rich and famous throughout the world. Uncle Thin was in his element. Who does not, at some time in their life, long to run away with the circus and fly through the air in a spangled costume?

When Uncle Thin sent his letters home we worried and we didn't know what to believe but we must believe because there was the proof in an artist poster. A beautiful painting of Pawah and the boys arriving in New York harbour. Daw Bu Ma read it aloud. First And Only Genuine Sacred White Elephant Ever Permitted To Leave His Native Land. We can see Pawah is snow white and smiling, descending the gang plank on an honourable red carpet. The public are there to welcome him and the photographers' cameras are flashing. Moora Aung, the black mother elephant, is there in the background. She waits politely not to steal Pawah's limelight. The Karen boys are wearing curious costumes of many colours which we have not seen before. Uncle Thin's parents were pleased to know Po Min and his boys were so well received.

You will not be surprised to know Uncle Thin fell in love with the circus and everybody in it. While his brother Lwin sat at his desk in the city and San Dwe was confined to London Zoo, Uncle Thin adventured all over America on the circus train. He observed how God blessed the people of America with great prosperity and the train was a powerful mark of God's blessing. He travelled hundreds of miles with hardly any trouble and no expense to himself, south into Mexico and north to Canada and eventually to Hollywood. When the circus arrived at a new place everyone sprang to action. Each one had a job, setting up candy-striped tents for the performance and living quarters for the animals and their keepers all according to a marvellous plan. It was a miracle of organisation.

Uncle Thin knew nothing about elephants or the circus when he left home but he was quick to learn. Moora Aung and Pawah were housed together in a gorgeously decorated tent. The Karen boys always showed respect to the status of their charges and made them as comfortable as possible in the animal prison. It was an honour for them to do the work. Pawah and your Uncle Thin began their daily routine with an early morning bath followed by walking for pleasure. It was gratifying to see how the animals along the way paid their respects to Pawah. At the end of the day, Uncle Thin sat with Pawah and rubbed his head with his hands, just how San Dwe showed him when they were on the boat. The baby elephant drifted into a deep sleep on his own special pillow, which was unusual because the other elephants slept standing up, but they didn't have the benefit of Uncle Thin's care. Pawah needed plenty of rest because his work was demanding. Huge crowds pushed and shoved to see Pawah twice a day, standing room only. Pawah was escorted on stage by two of the boys dressed as Burmese guards and bright spotlights illuminated the stage. Pawah gleamed like raw silver and Moora Aung was polished black and shiny. Both animals wore heavy shackles on their feet. The people gasped with astonishment when they appeared.

Uncle Thin got his promotion in a very short time and this was the way it happened. One day Po Min said, 'Hey, Pathi Kwa,' meaning Bassein Boy. 'What did the public say of my lectures? Go to the back, listen to it and report to me what they say.' Po Min was upset when Uncle Thin reported the bad news he heard. The people couldn't understand a word of Po Min, what with his loud shouting and poor English. They thought he was Chinese, so Po Min struggled hard not to be insulted. Po Min ordered Uncle Thin to take the stage because, 'Bassein Boy, you are good in English,' and that was the moment Uncle Thin found his true calling. When he stood in front of the audience the words flowed, falling like garlands of flowers around the audience necks. He could say anything he wanted and they loved him for it, laughing and cheering. They threw money to Pawah, who picked it up with his trunk and put it in Uncle Thin's pocket.

Pawah was so clever and obedient. Uncle Thin told the audience, in the old days the white elephants brought good luck and prosperity to the Burmese kings, and now Pawah had travelled across a big ocean and foreign land to bring good luck and prosperity to America. Their power and riches would grow. He told them Burma is a country in Asia where the morals are high because the people choose to live a simple spiritual life. A country where people are happy, being content with their lot. Uncle Thin and his stories lifted the spectators in spirit. They laughed with happiness and Uncle Thin had complete power over them. He could express whatever he wanted and everything went very smoothly for Uncle Thin and Pawah and the whole band of Karen boys.

Pawah was exhibited in the circus side show where the public viewed many different freaks of nature billed as Living Wonders And Human Curiosities. Uncle Thin played baseball together with the human curiosities, at least the ones who were able, and these strange people became his close friends. He never forgot them so I will let him tell you their story in his words for I cannot say any better.

In this side show there was a group of black people, a band and trumpet team. Besides there was a very tall Jew from New York. This tall man's name was Sky Hawk. In Burmese you would say Ko Mo Myint. Sky Hawk was twenty-four years old. His height was six feet six inches tall.

Near Ko Mo Myint was Major Mike. He was twenty-four years old also. He was a short man. He was twenty-four inches tall from head to foot but we could not think low of him. He had a wife. His height was not honourable but his heart was highly honoured. He had a family with a wife.

Near Major Mike was Kansas Giant. He was sitting Kansas Giant. His body was very big and his face was very frightening. He was dressed in American cowboy costume including his hat which was also a very wide cowboy hat.

Near Kansas Giant were two negro white brothers. They were called twin negro brothers. Their hairs were twisted like black negroes but their head hair colour was not negro. They had golden twisted hairs, their skin was also white. The two brothers' eyes were also blue. Their names were Aiki and Aiku. Nowadays, in modern language, I would say they were astronauts. They dreamed to becoming astronauts. Standing under the full moon those two white negro twin brothers looked up to the moon. With rope they are pulling up and trying to climb to the moon. It was their act. Seeing this, I could not stay in my place any longer so I went to ask them some questions. What is that you are doing? We are going to climb and visit the moon with rope. It was strange.

Near them was a tattooed lady. She was tattooed all over her body. She was a snake charmer. She showed strange and fearful ways of charming snake.

There was still another one. Both of his hands were cut short from the shoulder. Normally we would say he had no hands. His name was Joe. He would never give up his masculinity (humanity) until his death. He could hold a fork and spoon with his leg and take all his meals by holding the fork and spoon with his leg. He was able to write with pencil, with chalk and with a fountain pen with his leg. His leg written letters were very beautiful. He could drive in four inches long iron nails. Holding the iron nail with the left leg and holding the hammer with the right leg. He drove in the four inch nails very neatly and carefully.

Mr Rubber Neck. He had a very stiff neck and very strong. If you hold his head and twisted about six inches and let go the neck it would turn as freed rubber. It sounded 'Pop' on releasing the head.

Mr Rubber Neck was in love with the snake charmer woman. They loved each other no matter what. One day they were separated. One day Mr Rubber Neck hung himself and was found dead of suicide. No matter how much he had a rubber neck he hanged himself and died in his room. The reason for his suicide was his lover, the tattooed lady, was sleeping with her other man. She committed adultery. Just like other people they also had heartache trouble and sufferings.

We can find different kinds of people in the circus. We cannot leave without talking about a man with a very big head. He could not hold his head upright all the time. The top heavy head could not stand on the straight neck. The neck could not stand straight for the heavy head. I went to spend my free time with that big head man.

I played baseball with them all. We were happy playing and eating together at the hotel. We were all happy at the circus hotel.

They were all human beings first although strange. At first in front of the audience when many people looked at the strange people the strange people felt shame but later when it became normal they were not ashamed. They were happy performing in their duties. In that way our circus team approached Long Beach California and I met old friends and acquaintance there.

Uncle Thin learned many things by his experience at the circus in America. He arrived in Hollywood and shortly after he met with our friends, Mr and Mrs Dudley, the missionaries from Bassein who offered to sponsor his education. When he sensibly considered his future career he could not refuse their kind offer. Uncle Thin gladly returned to his education at Mr Moody's Music School and his mother was pleased to hear that news and made sure to thank Mrs Dudley, who had not forgotten about how Uncle Thin impressed her when he captured the runaway horse.

It was a sad day when Uncle Thin said goodbye to Po Min and Pawah. 'Look,' said Po Min. 'Pawah knows you are leaving and his tears are welling up from somewhere deep inside him.' Po Min began to shake with his own sobbing. It was plain to Uncle Thin that animals have feelings and understanding to match our own. When Uncle Thin looked back, Pawah was crying so much his eyes nearly came out of his head. It was a strange and sad sight to see. As if Pawah, the sacred white elephant knew how to tell the future.

Your ever loving
Adaw Gyi

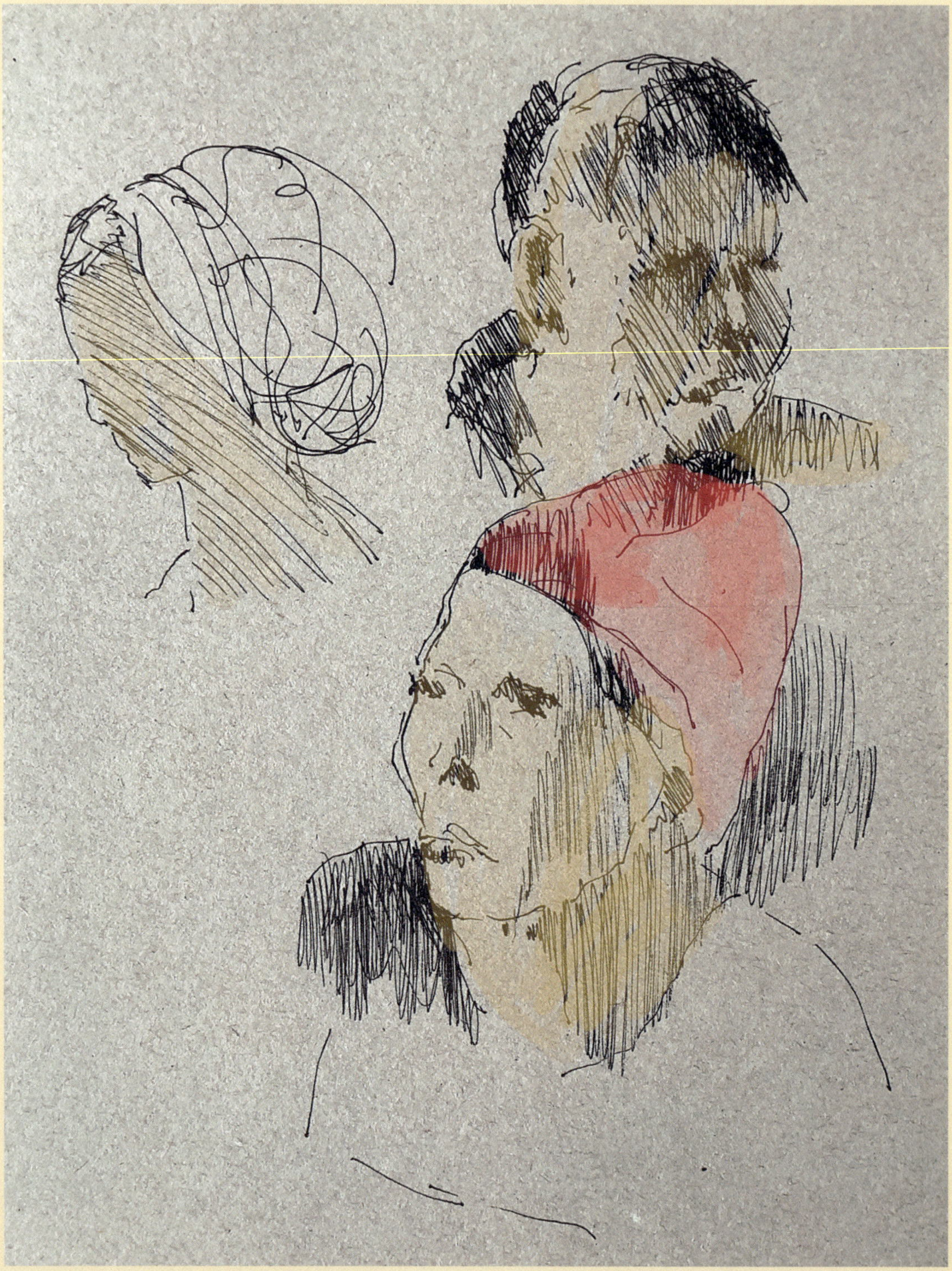

Village Portraits

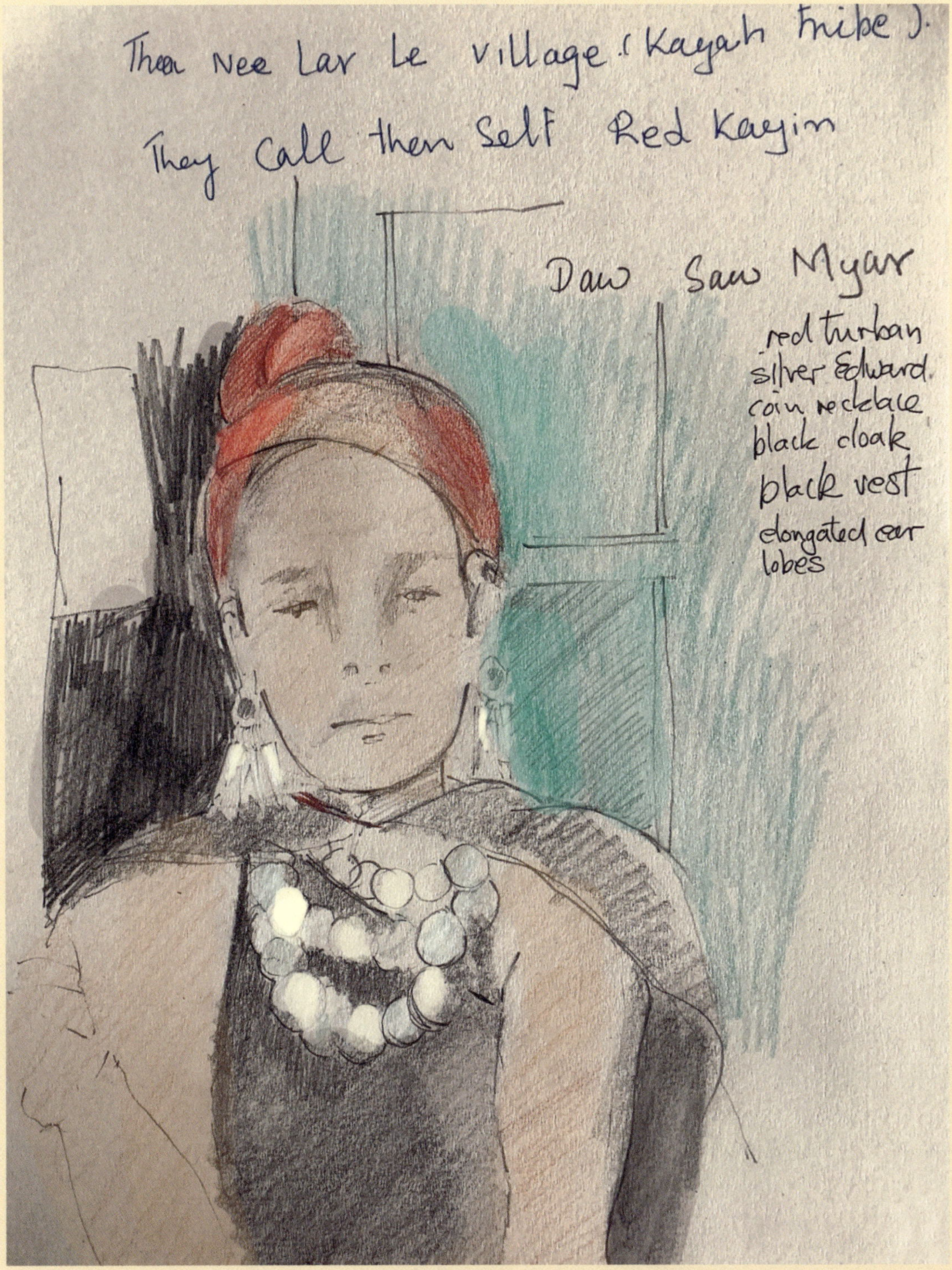

ethnic people with unique
culture, language and dress

San Po Lwin
Murder at the Zoo
Narrator: *Adaw Gyi*

My Dearest Darling Gazelles,

Tis strange – but true, for truth is always stranger than fiction. Lord Byron.

San Dwe slept alone in a narrow cot in a cramped room above the tapir house. He was twenty-two years old and never left the zoo compound except to go to church. Every evening he knelt beside the bed and recited his prayers with the sincerity and simplicity he learnt from his elders. He asked God to bless his parents and his siblings and give him strength to make his family proud. When he lay down and closed his eyes his hand instinctively reached towards the edge of the mattress, measuring the limits of his arms and legs in the unnatural, floating space above the floor. The fear he might roll over and fall out never lifted until he opened his eyes at first light and resumed the daily routine of hauling bales of hay, feeding and cleaning the elephants in their cages.

Po Min had chosen San Dwe to remain at London Zoo because he was the best trainer in the team, the best Karen elephant driver in his native division. The elephants trusted him, but when it came to relationships with foreigners San Dwe was painfully shy. His fellow zoo keepers were kind but they spoke too fast and teased too often. The furred and feathered beasts all had families around them but when San Dwe stood on a box and looked in his mirror he knew he was the only one of his kind. He felt ashamed of his small size and his poor English in the foreigner land populated by giants with noses sharp enough to plough a field. There was no one who looked like him, spoke his language or ate his food, he set his mind and took solace in his work and in the animals in his care. The keepers all had their favourites and San Dwe could always charm the birds of the air to sit on his shoulder but his favourite was the zoo's baby elephant.

In those days Londoners loved their zoo. They queued for hours to ride on the elephants and camels or take the llamas for a walk. The chimpanzees' tea party was a highlight and San Dwe laughed to see how daintily they shared the cups and saucers before tipping the milk over each other's heads, but at night, when the gates closed, laughter fell to silence and it was a different story. In dim parts of the compound shadows solidified, stalking from cage to cage. Trees rustled with creeping and crawling conversations. Nocturnal eyes dilated and hairs twitched on the backs of necks. An unnatural orchestra practised their parts, beginning with the high pitched avian singers supported by grumbling herds of ruminants. Sorrowful northern laments answered by roars from the savannahs. Captive souls slipped between the prison bars and flew over the canal. No one could say there was not passionate dancing in the night. The keepers said there were ghosts. If San Dwe had been asked he would have said there were Nats. On nights when San Dwe longed for a friendly touch he crept along the gravel path to lie in the sweet straw with the baby elephant. He sang lullabies and read passages from the bible to keep the Nats at bay. He recounted stories of life in the jungle, hot seasons and dry seasons and monsoon rains the elephants would never know and he prayed to be protected from temptations and see his village again.

When Po Min came to the end of his tour with Barnum and Bailey Circus he could see Pawah had had enough of entertaining the public. The responsibilities of Karen ambassador weighed heavily on the young elephant. From his point of view public life didn't suit him at all. He was sometimes mistaken for an African or Indian elephant: nobody seemed to know or care about the difference. Some of his American audience rudely accused him of being a painted white elephant. Nonetheless he remained polite and obliging, performing little tricks and bowing on demand, but he was sick at heart. He cried every day, longing for his native land. Fortunately he was booked for one season only at the circus and true to his word, Po Min made arrangements to return home. Po Min and Pawah broke their journey in London before taking ship for Calcutta and Rangoon but sadly, the journey was all too, too long. Pawah was destined never to set foot in his Burmese jungle again. He died in Calcutta. All the people of Burma mourned his death. On the last occasion a white elephant was removed from our country drought and famine followed and sure enough the monsoon rains were late that year. Pawah was just ten years old when he died, an elephant child.

San Dwe was desperately upset. He had loved Pawah since the first day he was captured in the jungle.

On the other hand, I can tell you, Lwin was the happiest twenty-eight year old man who ever set pen to paper in the Western Hemisphere. Life was on his side. Whatever he asked for, his mother gave it to him and her trust was well placed. He could do no wrong. That morning he had taken delivery of a black gown and a white horsehair wig, tailormade for him. He tried them on and admired himself in the mirror before hanging them on the back of his door. Then he set his work aside to write to his parents and thank them. His time in London was almost over. There was only one thing that could increase his happiness and that was his parents' blessing on his marriage to Lucienne. He had proposed and Lucienne had accepted. He knew, when his mother and father saw her photograph enclosed in the letter, they would celebrate with him and welcome her into the family. He licked the envelope with a flick of his tongue and closed it with a confident rub of his gold ringed finger.

He had not a care in the world... until the office boy thumped the evening newspaper on the desk in front of him. 'Bloody Murder at London Zoo,' 'Native boy San Dwe found half naked behind the tapir house.' 'Celebrated mahout Said Ali bludgeoned to death with a sledgehammer.' The article was lurid. Lwin read it through twice to make sense of the nonsense, without success. Early that morning San Dwe had been discovered cowering in his underpants, incoherent and foaming at the mouth. The dead body of his superior, the Mohammedan Indian elephant driver, Said Ali, was lying in a pool of blood on the floor next to San Dwe's empty bed and San Dwe was the only possible suspect. Every newspaper reader in the entire United Kingdom was fascinated by the exotic, bloody details of the case. They couldn't have made it up.

San Dwe needed help. Propelled equally by sentiment and duty, Lwin presented himself at the police station, where he found San Dwe wrapped in a rough blanket. There was less comfort in the white tiled police cell than in one of the cages at the zoo. The sweet smell of straw and elephant dung which habitually clung to San Dwe had turned acrid overnight, adding to the cloud of fear and shame which hung around his head. He refused to speak or look directly at anyone.

Lwin called for water and a clean white shirt to be delivered from his home. San Dwe was the same age as his brother Thin but looked even less. Lwin asked to be left alone with the boy. He worked quietly with the sponge, removing blood and dirt, and waited. When at last the two men spoke it was mixed English and Karen. San Dwe said it was not him who did the evil thing. It was Said Ali's fault. There were robbers and shameful women flaunting themselves on the banks of the canal and a man who had broken into the room demanding money. San Dwe had crawled under the bed to escape. His contradictory stories evolved over the course of the next few days but the evidence was against him. The bloody weapon and the doorway which had been broken on the inside when an intruder should have broken it from the outside both pointed at San Dwe. Although his acquaintance spoke well of San Dwe, there was no direct witness of events on the night of the murder. When the case came to court, judge and jury had no option but to find San Dwe guilty and condemned him to death. San Dwe wrote a letter to his parents saying he accepted his fate and he begged for their forgiveness. Please pray for my soul.

Lucienne could hardly believe it. The sweet boy she had met, the one with the shy smile who loved and cared for his animals as if they were his own children, it was impossible that boy could have done this dreadful thing. San Dwe had more friends than he realised. The great British public took San Dwe's side as they would a young David against a Goliath. After all, San Dwe was a devout Christian boy and the victim was a Muslim, twice his age and twice his size who was known to be a bully. The congregation at the Baptist church were shocked. The Karen community at home and abroad were shamed and angry. None could understand what had come over him to commit a violent murder.

Events moved quickly to a hanging but truth will out, in San Dwe's case just in the nick of time. The prison doctor discovered, by a curious conversation with San Dwe, that the boy had been assaulted, indeed raped, by Said Ali. As soon as San Dwe's defences were broken the truth poured from his tongue. He had endured weeks of torment in the small bedroom he shared with his supposed superior. Everything he said, everything he did was made into a mockery. He was forbidden to cook pork. He was forced, on his knees, in the place he said his prayers, to say and do unholy acts. The final cruelty was when news reached the zoo of Pawah's death in Calcutta. Said Ali tormented

San Dwe brutally, and the two fell into a fight over whether elephants have souls. Although the judge knew the awful details of this story he had not allowed it to be presented in the court. When the British public learned the truth they were outraged. They knew the boy had been pushed far beyond the boundaries any decent Christian young man could be expected to endure. Any young man worth his salt would have done the same.

San Po Lwin sat up every night, writing and rewriting letters on behalf of San Dwe. With only days in hand the judge was persuaded to reduced the death sentence to a prison sentence and the public rejoiced. Lwin's first case was a glorious victory and the pattern was set for his future career, but what pleased him most was that he was a hero to Lucienne (and her mother.)

I heard that San Dwe was a model prisoner who never gave up trying to improve himself. He was sorry for all his sins and wanted to make amends by helping others and he took every opportunity to further his education. Years later he was released from prison but what happened to him after that and whether he ever returned home I cannot tell because that part of the story is lost to my memory and you must forgive an old lady.

Your ever loving
Adaw Gyi

Hsin Gyi: Burmese Elephants
Narrator: *Linda Lewin*

When I arrived in Myanmar I knew as much about elephants as Loch Ness monsters and I certainly did not know how big a part they played in my family history or the history of the country. Elephants were the baggy trousered labourers and all-terrain transport vehicles of the British Empire in Burma. They worked in the teak forests, helped build bridges and in 1942 they willingly carried survivors of The Trek through the The Valley of Death to India. To know more about this you must read the wonderful *Elephant Bill*, written by James Howard Williams. A few elephants are still at work in Myanmar and rumour has it, they are still at war. I have photographs of them out and about with their boys, in processions supporting democratic values, but these days, despite their great size, an elephant is not always easy to find when you want one. I was entranced when an elephant appeared at the front door of my hotel in Pathein. An unexpected breakfast guest who liked bananas, but only with the skin on, and biscuits, also with their plastic packaging on.

The oozie mounted on the animal's neck with his legs dangling either side sat uncommunicative and nonchalant, fiddling with a mobile phone as any other youth would, but, I thought, ever the pessimist, what if the elephant runs amok between the expensive parked cars and the hotel guests? I could not think of any good reason why an elephant would agree to obey a boy who appeared to be more interested in his phone than in his animal. The elephant seemed small compared to the elephants of my imagination but still immense in comparison to a horse or a cow, and even they can do quite a lot of damage. It didn't bear thinking about, but fortunately it never happened.

At the age of twenty three Rudyard Kipling spent just three days in Burma but his descriptions of the country are exactly in accordance with my experience. He observed elephants working at the docks from a vantage point on board ship. This was his view of the giant beasts at work in Moulmein and I would like to think of them the same way.

A few narrow-minded folk with binoculars said that there were mahouts upon their backs, but this was never clearly proven. I prefer to believe in what I saw – a sleepy town, just one house thick, scattered along a lovely stream and inhabited by slow, solemn elephants, building stockades for their own diversion. Rudyard Kipling, 'From Sea To Sea, Letters Of Travel'.

My elephant visitor quietly agreed to do a walk about around Pathein. I saw him surrounded by crowds of onlookers when I went to the bank at lunchtime and then he paraded past the community centre where I was working. All the students turned out to cheer him on. He had some sort of advertising chalked on his side and he picked up a fair amount of free food and then, when I came out from afternoon class, I saw his backside disappearing down the road at a surprisingly fast pace. No doubt ready for supper and bed.

At Home in the Delta
Narrator: *Adaw Gyi*

My Darling Gazelles,

Your grandfather was very well respected and you are very well respected because he helped his people without asking for money. Aunt Nettie.

Lwin promised to love Lucienne like a princess, for ever and a day, but we know Lucienne was not a princess: she was unusually strong willed, a professional young woman who earned her independent living and needed nobody's advice or permissions. She courageously accepted to follow Lwin with all her willing heart. The young lovers married in Pimlico and honeymooned on the ship which carried them home to our native land. It was a magical journey and when Lucienne eventually stepped ashore her dainty feet landed on a red carpet.

Lucienne and Lwin set up home in Bassein. In those days our town was a wonderful place, not grand like Rangoon but a busy river port where delta rice was processed like gold dust, grain by grain, from hand to hand, from sack to sack, until countless mountains of polished white rice were dispatched to every country in the world. The fortunes won and lost went beyond imagination and the foreigners managed everything so efficiently according to their rules. Lwin worked day and night in the law courts and Lucienne managed household affairs.

Lucienne already had a London friend living in Pathein: Mrs Gyi, who had married her own handsome Karen barrister. She assured Lucienne that life in the colonies could be very enjoyable although the rainy season, which she had to admit lasted half the year, was a slippery Slough Of Despond. Undaunted, Lucienne set to, full of energy, to make her new home. I don't know if they had estate agents in those days but if so one might say Lucienne rented a traditional board house on a tree lined street, conveniently located within walking distance of the law courts in one direction and St Peter's Catholic Cathedral in the other. The garden bordered a pretty tidal canal on good days, otherwise known as a foul drainage ditch on bad days. The upper living rooms were large and airy, the office was downstairs, all supplied with electricity. Wiring in need of an upgrade and Western plumbing unknown. The kitchen was a separate building at the back of the house, equipped with modern charcoal stoves.

Lucienne bought new teak furniture from The Bombay and Rangoon Furniture Company, crystal glasses of which she was inordinately proud, and imported china from the department store. Daw Bu Ma arranged for a house boy, a cook and two maids to be sent from the village. The dhobi wallah called for the washing every week. The mistress-servant relationship was new to all concerned, including Lucienne, but she took comfort from the fact she had watched her father run a grand hotel in the south of France with absolute precision and attention to detail, so at the very least she could run a family home with occasional entertaining. At last, in the colonies, she was the acknowledged mistress of her household.

At first, the maids were too terrified to speak or even look their mistress in the eye. They knew nothing about Western ways so Lucienne put them through an intensive training course. Lessons included, 'Foreigners must not be requested to remove their shoes indoors' and, 'Peeping out from behind the curtains and giggling at visitors is strictly prohibited.' 'Bathing water must be provided at 7 o'clock precisely, piping hot, not cold, not even natural as nature intended, only hot water would do.' Between you and me, my dear patient Gazelles, none of those instructions made any sense, even all those long one hundred years ago, but our young Karens always tried their best to please and an amicable working relationship was established. Lucienne never lost her temper, even on the hottest days.

At that time you could buy anything your heart desired in Bassein and the pavements were so well laid it was perfectly possible to wear a pair of high heeled shoes on a trip to the new international department store, as long as you kept an eye open to avoid slipping into the dark depths of the storm drains. There were passable hairdressers on the top floor in the new market, right next to the gold jewellery shops, and the tailors charged next to nothing for film star fashions. If one cared to visit, the prison workshop sold a nice range of hand made household goods and one could buy genuine international luxuries by travelling up to town on the overnight ferry.

Lucienne's social diary filled up within days of her arriving, by hand written communiqué which arrived with her breakfast. If Lucienne and Lwin ever had an evening free, which was rare, there were two cinemas to choose from, both with up-to-date films. In her letters home, Lucienne described the air as beautifully fresh in the morning and delightfully balmy in the evening, preferring not to mention the in between, which was so dreadfully hot it was impossible to go outside or so dreadfully wet it was equally impossible to go outside.

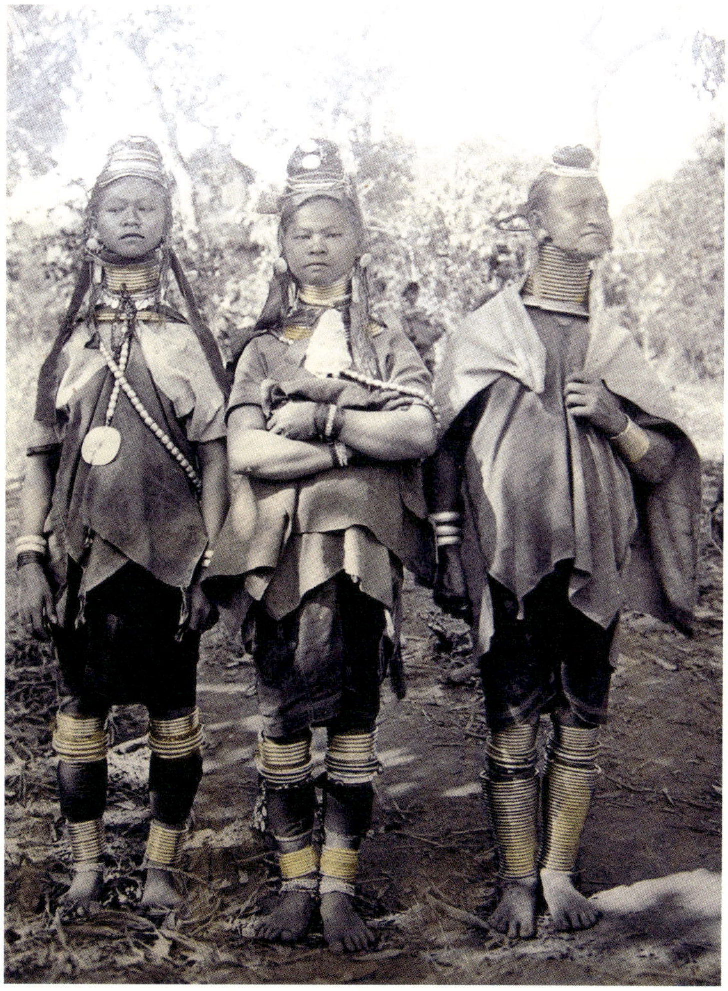

Mrs Jessie Hope – Padaung Women – 1914

Her pregnancy was progressing well and her husband was enjoying his work at court. She had joined the Gymkhana Club and once her baby was born she would consider the tennis or golf club. Most likely golf, it didn't appear to be quite so energetic. She loved the parties and felt welcomed everywhere she went.

Lucienne's first and most important invitation was to visit Lwin's family in the village. She was understandably nervous about venturing into the hinterland of the delta and had secret nightmares, worrying how to behave if she was asked to sit cross legged and eat her lunch off a communal palm leaf. An intrepid lady photographer she had met on the sea crossing had warned her about such things but Lucienne need not have feared. Our village boat which collected Lucienne from the dock was thoughtfully prepared with real chairs, cushions and a canopy to shade her precious complexion on her journey down river. A young boy dedicated himself to bailing out unwanted water from the bottom of the boat with an old petrol can and seemed to be very good at his job. Darling children in traditional costumes and yellow-painted cheeks vied with each other to waft cooling fans. Lucienne was not allowed to carry so much as her own hanky.

The river was broad, so much wider than the Thames in London, and appeared perfectly flat and calm but even so Lucienne was a little nervous of the hidden depths. Goodness knows how many unseen crocodiles might be lurking there. She did her best to put those difficult thoughts aside and concentrate on the delightful views of fishermen, local boats and families travelling to market along the way.

My Dear Gazelles, it is always difficult to disembark at the village where it is so muddy. I remember when the baby monkey fell in – even its own mother couldn't save it from drowning – but Lucienne was a foreigner princess. She was lifted bodily from the boat by small but remarkably strong boys and she was delighted to arrive on dry land looking just as clean and pretty as when she left home. Lucienne and Lwin's path to her mother-in-law's house was strewn with flowers and the villagers pronounced the new foreigner wife to be the prettiest wife they had ever seen, especially when they realised she was with child.

Daw Bu Ma had been preparing for days, discussing every detail of every

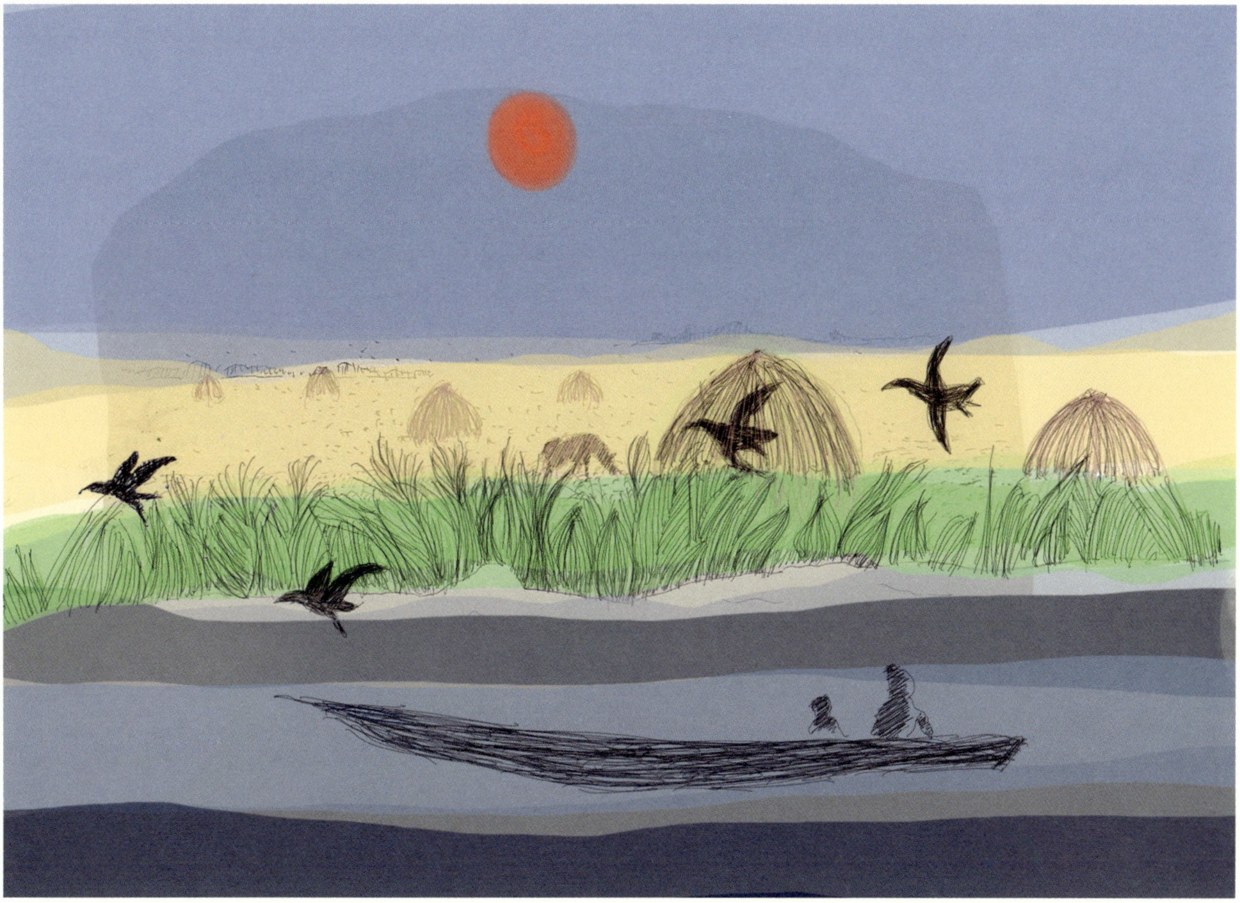

Sunrise to sunset – Land of rivers and rice

arrangement with all her neighbours, who were naturally fascinated. When Lucienne entered the family home Daw Bu Ma addressed her as 'Po Naw,' which was to say, 'My very own daughter-in-law with gentleness and meekness.' Since this was not an accurate description of Lucienne's character I can only suppose it was a diplomatic reminder on Daw Bu Ma's part, to Lucienne, of her status and required behaviour. Daw Bu Ma clearly illustrated her superior position by laying a dining table with cutlery and crockery which Lucienne's own mother would have been proud of. Daw Bu Ma refused to sit and eat with her daughter-in-law. Instead she fussed about, directing service from kitchen to the table, which soon threatened to collapse under the combined weight of chicken, pork, rice and vegetables, all well covered in oily juices. Daw Bu Ma knew for a fact that foreigners disliked curry so she left out the chillies. She assured

Lucienne, not to worry about the meat – it was quite fresh because they had killed it that very morning.

The senior family members, watching this perfectly-mannered performance from the best seats at the table, fell about laughing and apologising for their simple country ways, saying things would be different when they acquired a fridge and some electricity like their relatives in town. For now Lucienne must, 'Eat all because there is no use for left overs.' Lucienne had prepared in advance for the journey by eating a good breakfast so she was not quite ready for lunch at ten-thirty in the morning, but she performed as best she could. She quickly realised it was a serious mistake to empty her plate as she had been taught by her mother, for as often as she succeeded her plate was refilled abundantly. The only way to stop the inevitable was to leave a neat pile of rice conspicuously untouched in the middle of the plate. Only then was Daw Bu Ma's honour satisfied.

After lunch, the whole company settled in the church to receive the pastor's blessing. Hymns were sung and welcome speeches made. Lwin said he was the happiest man in the world and Lucienne made a thoughtful thank you speech to her mother-in-law in English which was translated into Karen by Lwin. My Darlings, you know Daw Bu Ma spoke very good English but perhaps U Tun Hla did not, and Lucienne never learnt Karen.

Daw Bu Ma presented the young couple with a special wedding gift – one of her own blankets woven with a mother's deep love and blessings for the future in every thread of its warp and weft. Finally, U Tun Hla recited a Karen prayer, 'May you sleep in peace and eat the fruits of the land. May you have long life, ten children and one hundred grandchildren. Amen.' The entire village lined the river bank to wave farewell as Lucienne and Lwin set sail towards home in the sunset. Tired but pleased at the end of the day, Lucienne decided to hang her mother-in-law's handmade blanket in the bathroom where she thought the jolly colours would brighten up a dull wall.

Your ever loving
Adaw Gyi

The Expensive Foreigner Wife

Narrator: *Adaw Gyi*

My Dearest Darling Gazelles,

Every morning the monks filed along the street, older boys in front, younger boys at the back, clinging to their precarious robes with one hand and a begging bowl in the other. Lucienne felt so sorry for the little ones. She instructed her head houseboy to fill their bowls with large helpings of rice, assuring good luck and merit for her entire family.

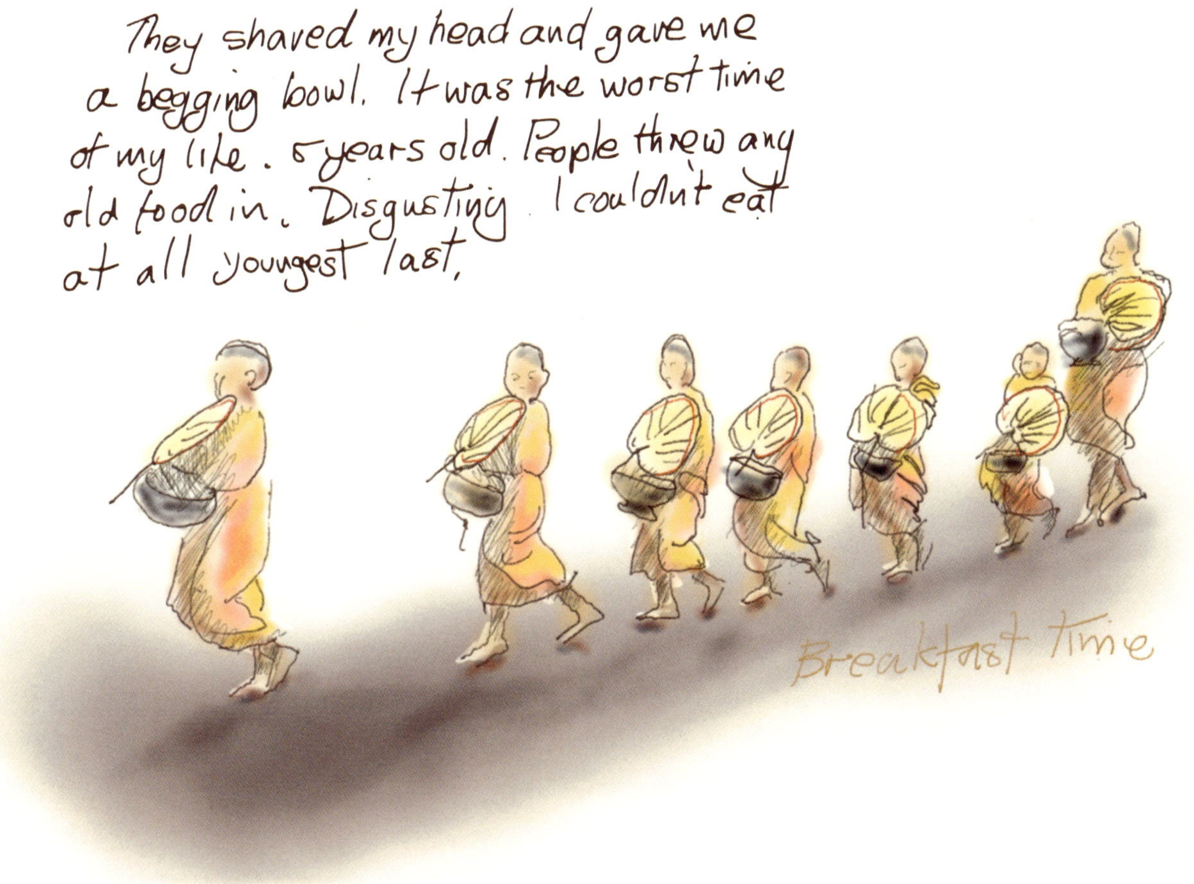

When it was Daw Bu Ma and U Tun Hla's turn to be entertained in town, Daw Bu Ma put on her best blue button shoes from the shop in Rangoon and engaged a horse and carriage to convey them from the wharf and deposit them at Lucienne's front door. All went sparklingly well until Daw Bu Ma had cause to visit the bathroom. At this point she forget all her good manners. My Dear Gazelles, I prefer to think that when Lucienne hung Daw Bu Ma's precious wedding blanket, which had been woven with so much labour, love and care, in her bathroom, she made an unwitting faux pas, but of course you must understand Daw Bu Ma felt it as a dreadful insult. At that point Daw Bu Ma forgot her beautiful manners and said exactly what she had been thinking and holding back from the beginning. She demand to know why her son had married a ridiculous and expensive foreigner wife who knew nothing and could do nothing, not even cook her husband rice. Fortunately these comments never reached Lucienne's delicate ears and as it happened Lucienne very rarely had any need to visit the village.

Lucienne settled into a happy domestic routine and delighted her husband by producing the perfect family, first a boy, Boh Lay Desmond, and then a girl, Marie. There was an occasion when the maid tried to please a little too much and sensibly tried to comfort Lucienne's crying baby at her own breast and that was the only occasion we can remember Lucienne losing her temper in all the time she lived in our golden land.

Over time, Lucienne taught the cook to make omelettes in the morning and chocolate cake in the afternoon. She spread her dining table with white linen and placed flowers in a silver vase. The guests were astonished by the chocolate cake, which they assumed she made with her very own hands, but Bo Lay assured me this was never the case. She invited the village children to birthday parties, gently requesting them, Please Darling, not to drink milk from the milk jugs or to eat sugar from the bowl – she would give them cups and plates enough for all. She hosted cocktail parties for her husband's colleagues, instructing them to help themselves to a French canapé or a Scotch egg.

Some of her younger staff were curious about the leftovers which arrived in the kitchen, tempted by the foreigner wine and whisky drinks. 'Why waste?' they thought, and downed the lot. Too late they realised their mistake, falling on the floor in fits of giggles. They never forgot making their way home on their hands and knees, in the dark, but never mind, no harm done.

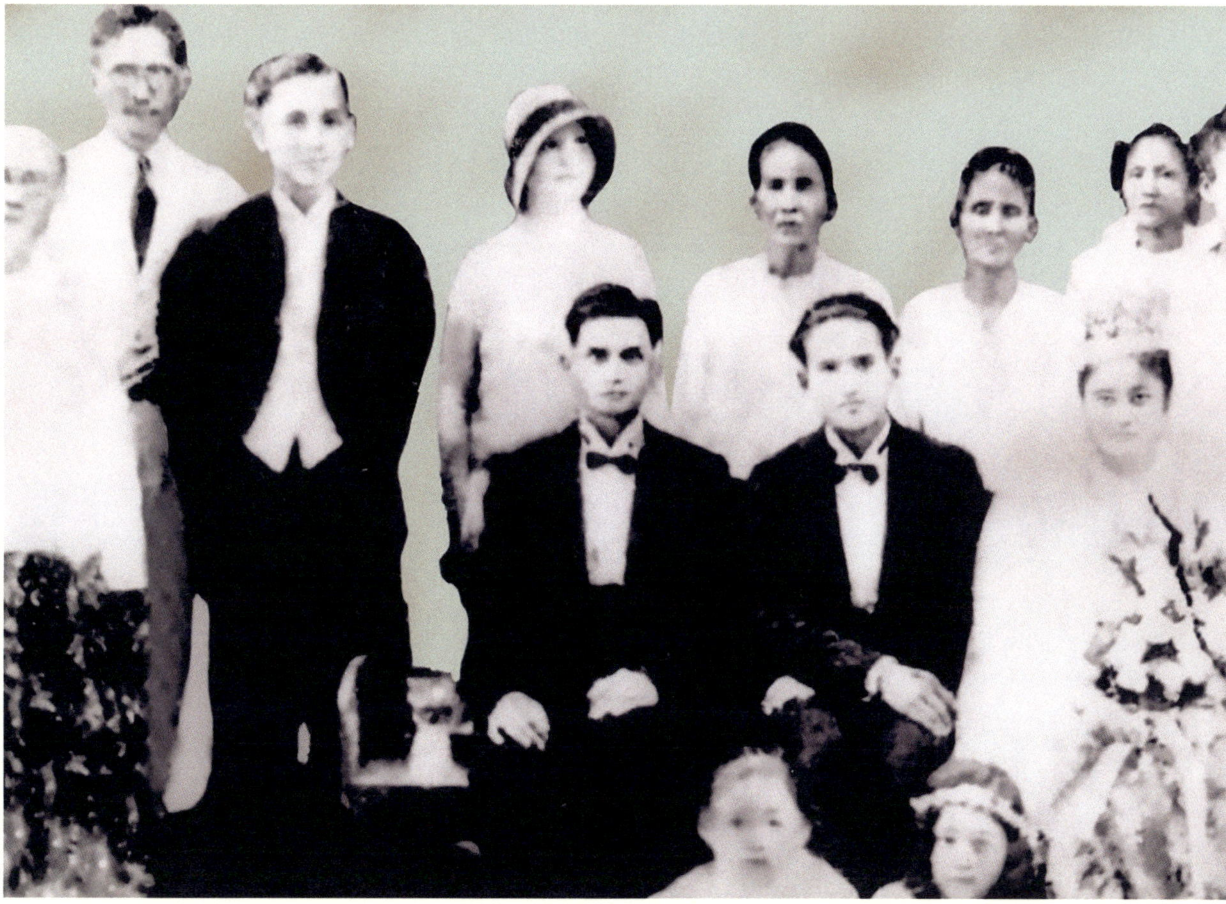

San Po Thin wedding. Unfortunate guests eaten by termites!

From left to right: San Po Lwin in dress suit, Lucienne, Daw Bu Ma;
Seated: San Po Thaw, San Po Thin, The bride.

Lucienne tried her diplomatic best to be even handed. She took the children to Mass in the cathedral one week and Lwin took them to Sunday Service at the Baptist church the following week. They were enrolled at the convent school next to the cathedral, wore crisp green and white uniforms and studiously presented their homework to the nuns on time. In short, Lucienne made life completely charming, strictly organised and as clean as is possible in a tropical climate, from the beginning to the end of every day. There was only one slight difficulty in Lucienne's household management and that was Uncle Thin. His enthusiasms made Lucienne nervous: he was liable to overexcite the children with rowdy tunes on the piano or wooden toys from the school he set up to provide employment for street children. Sometimes there were even less suitable gifts, such as the souvenir German bayonet which he presented to Bo Lay. Thin had married a local girl shortly after returning from America and Lucienne attended the wedding wearing a hat from her milliner days in London. Daw Bu Ma's three sons looked so handsome in their formal suits and the bride was a vision in imported white lace. If only Thin would stop attempting to lead her husband astray with his overexcited ideas of Burmese independence all would be well. One might have thought he would settle down to his family responsibilities now he had twin girls, Rose and Esther, just three months older than Boh Lay, but one never quite knew where or when he would pop up next.

My Faraway Country
Narrator: *Linda Lewin*

Legal definition:
The Anglo-Burmese people were legally named 'Anglo-Burmans' in the late 1930s, and the lawful definition of the community was described in Clause 13 (1) of the Third Schedule to the Government of Burma Act 1935. It defined an Anglo-Burman as 'A person whose father or any of whose other male progenitors in the male line is or was of European descent, but who is a native of India or Burma.'(1)
According to this definition, only the male line was given consideration, and the female line was neglected. Nemoto Kei.

I was drawn back to Myanmar and Pathein time and again, walking in my grandmother's and my father's footsteps. The past felt tantalisingly close but no one who knew anything really wanted to talk about it, they wanted to let go and move forward.

Over the course of her lifetime Lucienne moved from France to England to Burma to India and finally returned to England and whichever country she lived in she remained a foreigner with all the accompanying advantages and disadvantages. She made being foreign part of her identity, maintaining her glamorous, hybrid English-French accent to the very end. In the days I knew her she was short-tempered, a woman whose foreignness had grown threadbare, not glamorous in any way, but who could blame her? If we had understood more about her past, we would have been more patient. I was delighted when the Karen family told me Lucienne was 'always smiling' because that meant she was happy in Bassein. It was so unexpected and revealed a side of my grandmother which I never knew.

According to the legal definition of an Anglo-Burman, solely the male progenitors are taken into account. By marrying San Po Lwin, Lucienne had taken herself to a place beyond masculine legislation, but she had a circle of women friends in Burma in the same position as herself, married to men who were educated in England and had chosen to marry English women. I know it was much more common for white men to have relationships and formal marriages with local women but surely Lucienne and her friends were not the only female British Citizens married to male British Subjects. Men and women fell in love and children were born regardless of legal definitions. I certainly never expected to feel so well connected, so much at home, in a country where I could not even hold a conversation in any of the native languages.

From Lucienne's point of view her unconventional marriage was a great success. Aside from the fact she chose to marry the man she loved, her status in Bassein was immediately elevated, because she was European, because her husband belonged to an elite class and because she enjoyed the advantages of a colonial lifestyle well beyond the means of her life in London. There were always flowers in a crystal vase on Lucienne's table in Bassein.

On the other hand, Daw Bu Ma, the Karen family matriarch, would have had to overcome perfectly understandable reservations on the marriage of her oldest son to an outsider, an expensive foreigner wife, not least because Lucienne and her husband were dependent on family resources to set up home when they first arrived in Bassein and Lucienne made sure setting up home was done according to exacting foreigner standards.

I know there were cultural misunderstandings and language barriers within the marriage and within the wider family but Lucienne and San Po Lwin's exceptional relationship survived all of those difficulties. Lucienne did what other foreigner wives did when her children reached a certain age – she returned to England and perhaps she considered staying there with the children. Perhaps she found the monsoon climate tiring and realised her husband was not the prince she might have thought when she met him in London but she never willingly gave up. She refused to choose between her children and her marriage as other colonial wives did. Having spent a year in London with her mother and family she and the children returned to Bassein, where she planned to remain with her husband. If not for the calamity of the Second World War my family history would have been very different.

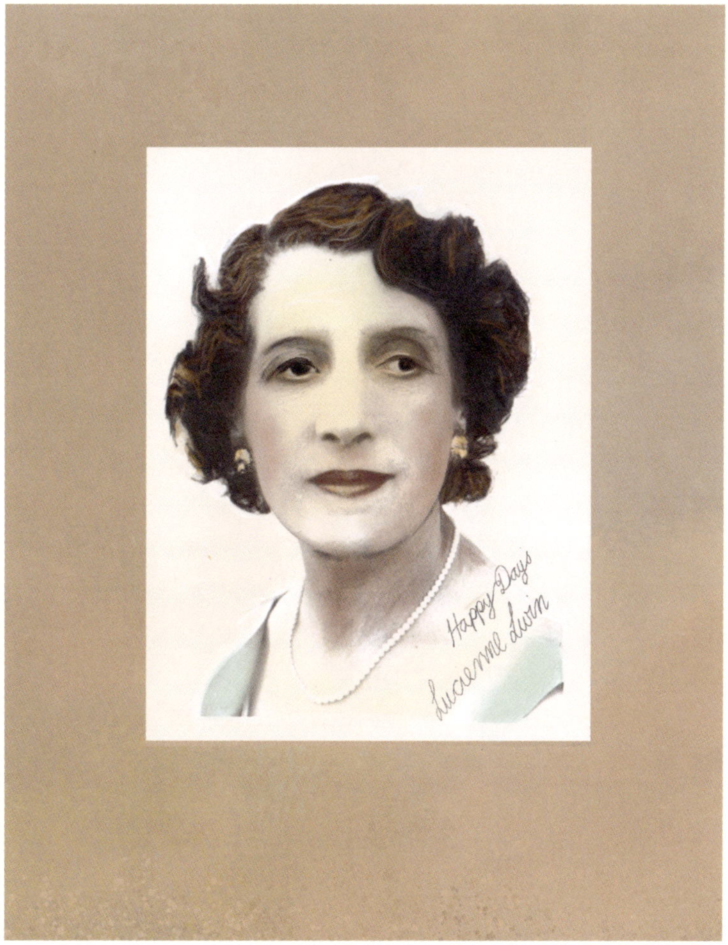

Lucienne. Always well turned out

My father claims he had prospects to marry a Burmese princess before he met my mother and if the princess's mother allowed it. However true or not that may have been, a woman does not need to be royalty to feel like a princess. When I arrive in Myanmar I become a princess by some magical process which is hard to understand and it happens just as soon as I exit the airport in Yangon. Perhaps my grandmother Lucienne had the same feeling. People I have no connection with will stop me in the street just to tell me how beautiful I am. I know it is simply because I am a foreigner and after so many years of being set apart from the outside world the Burmese are intrigued by my pale skin and to them, exotic way of dressing. They politely request to have a souvenir photo taken standing side by side and then, sneak in a little pinch just to see if I am indeed flesh and blood. If a similar thing happened in Edinburgh I would be outraged and suspicious, but somehow when it happens in Myanmar I feel quite differently about it. That is the lovely charm of the country and the people. They understand how to make visitors feel truly welcome. They love to laugh and smile today and never worry about tomorrow. Who would not want to return for more?

Aunty Nettie was able to take us straight to the site of the old family home in Bassein which, as it happened, was located directly behind our hotel. The original wooden building had been replaced but the occupants of the new house seemed to remember a foreigner family had once lived there. Across the road was a grand old wooden house with high pitched roofs, clinging on to life as it had been in the 1940's. It was surrounded by overgrown tropical trees and belonged to Richard, who rented out the ground floor to a private language school. One had to climb a flight of worryingly dilapidated steps to reach the first floor, where Richard and his ancient mother lived amongst piles of even more ancient and slightly rotting books. Richard was the custodian of these treasures, which I doubt anyone ever read, but they were important symbols of intellectual life and aspirations in past times. There were photographs of his parents' wedding on the wall and his mother spoke beautiful English in a frail voice. She was delighted to see us but I dare not stay too long. It was her bedtime. In Richard's house it was not difficult to imagine life as it had been in more gracious days.

Although it was seventy years since my father had left Bassein, he seemed to know more about the history of the place than anybody who presently lived there. He remembered everything perfectly.

From our hotel balcony we could see girls playing and doing their homework in the compound on the opposite side of the street. Father said the house and compound had belonged to a colleague of his father, a German family who donated it to the Catholic nuns when they evacuated prior to the Japanese invasion. It is now a girls' orphanage. The delta region was devastated by Cyclone Nargis and some of the girls I met in the orphanage were survivors of that disaster but there is never a shortage of orphans in Myanmar. Orphan is one of those English words that has been embedded into Myanmar culture because it is so useful and necessary but the meaning has been slightly diverted from the original. In Myanmar, it is no deception to say that some children who have parents are nevertheless orphans because their parents are too poor to feed and educate them. Some orphans have parents who dream of taking their children home just as soon as ever they can afford to.

We walked along to the cathedral. The street was in transition from bicycles to cars and no agreement had been reached on whether pedestrians had pavement priority so we fell into single file for safety's sake. Just beyond the gateway of the cathedral compound we found Dad's elementary school, not much changed in appearance, but it had been taken from the church and had become a government school. The vibrant green cathedral with white trim was an unexpected shock. Nobody could say why it is bright green. My theory is the misguided person who designated pistachio for interior use in Myanmar chose forest green for exterior use.

There was a plaque to a Karen martyr on the cathedral door but it made no sense to me at that time. We entered the compound, bounded by the cathedral on one side, the bishop's house, offices and an open air stage on the other three sides, all of generous proportions which implied money had once upon a time been available to invest in this country, where time seemed to have been stopped by some catastrophe which no one wanted to talk about. Nonetheless a spirit of calm and order endured within the cathedral compound and it was a welcome contrast to the hustle and bustle on the streets outside.

I invited Aunty Nettie to join us inside the cathedral. It was a lovely space with small birds flying in and out between the open windows and rows of wooden pews polished by use. The priest explained mass was said regularly in Karen and Burmese. Nettie managed to cross the threshold but when I attempted to explain the story behind the illustrated stations of the cross which lined the walls, as they do in every Catholic church, it was a step too far for her. She took fright and headed for the door. Given she proclaimed herself such a committed Christian I was surprised but the stations of the cross were obviously not to her taste. The Catholic cathedral was just as difficult for her to enter as the Shwe Dagon pagoda. The place might as well have been full of heathen idols. Her version of Christianity was obviously different from the one I had grown up with and I had to wonder where she learnt it.

Perhaps there were monsters in the compound which Nettie knew about and I didn't. A nun directed us towards a pair of students who looked to be perfectly innocent and smart young men in uniform enjoying an English lesson in the nuns' garden but there was a distinct note of caution in her voice. The atmosphere around the table was charged. It felt rather as if a family of mice were entertaining two cats at a tea party. It transpired the young men were Generals' sons taking advantage of the nuns' expertise in English. Entertaining the enemy was not an option, it was required.

The nuns were respected teachers, not only of English but were also a repository of genteel manners, needlework, music, gardening and Bible studies. All so charming and nothing dangerously political. Hilary and I admired their needlework and dutifully handed over a very few pennies for pillowcases that must have taken the novice girls hours to embroider with mottos such as Home Sweet Home and Sweet Dreams. The smiles on the girls' faces were worth so much more than the money we paid or the pillow case we received.

The nuns were preparing the girls for religious life. We were told they were poor girls from villages. It was implied they were very simple and perhaps a bit of a trial but I wanted to know if the charming girls, so full of life, decided not to take the veil, what would they do? I received an all too easy answer. These young women, in training to be maids of the church, would easily find jobs as maids of the wealthy. There was no talk of careers.

I was intrigued by everything and everyone I met but one trip was never going to be long enough to find out what lay beneath the surfaces of charming conversations or in the shadows of the gold leaf pagodas. The Myanmar light was simply too bright, too extreme for my Scottish sensibilities. I needed an excuse to stay longer and to get to know the place better but what skills did I have? I tentatively asked the priest if the community might like help with English lessons. I certainly was not expecting such unconditional enthusiasm or to find a fellow Scot, there and then, doing that exact thing – teacher Hazel, in the library, located in the very same building where my father had taken refuge during the war. I took a look around the bookshelves, more rows of out of date and broken spines treasured for no other reason than the fact they were books and in Myanmar books seem to equate with knowledge, regardless of contents, but Hazel's student were so delightful and so pleased to be there I could not resist the idea of working with them.

I returned to Pathein the following year and year on year began a teaching programme supported by exceptionally generous friends. I had to confess that although I was a native English speaker I was not an English teacher. Never mind, they said, you are always welcome. My qualification was Foreigner and the Burmese seemed to have a similar attitude to foreigners as they do to books. Foreigners are respected simply because they are foreigners, regardless of content. We were given joyful free rein on the curriculum and developed a creative, hopefully inspiring programme. Our students were shy young men and women from the villages, the most attentive students any teacher could ask for. They taught me how to be an English teacher, something I never imagined I could be and I will never forget them just as much as they swear they will never forget me. I am grateful.

On our way back to the hotel we met Snow White learning to ride her new two wheel bicycle with proud parents in attendance. Mother pinched her daughter to make her speak and the beautiful child sang out in a clear voice, 'Good evening, my name is Snow White.' We were astonished. She was radiant, perfect down to the last T, so rarely pronounced in Myanmar. She embodied everything I wanted for my students.

San Po Lwin: The Rule of Law and Order

Narrator: *Adaw Gyi*

My Darling Gazelles,

Email from Nettie Thin, formerly known as Snow White:
'I just came home from the delta this morning. I had to go after a murder case for a man is wrongly arrested and accused for some police men are very treacherous for pinning people for nothing just to squeeze the bribe. Bribery and corruption are almost everywhere, dear.'

The commissioner's daughter had a new box brownie camera and she took a photograph of Lwin in his garden, wearing formal court dress with his hand resting on an imposing law book or perhaps it was the bible. His white wig and black gown were bought in London. His shoes were beautifully polished but they were outshone by the smile on his face. Aung Htoo was in the garage and Boh Lay was called to put his bicycle away. That boy expected Aung Htoo to do everything for him, which is a fault Boh Lay admits.

Lwin's career prospered in Bassein because he was clever and honest in his work and people said that was a rare thing so they appreciated that and trusted him. Daw Bu Ma and U Tun Hla were delighted because he helped his Karen people even without fees and Lwin was pleased to see his mother was reconciled to Lucienne, the foreigner wife, by the two beautiful grandchildren, Boh Lay Desmond and his sister Marie. Life and business were running so smoothly most of the time but not all of the time. Lwin conducted his court cases exactly as he had studied, according to the foreigners' rules of law and order. He was conscientious and believed in moral principles and never accepted a compromise but My Dears, an honest man must be a brave man in the face of such abundant bribery and corruption, which are always rampant in our country.

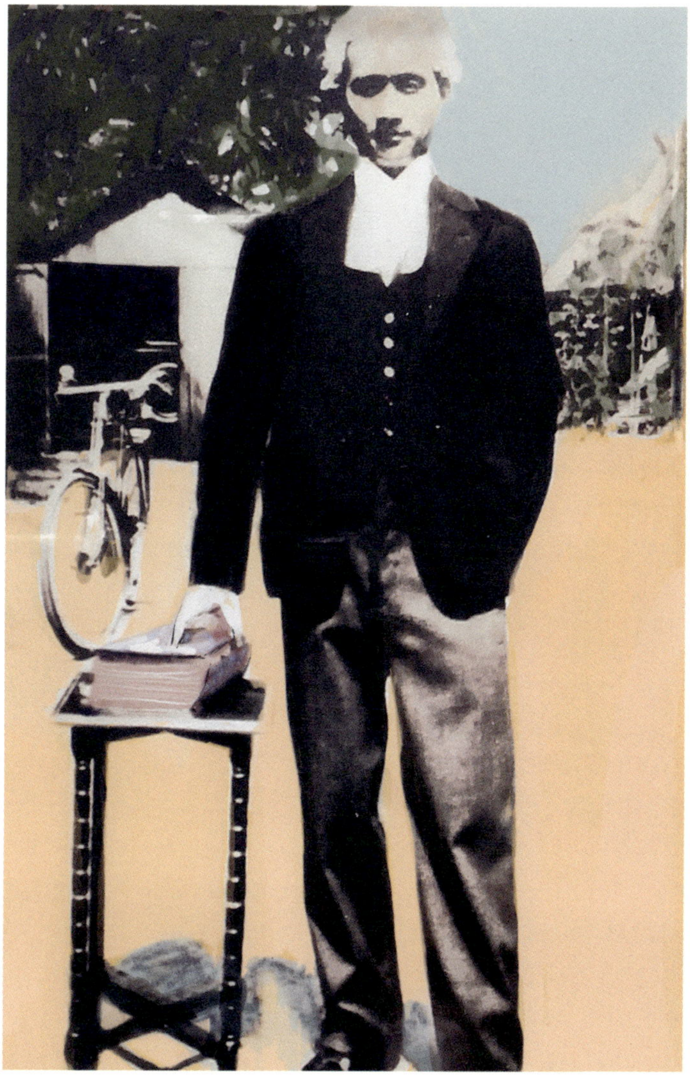

San Po Lwin.
A happy man
in
his garden

Lwin had just sat down at his well-polished dining table when Aung Htoo, the house boy, delivered a message that a client wished to see him. Lucienne sighed at the disturbance. Lwin worked such long hours and never got any peace. Lwin directed the man to come back the next day. When the client refused to leave, Lwin reluctantly descended the stairs and invited the man, who turned out to be several solidly built men, into the office. He politely explained that infinite amounts of fresh laundered money would never be enough to change his professional opinion on any case whatsoever. The rule of law could not be diverted from its smooth, just course of action. If the men did not leave Lwin would call the police to give them a jolly good thrashing.

These correct and stern words sent the vile criminals into an angry panic, which caused them to throw Lwin on the ground and hit him over the head with a fierce cudgel previously concealed beneath their lungyi. Thanks be to God, the naturally mild-mannered houseboy Aung Htoo, dutifully listening at the door, heard the thump as Lwin hit the floor. He rushed in, seized his master's Japanese sword which always hung on the office wall, and, swishing the blade around with great unaccustomed energy, he drove the attackers off. When Dear Lucienne and the children heard the commotion they threw their bedtime stories aside and came tumbling down the stairs. Lucienne heaped so much praise on Aung Htoo for saving the day he was beside himself with manly embarrassment and Boh Lay was a tiny bit jealous. He spent the whole of the next week secretly brandishing the sword, practising attack and defence moves, just in case he might get the opportunity to confront the evil dacoits and save his grateful family's life. He was quite sure he could do it. Fortunately, the blow Lwin received required nothing more than sympathy and a bandage. It was hard enough to prevent him attending court the next day, but fortunately not hard enough to make a permanent indent in his head or reduce his determination to do his duty according to the just rule of law and order.

Lwin was a clever man but of course he could not always be on the winning side and the case of Cyril's inheritance was an unhappy judgement against Lwin and his young client. This is a complicated story which was shocking at the time and made me weep to hear it so you must bear with me, my dears, to explain, because after all these years, I cannot say I am reconciled to the injustice of the situation.

Mr D'Attaides was a Christian. He had no legal wife or legitimate children, according to the foreigners' way of thinking, but Mr D'Attaides was highly regarded in the town and his wealthy ancestors were great benefactors of the Catholic Cathedral in Bassein. He attended mass without fail and when he fell ill he naturally confessed to all his sins so he had no secrets before the priest or God. His house boy, who was promoted to personal secretary, was named Cyril and the housemaid, who happened to be Cyril's mother, lovingly cared for old Mr D'Attaides right up to his last day, as if they were intimate family members, and they shed tears when death took Mr D'Attaides to sing praises before God on his throne in heaven. Mr D'Attaides' final request to Fr. Brun, his parish priest, was to write a note ensuring that Cyril and his mother would be well provided for. He signed the note in his own hand and with complete confidence he had done everything necessary to ensure his final wishes would be carried out. He drew his last breath with a clear conscience.

The whole town knew that Cyril was not just Mr D'Attaides' secretary. In fact he was Mr D'Attaides' son in 'the traditional way,' and one who loved and was loved by his father just as much as any foreigner's legitimate sons loved their fathers. Unfortunately for Cyril, when Mr D'Attaides died his entire estate was claimed by his foreigner niece, who was the legitimate heir, according to foreigner law. Cyril and his mother were afraid of being thrown out on the streets, penniless.

Lwin argued Cyril's case to benefit from his father's estate, according to his father's intentions and last wishes, as best he could through high and low courts in Bassein and Rangoon. Fr. Brun was his witness. Finally the high court judge ruled against Cyril's claim because Mr D'Attaides was a Christian and Christian laws were the legitimate laws which took precedence over all other traditional laws of the land. He awarded the whole of Mr D'Attaides' valuables to the foreigner niece, pronouncing that in the absence of a legal will, illegitimate children of a Christian father could not and would not benefit from their father's estate.

In my view, if Mr D'Attaides had been a Buddhist it might have been an entirely different matter. Lwin would have won the case for Cyril and the court's argument would have fallen flat on its foreign white face. Good will and traditional common sense would have prevailed and a dying man's last wishes would have been honoured as he desired, but that was not the case. The foreigners' judge claimed the estate in the name of the Christian God, who proved himself to be the most powerful god in the land and there was nothing more to be said on behalf of the young and penniless Cyril, a natural son who loved his father as much as a son possibly could.

How May I Help You?

Narrator: *Linda Lewin*

Outside every Myanmar police station there is a laudable, aspirational sign: May I Help You? Family, friends, students and complete strangers will all go out of their way to help you but not the police.

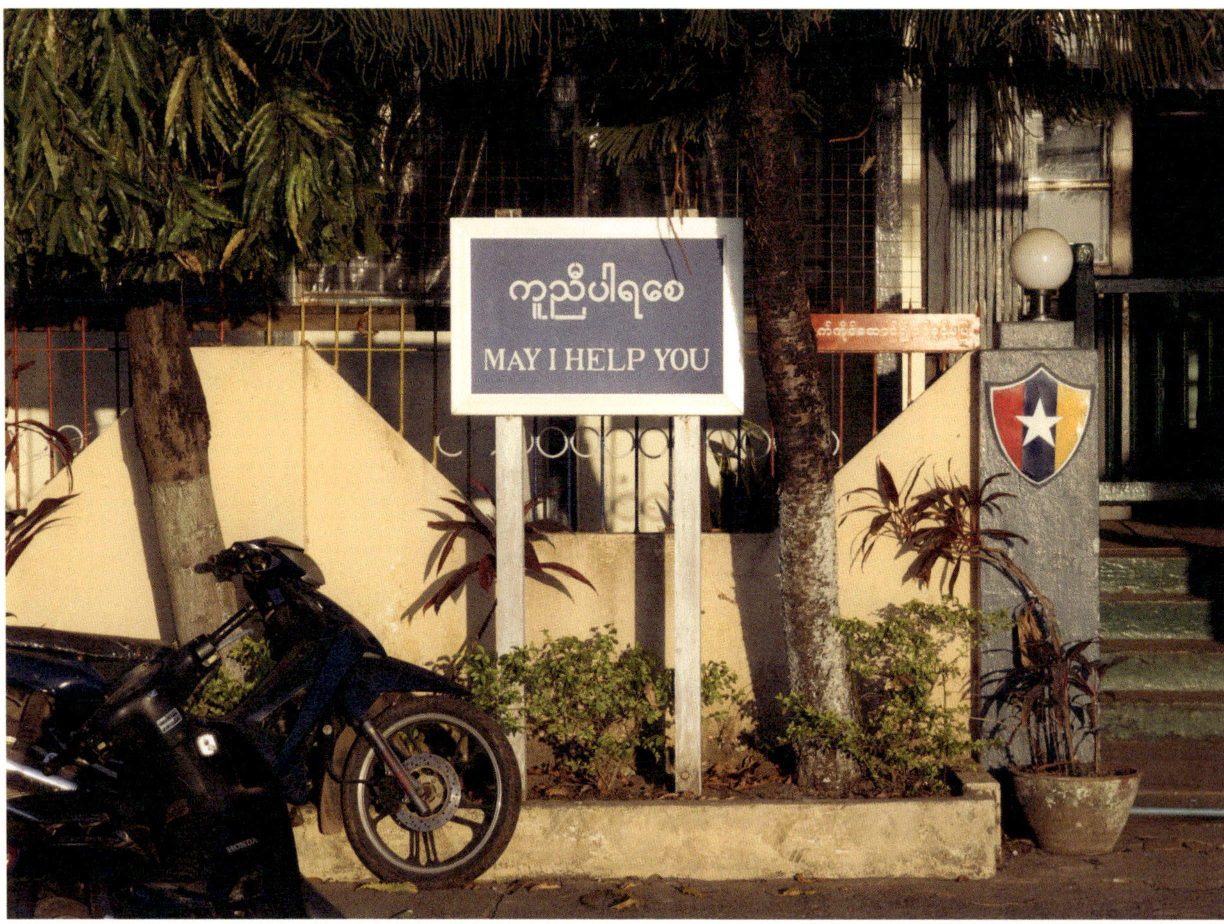

The Police Station – beyond ironic

How May I Help You?

You Are Welcome
How may I help you

I will carry your bags
If they are heavy and I am small, no matter
If you are lost I will find you
If you are hungry I will feed you

I will wash your feet when you are tired
I will be your voice when you need me
We will order the best food in the best restaurants
because it makes me happy just to watch you eat

I will save you from the sun with my umbrella
and never worry to cross the road because I am at your side
We will walk arm in arm to the night market

You are my mother and I am your child
I will always smile for you
You will never be sad or lonely in my country

I will never forget you

Boh Lay and the Ebb Tide
Narrator: *Adaw Gyi*

My Dearest Darling Gazelles,

Boh Lay Dasemi has forgotten nothing but he prefers to remember the good times and not dwell on the bad. I promise to tell you all, good and bad, because you know, the truth shall set us free. My Darlings, when wild elephants rampage through your village or fight their battles in your paddy fields, not one tree, not one single blade of grass will be left standing and Boh Lay is our witness to the facts. Boh Lay was born with rice in his mouth and if fate had not turned in the way it did he would have died with rice in his mouth.

Boh Lay was welcomed into Bassein Township, Ayeyarwady Division, on the 25th June 1930 by a Scottish midwife in a private room in Bassein hospital. We loved him deeply and his foreigner family loved him just as much. He was a strong and healthy boy with just a little too much energy to be entirely good, but he was certainly not bad. At seven years old his mother sent him to the convent school beside St Peter's Cathedral where his cheerful attitude prevented him from taking lessons altogether seriously. Sometimes he was top of the class and sometimes bottom but never in the middle. What Boh Lay failed to learn at school he learned from reading his favourite magazine Film Fun, going to the picture house and from his collection of DC Thomson comics which came from his friend Michael Gyi in London. Wherever he was and whatever he was doing, Boh Lay was extremely observant. He missed nothing.

Boh Lay naturally assumed the role of hero in his own adventures. His stage included all of the town, the port, and his grandparents' village. He knew who was coming and going on the daily ferries, and he kept an eye on the fishermen landing their catch. His fellow actors were our Karen people, the Bamar, the Chinese merchants, Indian coolies, French priests and

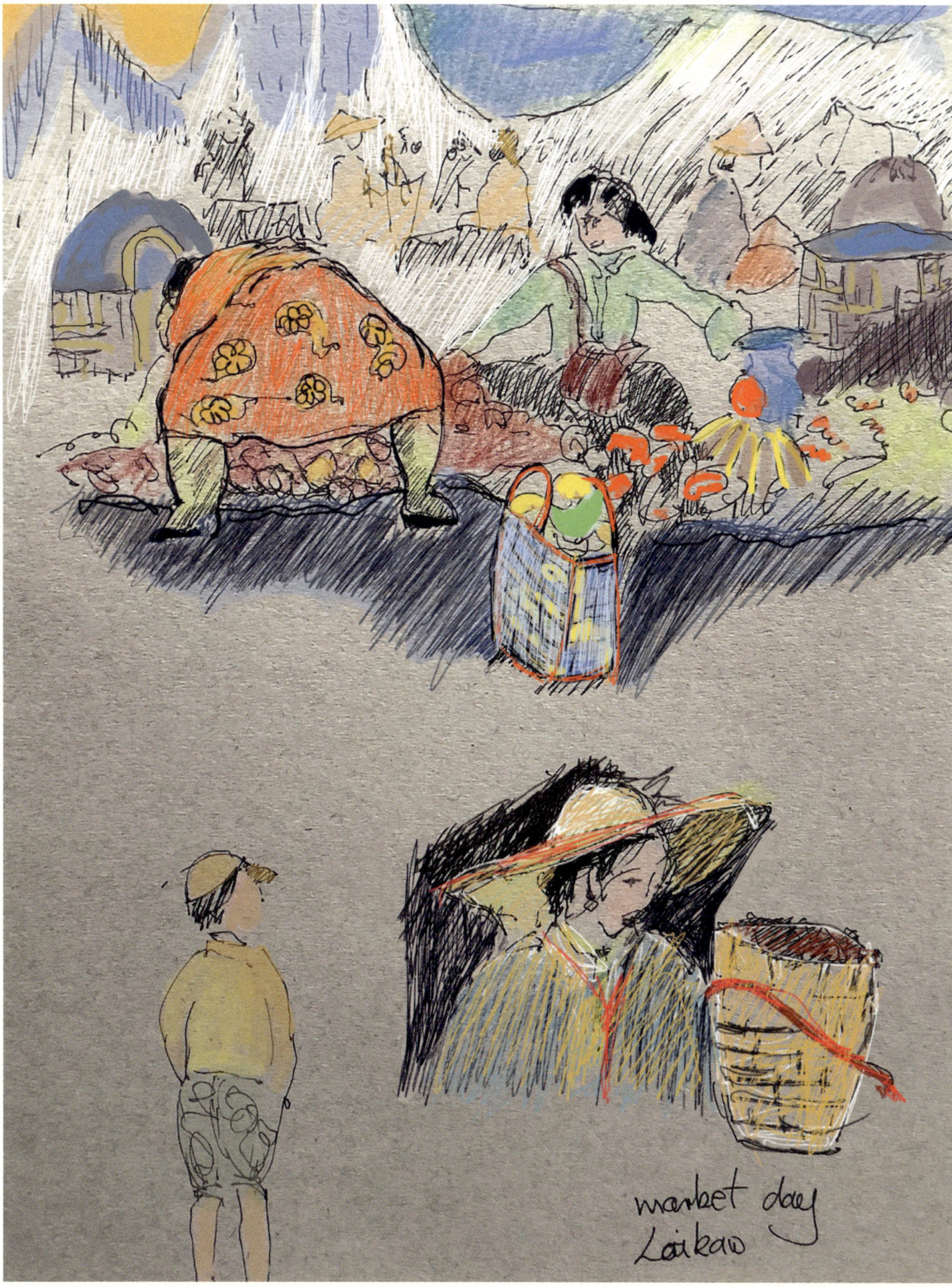

He spent his pocket money in the bazaar

nuns, British administrators, Scottish nurses and midwives. Merchants, tinkers, tailors, soldiers, sailors and spies. He knew them all. He played freely between caste and creed.

He grew up surrounded by the true wealth of our country. He watched it growing green in the paddy fields, drying in the sun, being poured into sacks and carried on the heads of beautiful young women quite unbowed by their burdens. It rolled past his door in carts, was loaded onto trains and boats, and finally, but only after vast quantities of money had changed hands, it sailed away to foreign countries down the muddy river. In those days we grew enough rice to feed the foreigner empire and all our family business depended on it because that was the way of the world and at that time it never occurred to Boh Lay that anything ever would or could change.

Boh Lay's most important possessions were the German bayonet, gratefully received from Uncle Thin, the sword which he appropriated from his father's office when Aung Htoo's back was turned, and a wooden catapult made from a conveniently-shaped tree branch. Aung Htoo taught him how to dig clay from the canal bank and dry it in the sun to make pellets. And if all of this was not enough to satisfy him, his grandfather, U Tun Hla, sent him a dugout canoe from the village, which he launched with ceremony in the tidal creek beside his house.

Sometimes Boh Lay's enquiring mind led him astray. The entire household was distraught when he slipped in the mud and fell into the charming canal, otherwise known as the foul drainage ditch, where he might easily have drowned or caught any number of fatal diseases. The doctor and the priest were called and – 'Thanks be to God' – between the two of them Boh Lay's life was saved.

Boh Lay was proud of his father's car but he equally enjoyed a boat ride. For instance, if Boh Lay's mother wanted to go shopping or visit her friends in Rangoon she booked a cabin on the overnight ferry which was so much fun the destination hardly mattered. The family sailed to Diamond island on The Louise where the children learned to live off the land, which meant fishing and collecting turtle eggs off the beach. One early morning Boh Lay terrified himself by catching a giant flying fish, as big as himself and quite possibly stronger. It flexed its muscles on the end of his line, threatening to drag him into the water. He accepted an offer to swap it for a bag of beans, which he proudly presented to Mama, who gave them to the cook. The beans did not grow into a magic tree but a fisherman's family enjoyed a welcome feast.

Boh Lay's father was a busy man, full of energy. He never stopped working. Lwin spent his days at the court house in Bassein and in Rangoon and whatever time was left over developing our family farm. To celebrate his family success and respect his parents he built this church, in this place, where we are sitting to tell our stories, just next to his parents' house. The solid brick walls, corrugated iron roof and bell tower remain standing. You can see them from miles away. To finish, Lwin commissioned a bronze bell from a London foundry. He wanted it to remind him of his student days in the city where he had met and married Boh Lay's mother, Lucienne. The foundry packed the bell in a wooden crate with straw and delivered it to the London docks by horse and cart. It travelled across the ocean in the belly of a liner by the same route Lwin had made his journey so many years before. At last, when it arrived on our shores, his mother sent a cart drawn by a team of sweet-eyed oxen to collect it from the wharf beside the rice mill and deliver it to the village. Boh Lay was given the honour of opening the crate in front of the entire family. He remembers pulling the straw and watching the village men hauling the bell into the tower with their strong arms taut against the rope. The bell called our people to pray and to celebrate their good fortune every day. When the congregation gathered together they sang their hearts out with pure joy, just as we do today. Lwin fulfilled his parents' dreams beyond their expectations.

When Boh Lay and his sister Marie were old enough to walk and talk and tie their own shoe laces, Lucienne said it was time to take them to England. She had left her family home with barely a backward glance and she surprised herself by how much she appreciated her family in their absence. Lwin worried Lucienne missed her London life. He knew she found the monsoon floods tiresome along with the heat and the endless mud which nearly claimed Boh Lay's life when he fell in the canal, and there was the question of the children's education. She should go home and refresh her spirits. The visit was overdue. Boh Lay's grandmother Daw Bu Ma willingly paid the expenses and Lucienne promised to return in a year and a day.

Alas for all fairy tale plans, once again a terrible war shattered the Western world in blood stained pieces beyond repair. Lwin advised his wife, if she and the children did not return soon they might not get home at all. Time was running out and the British government backed him up by advising all who could get themselves out of harm's way must do it. Returning children to the colonies was conveniently less mouths to feed in England and Lucienne could see the good sense in it. Burma was surely out of harm's way. Lwin was overjoyed to see his beloved family safely returned and promised to build a beautiful palace beside the Royal Lake. Lucienne fell in love with him all over again. Before long they were expecting a third child.

Twelve monsoons had come and gone since Boh Lay was born, hot and dry, Lent and Easter, Advent and Christmas to come again. Reliable and comforting as clockwork. Lucienne sat at one end of the polished dining table, Marie at the other end and Boh Lay sat in the middle. They each had a pen in their hand and a serious expression, except for Boh Lay, who was prone to humming Christmas carols under his breath. Advent was the season of waiting. There were letters and cards to write and invitations to send. Intriguing parcels and cards with pictures of Mary and Jesus and Joseph and shepherds and sheep and wise men with camels were arriving to the Lwin household from London, the capital of The Empire Upon Which the Sun Never Sets. Boh Lay was disappointed when he visited his French grandmother in London and discovered the only camels to be seen were the ones in the zoo and Mary and Joseph did not live there at all, but he was consoled with climbing a ladder onto the camel for riding on its back. After all, he could ride on elephants at home. He thought it would be nice to visit his grandmother and enjoy a 'White Christmas' when the Blitz his mother and father talked about in private whispers was over, but for the time being he was glad to be safe in his own home and his mother agreed, in a distracted sort of a way.

Lwin paused on his way to the court house and instructed Boh Lay not to bother his Mama because she was waiting for the new baby to arrive. Not Jesus of course, but a new baby brother or sister for Boh Lay and Marie and that required a lot of rest. Lucienne was not in a mood to rest. She insisted on keeping herself busy by wrapping Christmas presents for the village children, so many of them. It would be nice if the cook could make a Christmas cake. She would order the ingredients. Boh Lay was writing a letter to Father Christmas asking for a proper, grown up bicycle. He carefully wrote down the model number because he had done a lot of research and he would know how to ride it because Aung Htoo had been teaching him. For safety's sake he backed up his letter with a few evening prayers and was confident of a good result. Since Boh Lay already had a sister he did mention that he would prefer if the new baby were a boy. In the meantime he had the commissioner's Christmas party to look forward to. It was fancy dress. Marie would be Snow White and Boh Lay would be a pirate with his father's swashbuckling sword.

So much waiting was a tedious business but setting all that aside, Boh Lay had suspicions his parents were worried about something and perhaps that something was not what kind of Christmas presents to give their charming children. There were clues. Boh Lay observed the adults listening to the radio with worried expressions. The atmosphere all around town and at home was charged in an odd way. In the evenings Uncle Thin and his father spent hours talking quietly in their Karen language. That was what adults did when they didn't want children to know their secrets. They just changed language and they had plenty to choose from. Also, there were foreigners, dressed in military uniforms, who marched about the streets with ribbons and badges stuck to their chests. Some visited the house and he had to address them as 'Sir.' On Lwin's orders, a gang of boys Boh Lay recognised from his grandparents' village arrived early in the morning and started digging a large trench in the garden, big enough for at least six people to sit inside, as long as they were family or close friends. Down at the Gymkhana Club, the gossip was all about 'dacoits' and 'fifth columnists' and 'look how bad things are at home.'

A Sunday lunch party was ruined by a radio announcement. Pearl Harbour, they said, now we are in for it. The United States of America has entered the war against Japan. Boh Lay's mother made him an appointment at the Japanese dentist who treated all the best people in town, but before the man could get his drill turning on Boh Lay's teeth, he mysteriously disappeared. In the kitchen Boh Lay overheard the maids discussing whether it would be safer to head for the village or run to the jungle if fighting began. Despite all of this, he was not unduly worried. He knew, that in the unlikely but exciting event of war coming his way, the British Army, supported by the plucky little Gurkhas and possibly a few glamorous Americans, always won the day. He had seen it in the cinema and everyone agreed. He patriotically raised the Union Jack in his garden, only to tear it down when he received a row from his parents.

The baby arrived two weeks before Christmas and it turned out to be a healthy boy with a sweet face just like his father, which pleased one and all. He was christened in St Peter's Cathedral, Bassein, on the 22nd December 1941, attended by all the family and friends. On the 23rd December 1941, Christmas shopping and invitations to parties in Rangoon were cancelled without notice by a Japanese bombing raid and on 25th December it happened all over again. Dead bodies lay in the streets, rotting in the tropical heat. The wooden go-downs which lined the docks went up in flames as quick as dry leaves in a forest fire. In the face of such an outlandish, impossible to comprehend, catastrophe, the only possible thing to do in Bassein was carry on as normal. Christmas was Christmas – there were parties and presents and they were very good ones. Boh Lay's letter and his prayers were answered. He was delighted with his new bicycle, undoubtably the very best model available from the international department store.

In the New Year the Japanese bombing raids extended into the delta and Bassein suffered the same fate as Rangoon. The first plane flew so low our young Boh Lay ran into the garden and waved at the pilot, who was not much older than himself. A friendly lad who waved back with his silk handkerchief. It was printed red and white with the rising sun, autographed by all his friends and family for good luck and a safe return. For a moment the pure adrenalin of flight united the spirits of both boys. The pilot forgot he was on a noble mission to rescue his fellow Asian citizens from Western imperial domination by dropping bombs on civilians and our innocent Boh Lay, who had never had one enemy in his entire life, thought it was a game.

Things changed. Desperate news filtered along the road from Rangoon. Family friends, Karen husband, English wife and children all died in their beds in a bombing raid. People watched the sky for omens. Some said that when the planes came they would be guided by moonlight. Others said they would come under cover of clouds or with the sun at their backs. In the event, they came at all times and in all weathers. The slit trench in Boh Lay's garden received a tin roof and it turned out to be an excellent air raid shelter. Lwin and Lucienne insisted their children learn one life-saving lesson: when Boh Lay and Marie heard the terrifying sound of the air raid sirens wailing across town from the fire station, they must immediately run to the shelter with Mama and Papa and their baby brother. Do or die. The emergency suitcases were packed and ready. Boh Lay never again made the dangerous mistake of waving at an enemy bomber. He quickly learned how to distinguish friend from foe by the sound of their engines.

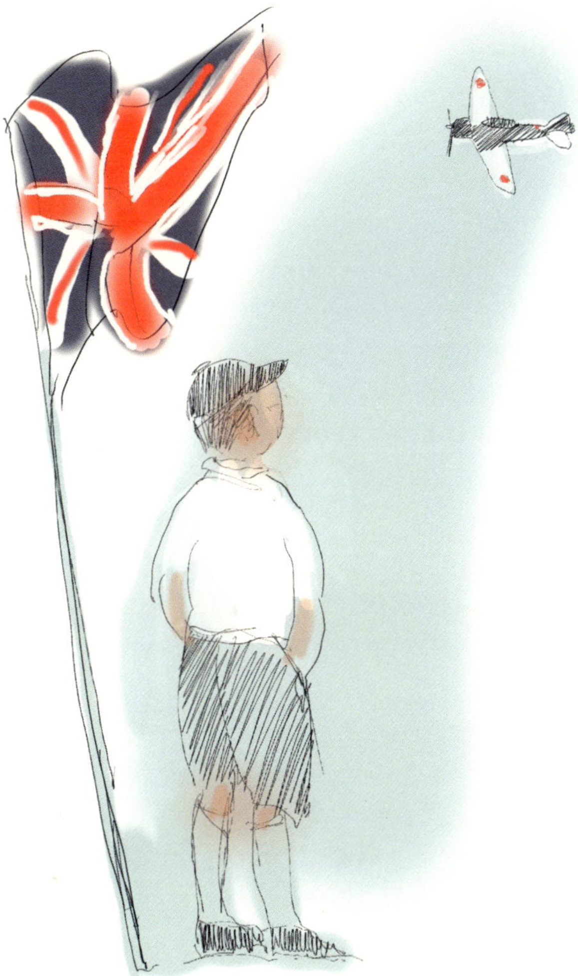

Boh Lay could hardly contain his excitement

After weeks of bombing raids the schools were closed and the most ordinary things were rationed. Farmers and fishermen stopped delivering food to market. A nighttime curfew and blackout prevailed across the town. Shops were boarded up.

The missing Japanese dentist and his wife were confirmed as spies and people suspected they were not the only spies in town. We were so terrified that all trust was broken and we were ready to fight anyone, including each other.

Very soon Lucienne realised she was the only white face left in town. While she was busy having a baby her friends had all left for home. Daw Bu Ma wanted her grandchildren to join her in the village but Lucienne told her husband she was not prepared to go and live in 'a jungle hut,' however well intentioned the offer.

If the news was not bad enough in Bassein, Lucienne received equally upsetting letters from her family in London: a bomb had landed right outside the local tube station and an omnibus fell directly into the crater. It lay there for days with its wheels in the air and its greasy belly exposed like a dead animal. Her mother warned her against crossing the ocean. She was terrified her grandchildren would be torpedoed and drowned by a U-boat. When Fr. Perrin invited the family to billet in the cathedral compound, Lucienne accepted. There at least the family would be secure from dacoits and it suited Boh Lay to be with his school friends.

But nothing was safe. Death spread like disease unchecked. Boh Lay's friend, the teacher's son, died by the bomb which landed on the street corner beside the cathedral, next to the school, caught before he could get into the air raid shelter. Boh Lay could hardly believe his friend was gone, alive one minute, dead the next. They laid the body out in the aisle of the cathedral and a scientific curiosity prompted Boh Lay to examine it up close, looking, hoping for signs of life, but there was no life and no sign of death except for a small bloodless hole in the forehead. Was that where the souls leaked out and ascended to heaven like the pictures on the cathedral walls?

One evening, Boh Lay and the dhobi wallah's son emerged from the air raid shelter, as always relieved to be alive and keen to know what damage had taken place. Their eagle eyes spotted columns of black smoke billowing

The streets were deserted except for
the dogs
who sauntered out every evening
on private business
of their own

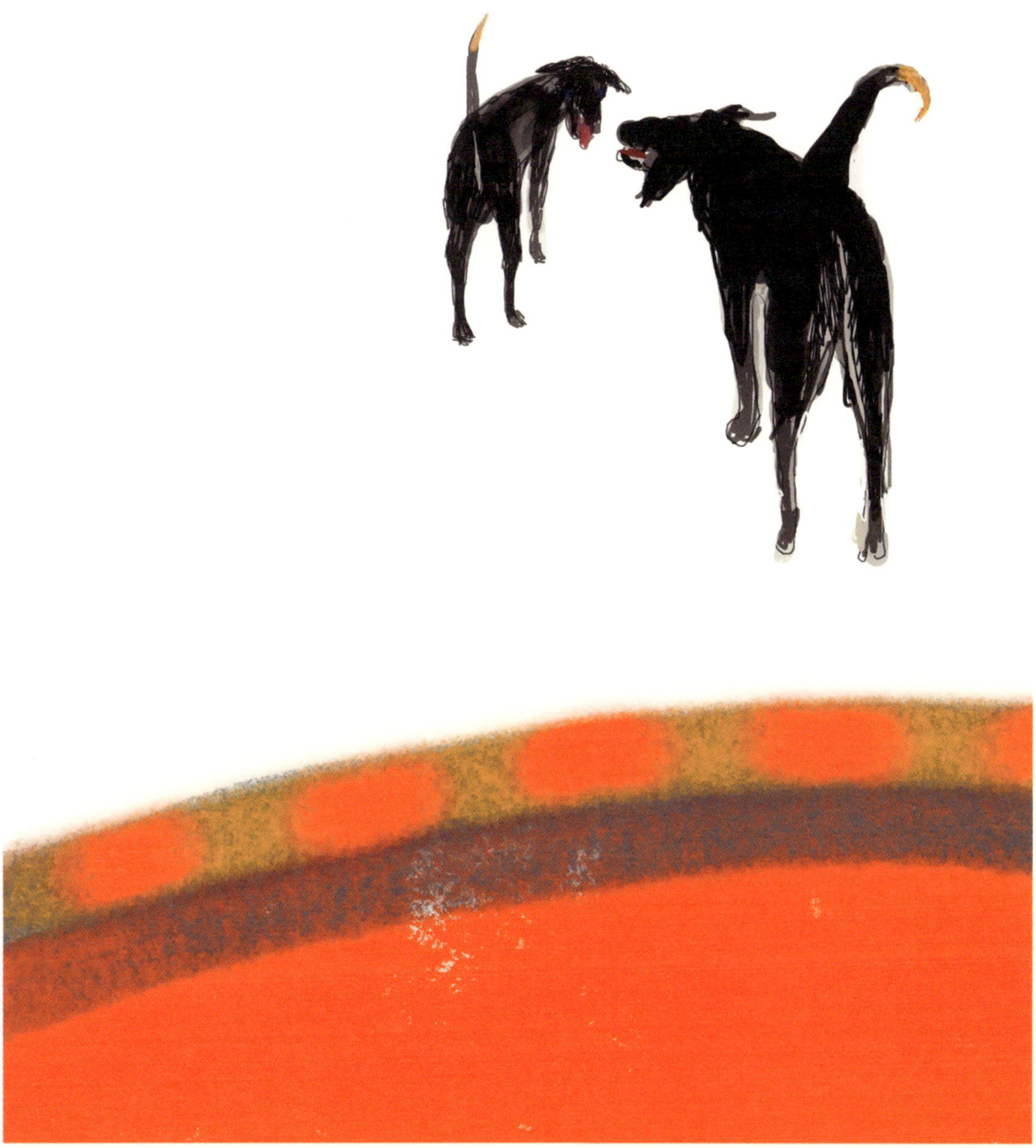

into the sky from the military airfield beside the railway tracks. The enemy bombers had scored a bullseye. Fear was out of the question and time was of the essence. Boh Lay jumped on his bicycle and the dhobi wallah's son got up behind, clinging round his waist. They raced along the road. Getting closer to the airfield, the air was thick with the acrid smell of burning parachute silk. Boh Lay could never ever forget it. Two planes, caught in the act of takeoff, lay smashed to pieces on the runway, one still occupied by a pilot in his flying jacket and leather helmet. Dead of course. A couple of dacoits took fright when they spied our boys and ran off, leaving Boh Lay and his young friend to take whatever they wanted. The boys filled their pockets with live ammunition then set to with their penknives to gather as much parachute silk as they could carry. They cycled home, delighted with their treasures – two barely visible shadows on the deserted streets. The next morning Mother Superior discovered their loot in her wash house. She grabbed the boys by the collars and hauled them round to the police station for a proper row. The sergeant in charge simply laughed and let them off with a caution. Boys will be boys.

Lwin had given up going to the courthouse. He was busy organising fire fighting teams and civil defence. He would never abandon his post or any of his responsibilities but time was running out for his family. If the enemy's attention turned towards Bassein, they were barely twenty-four hours march away and if Lucienne and the children were captured, the consequences were too awful to imagine. They said the enemy was merciless, even to captured women and children. As for himself, Lwin had no fear of death. He would fall on his sword or slit his own throat with a tin can rather than be captured but visions of internment camps kept Lucienne awake at night. Her escape options appeared to be, a sea voyage at risk of torpedoes or a formidable jungle trek, across the Yoma mountains to reach safety in British territory in India. Surely that would be far enough, but evacuee trains could only take them so far and were being bombarded by Japanese aircraft everyday. The last plane had already left. The only road transport was the bullock carts which Lucienne watched leaving town every day, loaded with families, children and possessions piled high. Lucienne shuddered at the thought. She and the children, including her new baby were embroiled in a deadly game of snakes and ladders with slim chance of winning.

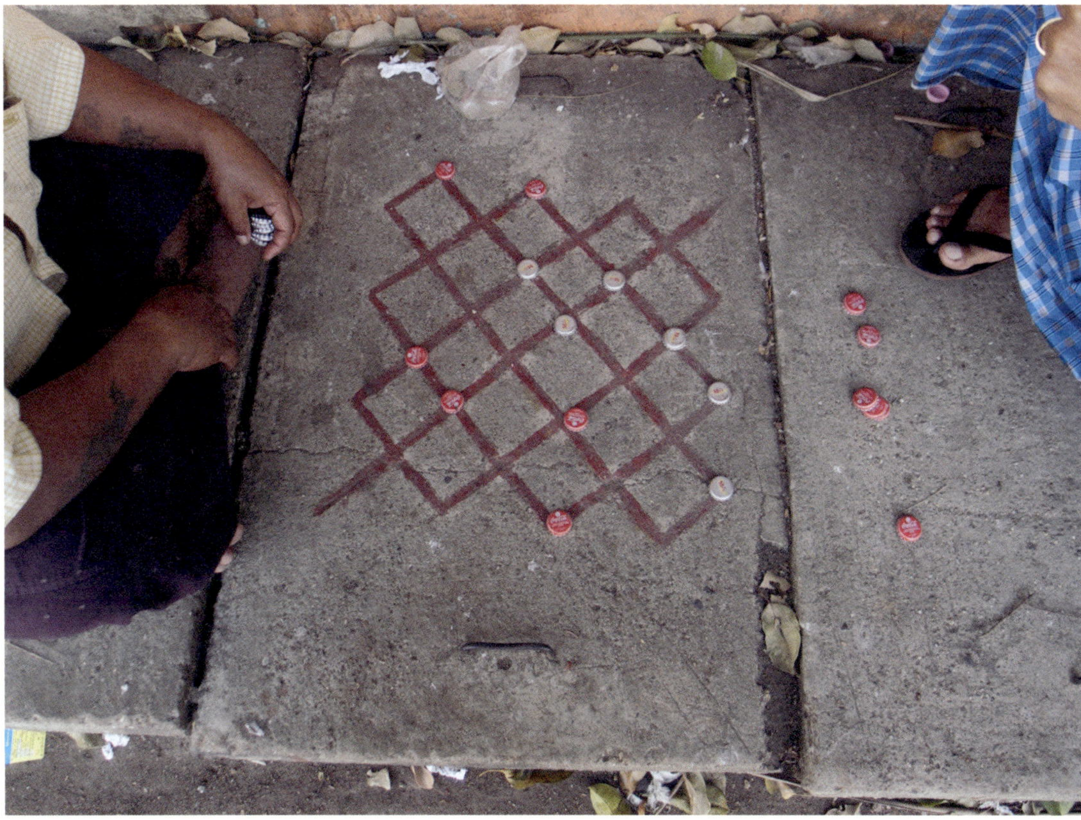

A game of chance at the docks

A decision must be made. Lwin was occupied with the harvest in the village. He had taken Boh Lay's bicycle because there was hardly any petrol left. Lucienne put on her best dress, carefully applied her make up and went visiting. She called Boh Lay to accompany her to the District Commissioner's house, where he sat on the doorstep playing with the commissioner's cat and she spent an hour in conference with the commissioner's wife. Their next call was to Father Perrin in the cathedral office. 'I have been told there is a boat leaving tonight on the ebb tide,' she said. He looked her straight in the eye. 'It is a wife's duty to be at her husband's side,' was his stern reply. 'But she also has a duty to protect her children. This is your last chance.' Mother and son left the priest's office and walked across the cathedral compound. Overhead, in the gentle sky, the egrets were returning to their nests, and in the short time it took the birds to settle, pink sunset turned to black night. The only light left in town was the gentle moon shining down on the one thousand years old golden pagoda. In silence.

Lwin failed to return home. Boh Lay watched Aung Htoo and the maid carrying suitcases down the garden path and heard his mother instruct Aung Htoo to use the last of the petrol and bring the car to the door. He prowled around the house taking a last look at his bedroom and in a slightly cross voice ordered Aung Htoo to make sure his father put the bicycle away safely when he eventually returned home. Meanwhile he strapped the sword around his waist and added the bayonet for good measure.

Boh Lay was prepared for anything he had seen in the films or in the comic books but the scene he entered at the dock was astonishing. Nothing could have prepared him. The wharf was crowded with foreigners desperate to escape. Businesses, pretty houses, loyal staff and pet dogs, possessions and obligations were all abandoned. Respectable adult men, pillars of the community, turned pirate in an instant, wielding crow bars, looting supplies regardless of law and order, removing tinned food, rice, tea, sugar, Ovaltine, and tinned peaches and condensed milk from the broken warehouses. These humble items had suddenly become the most precious commodities left in town. One man could not bear to be parted from his new fridge – he carried it on his back. Was it stuffed with food and drink for the voyage? Boh Lay refused to relinquish his bayonet but his mother persuaded him to leave his father's sword behind. Lucienne carried baby milk and nappies and a suitcase full of legal papers she could not afford to lose. She wore Lwin's gold signet ring beside her wedding ring. An Indian servant chose to take his master's silver plate.

Boh Lay counted twelve boats pulled up tight and dark against the river side but only 'The Louise' and 'The Sandeway' were properly fit for a sea journey. The nursemaid cried desperately, not knowing whether to stay or leave. She had no clothes to travel. There was no time left. She clung to the baby until Lucienne forcibly took him in her own arms. Boh Lay followed his mother down the narrow gang plank, feeling it bounce beneath his feet. The river pilot was one of the few who kept his head, he calmly directed Mrs Lwin and children to the saloon as if it was the most natural thing in the devastated world. His plan was to sail on the ebb tide in pitch black secrecy. Shortly, 'The Louise' weighed anchor and led the makeshift flotilla downriver towards the coast. Boh Lay's last view of Bassein was the flaming warehouses, accompanied by the low calls of the river pilot as the boatmen struggled to navigate their way between the sandbanks in the blackout. He noticed a brass plate in the cabin, 'Built on Clydeside.' Despite all precautions the boats were caught in a searchlight. They thought the end had come but fortunately, it was friend not foe. Everyone put on their bravest faces, determined to keep up morale no matter what happened.

'The Louise' was not fast but she was robust, she put her prow to the waves and sailed north along the coast with all the determination of the Clydeside men who built her. It was never safe to stop for long. Every evening Boh Lay stood out on deck listening to the ship's sirens calling to shore and longing for his father to come and join him, but nobody answered and no-one came. One morning, after a stormy night, Boh Lay realised that half the boats they had set out with had vanished without trace. 'The Louise' and 'The Sandeway' were lonely survivors.

Boh Lay and his family landed safely in Akyab, a town overwhelmed by men in military uniform, every nationality: white men from cold northern countries, black men from hot desert sands, and tough men from the high mountains. Some were cheerfully preparing for war but others were already in retreat. The King's army were busy unloading weapons from their ships. Vehicles, machine guns, stores, radios and canvas tents for the jungle camps. The enemy had taken the King's men by surprise with their devastating bombing raids and by marching up country as fast as 'The Louise' had sailed up the coast. They were uncomfortably close.

A lone woman and three children were a liability on the battlefront but chivalry prevailed. The family were allocated lodgings in a convent, conveniently overlooking the airfield. Boh Lay was delighted. The runway was a construction site with lorries kicking up dust in every direction. The heat was hard on the foreigners struggling to fuel their aircraft on the jungle strip. Boh Lay spent hours and hours studying planes in his comic books so he knew every one by name and technical detail. Sergeant took him in hand. A boy like Boh Lay, without a father, would have to grow up fast. This war could turn a boy into a man faster than anything, if he survived. He sat Boh Lay down for a facts of life lecture. The enemy could be anywhere. The little yellow devils were small enough to hide behind a bamboo stick. Never underestimate him. He was a better fighter than the German and the people at home didn't know that. The soldier's job was straightforward – kill the enemy – but easier said than done. It had to be done properly. It didn't matter if you riddled the Jap with bullets, ran over him in your jeep or cut off his head with a carving knife, he had a habit of resurrecting. As many enemy as you killed in one place, twice as many would pop up in another place. You had to hand it to him, he had courage. Every one of them would get a medal if he belonged to our lot. In Sergeant's opinion Boh Lay was quicker off the mark than some of the other lads just arrived. Half of them caught malaria before they got off the beach. Sergeant gave Boh Lay a job loading ammunition into anti-aircraft guns and awarded him a special rank: Youngest Gunner in the British army.

Lucienne directed a boy to fetch water and firewood and she sent him to market to search for food and baby milk. Boh Lay and Marie tried to help their mother by looking after baby brother, changing his nappies and warming the milk for his feeds. The nuns sent a sweet girl every morning with fresh eggs but the bungalow beds were bare wood planks and there were no mosquito nets. When dark fell, Lucienne and the children tossed and turned, being plagued by insects. The baby cried.

One restless night Boh Lay and Lucienne were disturbed by a strange noise coming from the nuns' sitting room. Lucienne thought it might be the enemy, who was so close that some of the soldiers said you could hear him whistling in the night time. At first, Boh Lay thought it might be the Nats. He had never seen a Nat but he had heard about them from his friends. Even Christians offered food and trinkets to placate the temperamental creatures. Of course the Nats were angry because of our burning houses and the broken cooking pots. The foreigners were no better than marauding elephants deliberately destroying everything in their path. The land lay bare. The foreigners said their scorched earth policy was a tactic to win the war, but it was our earth and their war. Boh Lay held his breath to hear better. He wished he had been allowed to bring his father's sword but he bravely picked up the bayonet and crept forward, with his mother following close behind. They cautiously opened the sitting room door. There was nothing to be seen or heard so they watched and waited in the dark, terrified. When the cause revealed itself: it was not the enemy or a Nat, it was a plague of hungry rats skipping over the nuns' dilapidated piano keys and playing out of tune.

Dear Lucienne did not know she was heartbroken, she had no time for that sort of thing. The one thing she knew was, the awful prospect of leaving

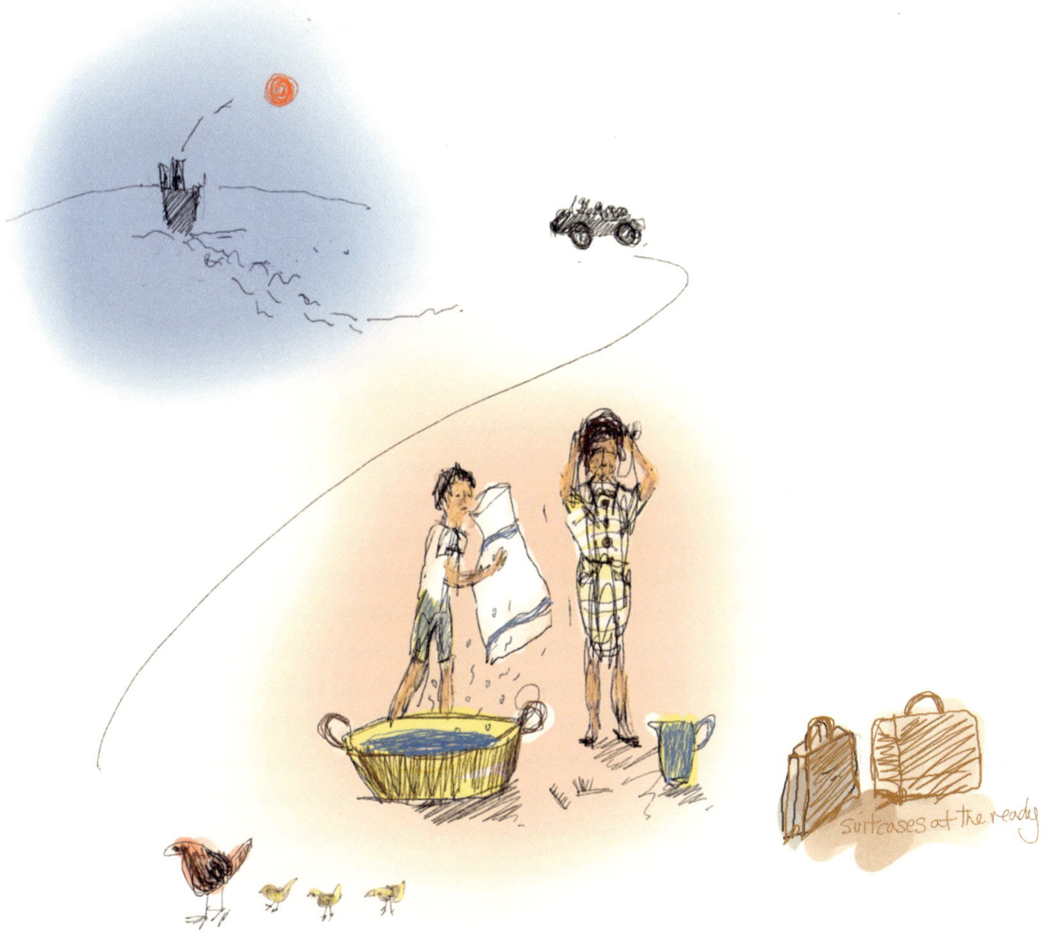

Darling, we missed the last boat because mother was washing her hair but thank god we did because we heard later it was sunk by a torpedo.

Dad xx (youngest gunner in the British Army)

her husband behind and risking her three children's lives on the ocean infested with U-boats was preferable to the risk of remaining in our country. Lwin had given her responsibility to keep the children safe. It was their unspoken agreement. Almost everything had been left behind but she had one valuable asset she relied on. Her appearance. Maintaining appearances was the last thing she would give up even in this primitive place. When a transport arrived at the bungalow, she was washing her hair in the scant privacy of the outdoor wash house. Where she got the hot water and soap from was a mystery. She emerged with a towel wrapped around her head and refused to leave until she was ready. The driver hustled the family into the truck and hurtled along the dirt track as fast as ever he could. They arrived at the dock in time for the children to observe the stern of the last boat to safety disappearing over the horizon. Boh Lay told me, in his own words, 'We missed the last boat because Mother was washing her hair.' Fortunately, in those days when the sun was just beginning to fade over The Empire Upon Which The Sun Never Sets, there remained gallant men who put women and children first. The family were successfully evacuated on the next 'last boat.'

For the last time Boh Lay stood out on deck, watching his past recede with the shoreline until the very tallest golden spires dissolved from sight. His lifelong sadness was that he never saw his beloved father again. Boh Lay resolved to put away his childhood memories, like photographs in an album, and trapped between the pages lay a perfectly preserved venomous snake which longed to sink its teeth into Japanese flesh. Boh Lay refused to open the album for many years, because, as he said, 'Who would believe me?'

My Darlings, I am happy to tell you, the silver plate was returned to its rightful and grateful owner by the honest Indian servant when he eventually reached safety in India, which was after all, the servant's native land and in a way, it seemed right and fitting. I wish I could say this was the happy ending to our story but that was not the case.

Your most loving
Adaw Gyi

'Yet Beautiful and Bright He Stood': The Last Days

Narrator: *Adaw Gyi*

My Dearest Darling Gazelles,

Email from Nettie Thin:
So my dears, while reading your letter and your snaps I felt very sorry for the death of your grandfather. That's why I recall what my father told me. After the bomb dropped by the Japanese invasion and the building caught fire and your grandfather is one of the person who put out fire by pouring water with buckets and followed by typhoid.

Lwin did not spend all his days in court. He wanted to see Western scientific ideas implemented on the family farms so he read all the latest books and invested in irrigation and drainage schemes. Swamps became dry land. Fresh water wells were dug. Mangrove trees were cleared and replaced with new paddy fields. He introduced a pineapple crop and teased his wife not to enjoy too many fruits of the land.

Every year more and more boatloads of paddy were delivered to the steam-powered rice mills. The paddy was unloaded by day labourers from the villages, barefoot men, deprived of land, who lived by the weight they carried on their bare backs. They submitted silently to climb the milling machines, balancing on rickety steps, bending double under the weight of rice, pouring sack after sack into the vibrating, open-mouthed engines which never slowed their mechanical pace. The noise and dust and hardship were colossal but there was no shortage of labour. Somewhere in the depths of the mill, caught between the sieves, belts and pulleys, the brown-skinned paddy turned into never ending rivers of polished white rice. Every sack of best quality paddy sold to the mill was noted in Daw Bu Ma's account book and added to her profits. The Baptist missionaries taught that prayers are rewarded and God will bring prosperity to the just men but in our land of plenty God struggled to hear poor men's voices because there was just too much of a greedy clamour.

From Lwin's point of view the successful order of life collapsed on that dreadful day when news of the Japanese invasion arrived in his office. His first thought was of Lucienne and the children. It seemed to him that all he had worked for, everything he believed permanent, including the rule of law and order, was revealed as flimsy as the Christmas lanterns the children hung around the house and garden. Lucienne was busy making final preparations for her traditional Boxing Day party and the maid was rocking his new baby in a hammock on the veranda, singing. What could he say to Lucienne? He had promised she would be safe in their new house by the lake and she had believed him. The foreigners' war in Europe had turned to a war in Asia, flown around the globe, and landed monstrous, bloody and screaming in Rangoon. The white-faced figures of authority were caught out, all unprepared. They immediately dispatched their wives and families on the last planes and watched them sail away on the last boats, counting themselves lucky to escape with their lives, their servants abandoned, left to the mercy of the invaders or to make their way upcountry by any means possible. On foot, barefoot if necessary.

The Japanese delivered their New Year message to Bassein by way of pretty printed invitations. Paper Nats fluttering from the sky, nipping the people's ears, whispering, 'Asia Unite. Freedom Rises With The Sun in The East. Asia Unite.' Our freedom fighting Burmese brothers joined with the Imperial Army and threatened to come marching down the delta any day. Every man, woman and child must look out for themselves because there was no one left to do it for them. Friends and neighbours remembered old quarrels and took knives to each other's throats. A young man was shot dead at the crossroads. People abandoned their homes and took to the roads carrying nothing but fear in their hearts.

Lwin knew he could not keep Lucienne or his foreigner children safe in Bassein, but neither could he make the awful decision to part from them. He set his papers in order and wrote a letter for Lucienne, leaving it on his office desk along with his gold signet ring. Lucienne must give the ring to Boh Lay when the time was right. He locked the office door as usual when he was away from home and gave Lucienne the key, saying it was harvest time and he had important business to attend to in the village. It was a gallant action. There was no petrol so he took Boh Lay's bicycle.

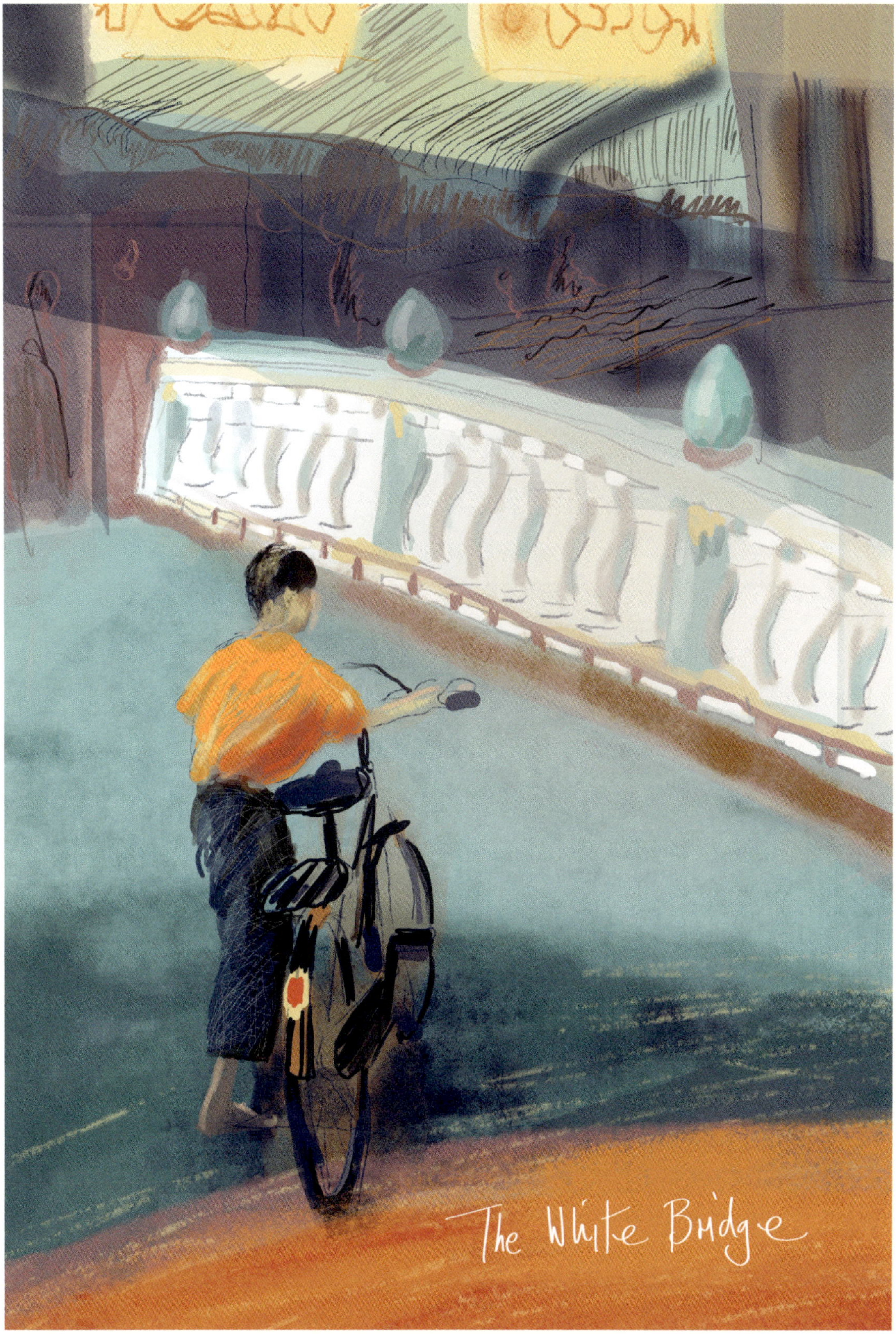
The White Bridge

On that terrible night, when the bombs were falling and the town went up in flames like a furnace, Lucienne remembered her father. She watched him march off to war with a battalion of men who promised to fight a war to end all wars. So few returned. She crossed oceans to put her memories to rest, to laugh and dance with her husband and children in a far away country. Her life, which had begun in one war, threatened to end in another. She would rather have died alongside Lwin than give him up but that choice was never hers to make. Necessity forged her courage, a mother's courage to protect her children. It drained her heart's blood. Lwin had left her so she could leave him. He knew she would do the unbearable right thing, for the children's sake.

That terrible night, floating away on the ebb tide with a new baby in her arms she left her husband and the best part of her life on the wharf. My Darling Gazelles, it is sad to say there are brave birds of passage who fly thousands of miles without coming to harm but however strong and resilient they may be they cannot fly against the wind. They must accept their fate.

Prayers went unanswered. The ancient pagoda proved to be nothing more than a convenient beacon for the Japanese bombers. It suffered a direct hit in the days following Boh Lay's departure. The golden mirage lay shattered in the dust with its dusty feet of clay exposed. Looters scraped away at the bricks, helping themselves to the precious gold fragments. An upturned cart and the bloated bodies of two horses blocked the entrance steps.

Lwin continued to do his faithful duty. When an air raid set the tobacco warehouses on fire Lwin directed his men to pour water on the flaming buildings, and when they ran out of petrol for the pumps and hoses they broke locks and requisitioned supplies from the last petrol store in town, and when even that supply ran out, they risked their lives with chain gangs and buckets. They fought until there was nothing left to save. In the short space of a few days, warehouses, shops and tree-lined streets were reduced to sheets of blackened corrugated iron and fragments of charred wood. The skeleton of Boh Lay's bicycle remained leaning against a brick wall, but the tyres and handlebars were melted away to nothing. Debris and ashes rolled away on the outgoing tide, only to return with the incoming tide.

Lwin had one remaining task. He signed the order releasing the starving convicts from the prison. It was his last official act. Guilty men were set free to roam the streets and fight the scavenger dogs for food. Lwin's mentor, San C. Po, the man who had given him his good name, stood unarmed on the road to Rangoon and called on the invaders to spare the women and children. For the moment they agreed to respect an old man's sincere wishes.

Lwin returned home expecting to find the house empty but Aung Htoo was waiting for him. The kitchen fire was lit, rice was cooked and warm water prepared in the bathroom just as Lucienne liked it. Aung Htoo took a cloth. He washed his master's scalded body like a parent tending a child and wrapped gauze bandages around Lwin's burnt hands. Lwin imagined he could hear Boh Lay chanting his homework. He went upstairs and paced around the empty rooms. The baby cot stood waiting with a mosquito net ready to unfurl. The children's sandals were laid out neatly with their green and white uniforms and school books on the shelf. Lwin stroked his hand over the fine foreigner clothes in his dressing room. The best linen and tweed any man could buy. He could see his face in his beautifully polished shoes but he could not bear to think of inserting his tender feet into the leather prisons. He pushed aside the evening suit and the horsehair wig and gown which Lucienne had maintained so carefully with brushing every week and picked up an old coloured longyi like the one his father wore in the fields. Aung Htoo knotted it firmly around his master's waist.

The night was cool. Lwin crossed the pretty canal otherwise known as the foul drainage ditch, remembering where Boh Lay had narrowly escaped drowning. He felt himself breaking into a fever. His head and bones ached. He walked down to the white-painted bridge beside the wharf where Aung Htoo liked to buy bread from the Indian baker. Everywhere deserted. He considered he might be the last person left alive in town but no, a boy pushing a bicycle appeared on the bridge walking towards him and pulled at his longyi, refusing to let go. The boy was smaller than Boh Lay and the bicycle was too large. Perhaps he had borrowed it from Boh Lay. He was too young to be out alone but he seemed to understand Lwin's needs. Without speaking, he escorted Lwin to a ferry boat and Lwin appreciated his help. The aches and pains had dulled his brain, spreading throughout his body. He shook, and tasted the salt sweat running down his face, shuddering in hot and cold waves. As cold as a winter wind on the Thames embankment

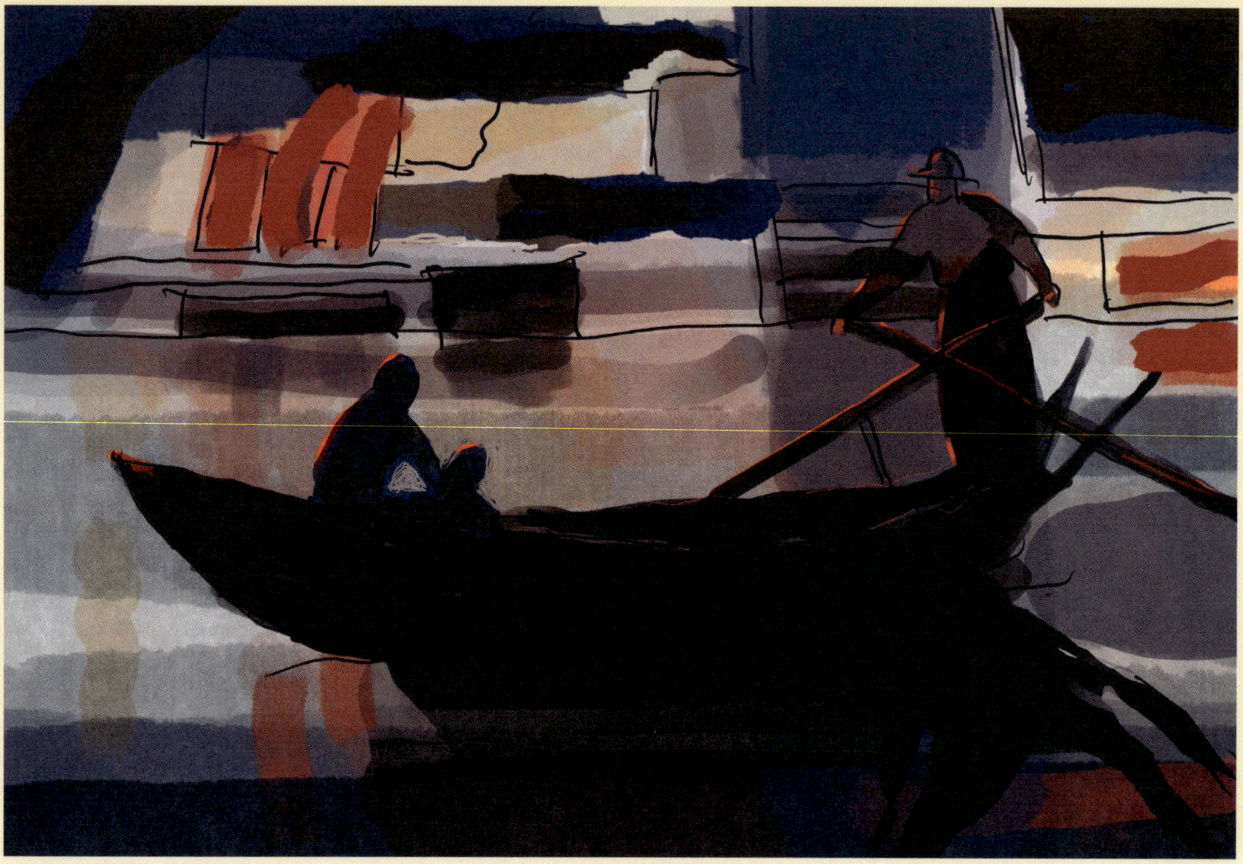

In the black night, the great tide of the Irrawaddy river, which rose and fell every day of Lwin's life. Which carried him around the world, returned Lwin to his village. He never knew his dear sisters ran to greet him. Dressed in moonlight, pretty as angels with tears in their eyes, they lifted Lwins body from the boat.

when the ground was covered in snow diamonds. Boh Lay threw a snowball in his face. He felt it trickling down his neck as he floated downriver to The Temple, where Lucienne was waiting for him. He did not think it strange when the boy opened his mouth as wide as a boa constrictor and exposed his pink tongue with a glittering silver coin balanced on the tip. Lwin accepted the coin and paid the ferryman.

Saw San Po Lwin was the oldest son and first in everything, including death. Lwin breathed his last in the place where he was born. Perhaps he died of typhoid after fighting the fire, when Bassein turned to ashes. I say he died because his faithful heart was broken but your Aunty Nettie said he died from eating a pork curry cooked by his unlucky sister. What nobody can say is where Daw Bu Ma and U Tun Hla buried their best beloved son. Many years later Boh Lay told me, with the slightest pain of resentment in his voice, nobody ever told him anything, but when his father turned the bicycle round the corner by the white bridge over the pretty canal he knew that would be the last he saw of him.

Your ever loving
Adaw Gyi

Where is Aung Htoo?
Narrator: *Adaw Gyi*

My Dearest Darling Gazelles,

'*Well done thou good and faithful servant.*' King James Bible.

I beg your patience for an old woman because out of respect for Aung Htoo's relatives who are good honest people and some of his children and grandchildren, who are our guests in the village, I need to inform you what is known of Aung Htoo history, which is a short story but that is a good thing because most often the short story is the one with the happy ending. The foreigners might say he was just the house boy but he was the most important, responsible person in the daily life of San Po Lwin household and no one could do anything without his help.

He was born in Chaung Zauk village and his mother requested Daw Bu Ma to get him a position in town. When he arrived in the Lwin household he had passed matriculation but his parents could not afford for him to continue studies so he went to work for the household and that was an excellent position for him.

He was fourteen or fifteen years old at that time. Of course Lucienne said he knew nothing and she had to start right at the beginning, teaching him to make French omelettes and later chocolate cake so she could impress her foreigner friends with entertaining at tea parties. He was a clever student, so he accumulated experience and quickly got promoted to managing the household.

Aung Htoo's skills increased in English. He learned how to drive the car and how to take notes and manage office affairs for Lwin. We can even say he saved Lwin's life when the intruder tried to hit Lwin over the head with a big stick. He was an excellent patient man and he put up with the naughty tricks of Boh Lay without ever complaining, and taught Boh Lay a

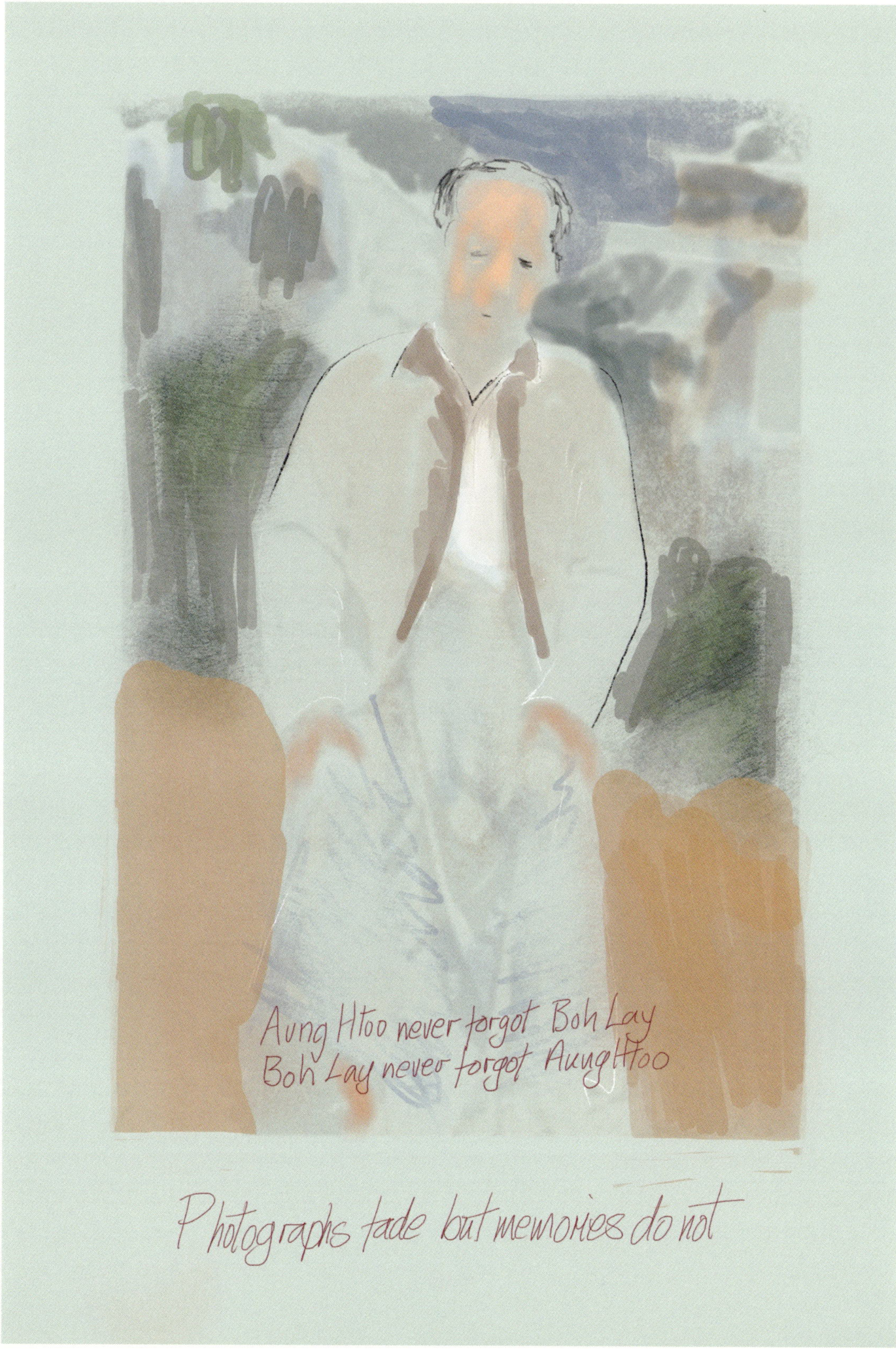
Aung Htoo never forgot Boh Lay
Boh Lay never forgot Aung Htoo
Photographs fade but memories do not

few things, like how to make ammunition for his catapult with little balls of clay from the river bank and how to ride a bike. He did not even complain to Boh Lay's father when Boh Lay stole the pens and papers from the office.

Well, Lucienne never learned to drive and Aung Htoo took care of everywhere she wanted to go. Lwin was not at home to take Lucienne and the children to the wharf on the last night so Aung Htoo drove them and carried the bags. He was the last person to say goodbye to Boh Lay when Boh Lay and his family left town and the warehouses were in full flame with bombs falling all over town. Boh Lay never knew what happened to Aung Htoo after that night and he spent the next seventy years worrying about him, even repenting the sins of his youth and being sorry for the number of times he had made Aung Htoo's life an absolute misery. We can also say Aung Htoo never knew what happened to Boh Lay and he would have been worried about that, as a senior Karen brother always takes responsibility for a younger Karen brother.

Boh Lay never cried about anything that happened to him and was always grateful for his good luck until seventy years after he left the wharf he cried with happiness for Aung Htoo's memory. When Boh Lay returned to his native land Aung Htoo's daughter made herself known to him, and then Boh Lay discovered that Aung Htoo had survived the bombing raids and the Japanese invasion and the terrible insurrection which killed so many of our Karen people. He had benefited from all the skills he learnt in the Lwin household, such as car driving and book keeping and so he was in a good position to marry and provide for a family. When the family grew up they were respectable and they became technicians in our hospital so, to this very day, they all benefit from the skills and education of their father, who had a good attitude.

Boh Lay dried his tears of happiness and relief and presented Aung Htoo's daughter with a new fountain pen, which she accepted in her two hands and she appreciated the gesture very much although she did not quite understand the full significance. These days Aung Htoo's grandson is very proud to bring his car and drive Boh Lay's daughter to the village when she returns to bring good luck and love from her relatives in the foreigner country.

Your ever loving
Adaw Gyi

Shakespeare in Myanmar: Falling in Love

Narrator: *Linda Lewin*

Under a dictatorship you forget how to ask questions, you just do as you are told. Suu Kyi.

English has been spoken in Myanmar long enough to be embedded. You will find English on products and in advertising as if it is a certificate of quality assurance and there is always someone who can speak English or who wants to practise so I am never stuck for an interpreter. Boh Lay listened to World Service radio in English, watched English language films and received letters and comics from London. He felt pretty well connected with the world. He was confident of his position at the centre of the universe, underpinned by the fact he was an English speaker. If English is your mother tongue thank your lucky stars, because English is a global language which grants English speakers free access to learn anything and do everything. English connects us to the World Wide Web, a digital wonderland which Western students take for granted.

Myanmar students struggle to access information in the free and easy way of their Western counterparts and one of the reasons is quite simply a language problem. If they want to access higher education, even within Myanmar, they are required to pass an English exam. If they want to read textbooks which have not been translated, to qualify for professional jobs or to study abroad, all that will be through the medium of English. All too often in Myanmar, learning English means learning script and vocabulary from old fashioned text books and learning pronunciation from poor teachers. No small task. I suggested to Aunty Nettie it might be easier and make sense for the children to learn Chinese, since the two countries are neighbours. Surely it would be useful for them to know what's going on next door, but that idea was poorly received. Everybody wants to learn English.

Our Myanmar students are all eager to learn but in the beginning they are extremely nervous. They clump together on their seats for mutual support. We try to gently tease them apart but they seem to be under the influence of a magnetism which pulls them back together. They all have beautifully neat handwriting, I think for many it is easier to write in English rather than in Burmese script, which appears complicated, at least to me. Within Myanmar there seems to be a hierarchy of those who consider they read and write Burmese well and those who can't. I'm sure politics are involved. Even though their English reading sounds fluent I never assume the students understand equally well because they have an extraordinary ability to imitate and rote learn. If you go out walking in the evening, you will hear the scholars in their dormitories chanting from textbooks like religious zealots. That is the way they pass exams, but ask them for an opinion or to answer a question on the meaning of a text and they will struggle to find an answer. I found a girl in the orphanage learning from a textbook that would have looked out of date in my old fashioned primary school. A simple question was answered with blank silence. Students have been trained to think that questioning the teacher or asking for help is disrespectful. We push our students hard to express opinions by making simple choices but games involving choices swiftly turn into follow my leader so we evolve to secret ballots.

When they gain confidence some students are surprisingly talkative. One young man told me, 'quite frankly,' that he had only one fault and that was talking too much. However, he was the odd one out who did ask questions and that could never be too much in my class. At the end of one course, a young man bowed in front of me with his hands folded and apologised for being a bad student. I could not have been more shocked. Every one of our students was a delight. I wish they would all rebel.

It was obvious some students were not accustomed to handling anything printed on paper. They thumbed the pages of a book in a disturbingly destructive way. Sharing Western art with our English Language students resulted in some extraordinary moments, simply because they had seen nothing like it before. Although reduced to postcards and photocopies, the power of imagery, magnified through the lens of being seen for the first time, persuaded students to become eloquent.

A photograph of Anthony Gormley's *The Angel of the North* was not to their taste, far too cold-hearted. Van Gogh's bedroom was their dream come true, every detail a delight, including the colour of the curtains. They could see just how much he loved that room. A sweet, motherly boy who adored children was overwhelmed by the emotion of a blue period Picasso, *Mother and Child*. He absolutely identified with the despair of a starving mother and the innocence of her child, who he described as being too young to understand. I suspect my student had first hand knowledge of circumstances and emotions that are difficult to express in any language, but Picasso persuaded him to try.

I began teaching in Pathein at a time when the sight of a foreigner on the street was an unusual event so it was particularly exciting for the students to have a real, live, foreigner teacher in class. Everyone was curious. One evening I was invited to speak to a class of about forty students I had never met before. Our classroom was in the cathedral compound and the students were a mixed bag who came straight from work or their full time studies. The task was daunting for a novice teacher, but an invitation I was pleased to accept. Thankfully, at that stage I knew very little about lesson planning so I did the best I could in the time available, which was to gather a big pile of pictures under my arm.

When I arrived in class I was warned we had an unexpected guest and I was slightly taken aback by the sight of a man in a military uniform seated in the corner of the room. I had no idea how to read the emblems which might have told me his rank or even which army he belonged to, and there were several possibilities. I tried to explain he was welcome to be in the class on condition he participated and then I tried to forget he was there, lurking in the corner.

Guided by beginners' instinct, I asked the students to process around the tables, where I had laid out a selection of photographs, and choose one to talk about in English. The simple instruction to 'stand up' took them by surprise and they tripped over each other's feet in confusion, but once they got the hang of it they had a lot of fun, getting more bold as the evening wore on. A couple of bright sparks did a quick research on their phones which, at the time, were new technology in Myanmar – full marks to them. Finally, it was the turn of a smart young man. He deviated from the instructions and demanded to know what kind of watch would I recommend, then he picked up a photo of my horse and asked, a boy or a girl? A gelding was my answer. They understood perfectly.

But the best was the last. The soldier in the corner was so impressed by my performance and the jolly atmosphere, he changed his mind and decided to participate. He had no English so his sister acted as interpreter. He chose a photograph of the beautiful apple tree in my Scottish garden, laden with bright red fruit. He said it reminded him of the tree in the Garden of Eden. This was a revelation because it implied he was a Christian Karen, unusual in the Burmese military.

At the end of class I was laden with presents and students desperate to escort me back to my hotel. The younger ones were curious to touch and even cuddle. The soldier insisted on having his photo taken with me, arm in arm. Desperate to offer a gift but unprepared, he hit on the idea of removing one of his collar studs, a brass star combined with an anchor and a pair of wings. He presented it to me as if it was a medal. Despite everything that has happened since then, it remains one of my most treasured souvenirs from Myanmar.

Finding good and appropriate reading material for the Pathein English class was a tricky task. The students encompassed a wide age range and it was hard to second-guess their life experience, their interests. They might have family responsibilities. Some had suffered traumas. In the early years of the project we had to cater for students with no experience of the physical commonplaces of Western life – trains and planes, high rise buildings, escalators and conveyor belts, plumbing and electricity in every home, a kitchen with a cooker. That ruled out rather a lot of conventional Western texts normally considered appropriate for their age group. I needed something that would cross cultural barriers and make sense in the context of our students' lives without treating them like children. I self censored anything which might be construed as politically subversive with one exception, which was the coal miners' strike in *Billy Elliot*, but the students failed to understand the concept of a strike. We tried to act out a picket line but they were reluctant.

When I asked the students or almost anybody, 'What has changed in the new democracy?' their answer was always the same. 'Roads.' It was true, roads and transport were making enormous differences to peoples' lives. The road from Yangon to Pathein was getting easier with each passing year. Taking a bus was less of an open-ended adventure. Timetables existed. Passengers were more certain of reaching their destinations without breaking down. Service stations were furnished in stainless steel and the cloths used to wipe the tables looked a lot cleaner, but I missed the women and children with their thanaka faces and trays of miniature snacks. Especially the little quails' eggs in their spotted shells. They seemed to disappear at the same rate as the big business franchises appeared. I certainly appreciated some of the motorway changes. As I was returning to Yangon from one of my regular trips to Pathein, a delicate hand tapped me on the shoulder, directing me to an unmarked door which opened onto a Western bathroom heaven. A brand new ladies' 'latrine,' as Nettie would have called it. I reported back to my disbelieving family, but when I tried to retrace my steps it was impossible to find.

Thinking about all of this and how a walk around the streets of Pathein seemed to be a step back in time, a step several centuries long, I realised Shakespeare was my ideal man. Shakespeare would have been perfectly at home in almost any small town in Myanmar. He knew about the wood and thatched buildings, the workshops and family businesses opening on to the street. I am sure his actors slept on bedding rolls stacked at the back of shop counters and listened to the cries of street hawkers selling their wares. They had their water delivered by the bucket and cooked their meals on charcoal braziers. Shakespeare's characters were woken by cockerels crowing in compounds where pigs and dogs and goats lived alongside their human owners. Aunty Nettie said the political situation in Myanmar was 'like The Wars of the Roses.' Shakespeare knew all about the rivalry, the scheming and plotting, arranged marriages, the assassinations and murders and so did my students. No melodramatic plot is missing or unappreciated in Myanmar.

I chose an adapted text of *Romeo and Juliet* and asked 'Sister' if she was comfortable with her girls watching the film, which might contain one or two adult moments. 'Of course,' she said. She had studied *Romeo and Juliet* when she was a girl. She knew all about it. Well, thank you, old colonial education system. I was not the first in with *Romeo and Juliet*. The students loved the film. I sat in the back row, watching them watch the film. They lived and breathed *Romeo and Juliet*. It was nothing to do with the language and all to do with the plot, which made absolute Myanmar sense. First love, gang rivalry, the political role of the priest, family duty and the ultimate sacrifice, living and dying for romantic love.

Looking back at my photos, which cover the ten years of supposed democracy in Myanmar, they are all happy memories. If anyone asked me what changes democracy brought to Myanmar I would have said shopping, simple things such as fresh Myanmar grown coffee for breakfast, no more three in one. If you have never tasted three in one it's hard to explain but it has nothing to do with coffee as it is known in the west. More seriously, when I began teaching it was hard to buy a roll of sticky tape. By the time I finished there were bookshops full of educational, exam-passing text books and computer shops. I found my way to the book binding quarter in downtown Yangon and bought paper for art projects and painting materials. I was no longer reliant on whatever could be carried in a suitcase.

Below the surface I knew there were continuing difficulties and under-currents. One student was an IDP (Internally displaced person), dressed in borrowed clothes, very obviously in a state of shock. Another student was exceptionally shy to speak. We discovered her father beat her whenever she spoke Burmese, the language of his worst enemies, the Bamar. For the most part the students were excited about the future, distracted by newly imported Chinese motorbikes and mobile phones. They had aspirations to be teachers, nurses, doctors and run their own businesses. They loved making new friends in our classes. I keep in touch with some of the students through Facebook and from a distance I watch them grow up. One emigrated and has acquired American citizenship. One who tried so hard to be a nun has changed course, married and has a beautiful baby boy. Sadly, one that I know of died and is badly missed by a handicapped boy who needed his very special loving support. The missing student was killed in a road accident – too many drivers took to the new roads, too quickly and with disastrous consequences. In Myanmar democracy changed the pace of life dramatically. There were a lot of distractions and it was hard to think clearly.

At the end, when I walked through the cathedral compound to my classroom – which happened to be in the very same building where my father had

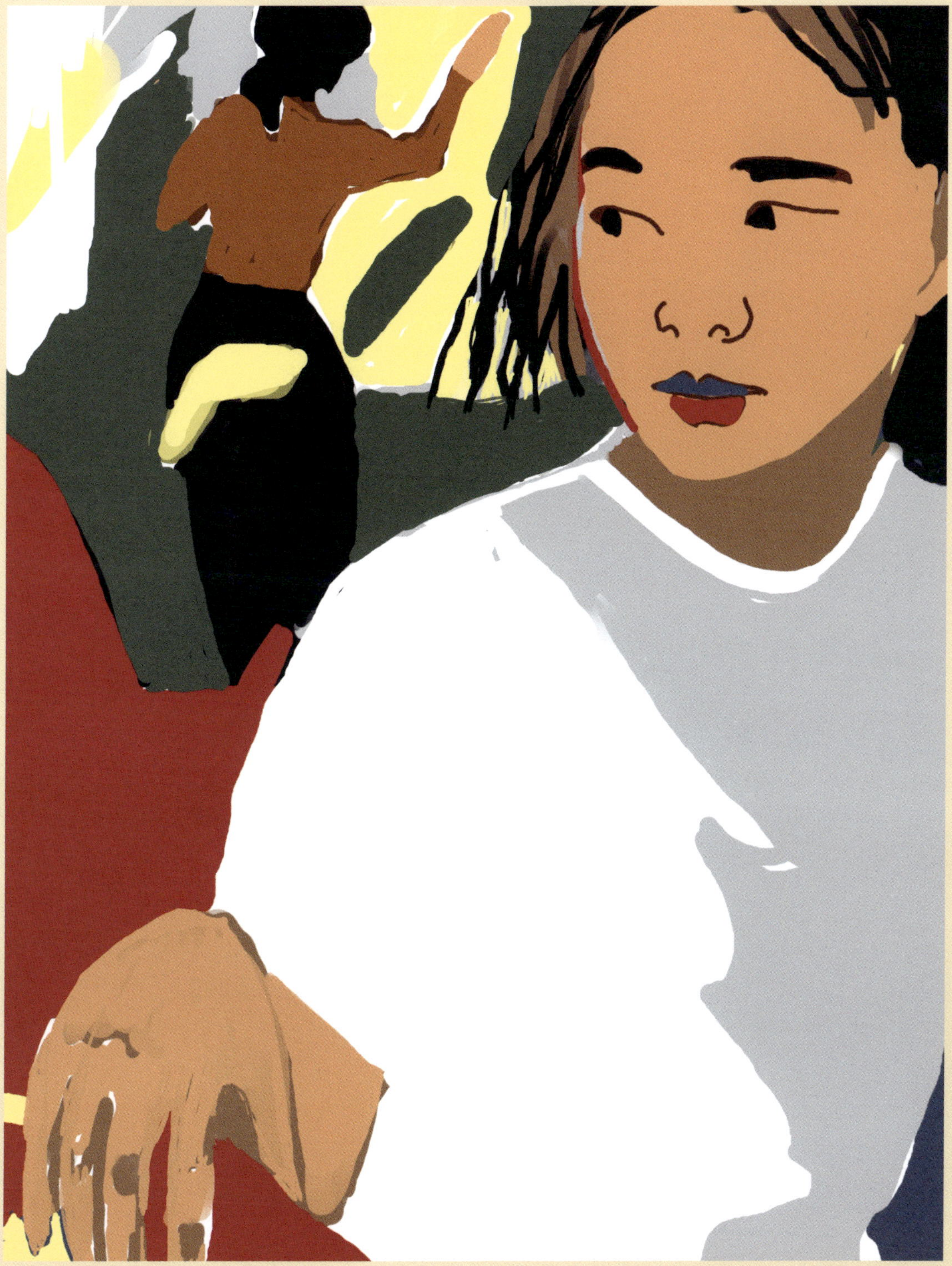

Juliet in class. Daydreaming of Romeo

taken refuge so many years before – I knew I was privileged to pay back to my family and community in Myanmar by creating something useful, a volunteer English teaching program. In doing so I was supported by many, many friends and their families in Scotland, all helping out with practical skills and generous fundraising efforts. It was hard work but it was always fun and fulfilling. There was no reason not to carry on developing the project, building on success. The students loved it and we loved it.

My memories of Myanmar are sometimes confusing, fast, shape shifting, bright colours and dark shadows but taken all together they are happy memories so why, on my last day of teaching in Pathein, having said goodbye to the students, standing alone in the peaceful cathedral compound, should I feel such a strange sense of sorrow and foreboding, quite out of keeping with the day? Somehow I knew it would be the last time but I did not know why until two years later.

San Po Thin: The Survivor
Narrator: *Adaw Gyi*

'If I speak the truth, may the thunderbolts and lightning, the Nat of the waters, and all sea animals love me, that I may be safe from them. May my prosperity increase like the rising sun and the waxing moon and when I change worlds may I attain the happiness of men and nats and realise merit, reward and perfect calm.' A Burmese oath.

Uncle Thin was not Buddhist, but perhaps he spoke the truth because the Nats of the water loved him and kindly saved him from drowning. He faced many difficulties in his long life but he overcame all and survived countless death defying adventures until finally enjoying life with his wife and children and grandchildren. That was his good fortune. Depending on your point of view, he was a politician, a soldier or a spy, or maybe an insurgent. At the very least he was a lucky man. That much could be seen in the jaunty angle of his hat and the curl of his moustache. Uncle Thin's grandchildren will show you his famous photograph when you like.

In the early hours of 19th July, 1947, Uncle Thin was standing on the top deck of the Irrawaddy ferry from Bassein to Rangoon with the first class passengers. It was wet season and the ferry was late due to an overnight storm. All night long the boat rocked and rolled in a terrifying way and some wondered if they would survive to greet the dawn. None forgot to say their prayers to whichever gods they believed in but as always, the storm blew over. The more courageous, more robust passengers appeared on deck and began to consult their watches, but no matter how many times they checked it made no difference. They would be late.

The engine pushed on steadily against the tide. The boatmen, who had been up all night battling the storm, continued their routines without making any hurry, huddled inside layers of wet clothes, faces obscured by hats pulled low against the morning cold. In due time the sun rose above the

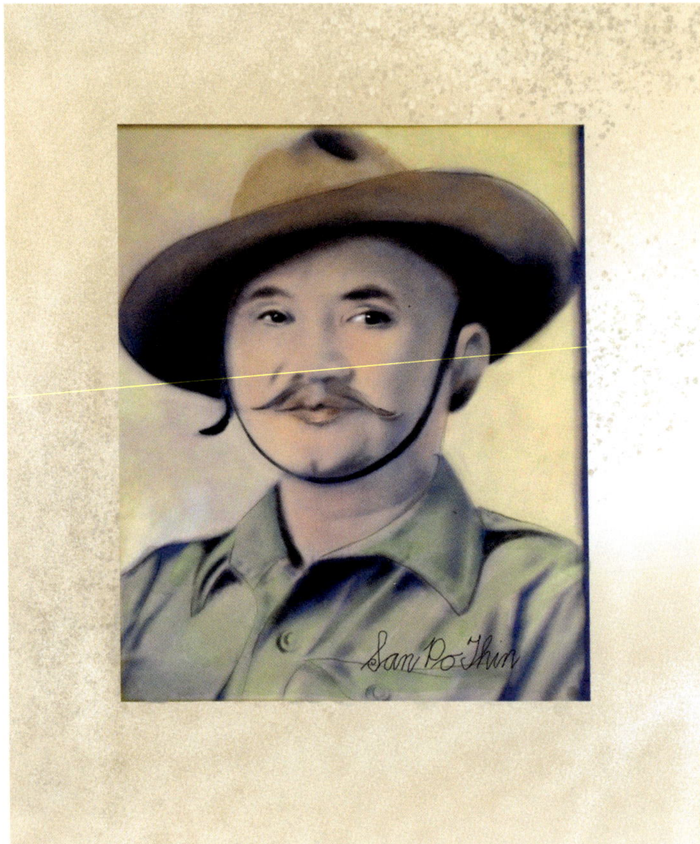

San Po Thin.
Never defeated in boxing or in life

horizon, colour swelled in the trees and in the distance, the great pagoda awoke with a golden wink. Uncle Thin felt the warmth of a new day on his face but his mind was elsewhere.

He was forty five years old. In those days, when so many of our bravest and best were lost to us, Uncle Thin was a senior man ready to write a handsome book of stories for his children to tell his grandchildren. For instance, the morning he captured a runaway horse on his way to school. He was eleven years old and fearless. He jumped on its bare back, only to be thrown off, landing unconscious on the ground. The American teacher picked him up. The day he sailed into New York harbour past the Statue of Liberty and they put him in detention with the poor unwanted souls of Europe. Barnum and Bailey's circus and Pawah the white elephant who cried such sorrowful tears. The strange circus performers he learned to love. Mr Moody's music school and memories of the burning villages and the night of Japanese interrogation. British military letters he had been compelled to bury and then destroy because, as they say in the films, they were too hot to handle. One day even he would find it hard to separate the fact from the fiction of his own life.

He was on the boat that morning because he was returning from his sister Charlotte's wedding to Captain Ma Lone in Bassein. At his mother's request he had walked the bride down the aisle. All the family had been there except for Lwin, who had died of typhoid during the Japanese invasion. Lwin's death broke Daw Bu Ma's heart, especially when her grandchildren, Boh Lay and his baby brother and sister, were forced to flee overseas. Everyone else survived. Simply surviving was a remarkable achievement in a country which had endured more than a century of British colonial rule followed by the Japanese occupation followed by political turmoil and armed insurrection. People were at their wits' end.

Uncle Thin and Lwin both wanted to make prosperous and peaceful dreams come true for their Karen people but that was not a straightforward thing. Lwin remained steadfast and loyal to the British Empire right up until his last breath, whereas Uncle Thin preferred independence. Independence for Burma and prosperity for the Karen People in Burma. Uncle Thin fought bravely for his principles all through the Japanese occupation but not everything he had done or how he had risked his life for the British officers was known to the public. In the end it had taken all his courage to march into the Bamar General Aung San's office with the words, 'Sometimes your greatest enemy can become your greatest friend,' but Aung San understood perfectly. After all, the general had supported the Japanese to eject the British and then supported the British in order to eject the Japanese. All is fair in love and war. War compelled soldiers and politicians to take devious paths and there were many unsung heroes.

Uncle Thin wished his brother was there to approve the course he was taking. He was ambitious for himself and his country and he was ready to lay aside his British uniform along with his Japanese sword in exchange for a business suit. That morning he wore modern European style, a man to be taken seriously. If the country lay in ruins he intended to be one who would rebuild it and if necessary he would be ruthless in the application of common sense. His Karen comrades called him a traitor when he accepted a ministerial post from the Bamar General, Aung Sang, but nonetheless he was on his way to a meeting in the Secretariat, where he had an appointment to keep with the future cabinet members, and he would have preferred not to be late.

His mind returned to the present when he heard the sound of the ferry engines manoeuvring towards the wharf and caught the whiff of garlic and fish paste from the mohinga stalls. The boatmen were poised with the mooring ropes in hand. At 10.30 it was already more than half way through the morning so he would engage a taxi to make up for lost time.

A familiar sound came pattering over the rooftops of the foreign embassies and grand hotels, falling to ground between the market stalls on the wharf. No one else seemed to hear it. It was not loud enough to disturb the mothers and children doing their shopping or the unemployed men playing board games with bottle tops on the pavement, but it was loud enough to alert Uncle Thin who knew it from old. Loud enough to alert a man whose life-saving good luck depended on his quick wits.

He arrived at the Secretariat building just in time to experience the spellbound moment of silent paralysis which precedes earth-shattering events such as great storms or earthquakes or volcanic eruptions. In that moment the history of our country cleaved apart and realigned, changing course for ever. The spell was broken by a white hanky fluttering from a window. Uncle Thin walked across the lawn and entered the grand hall just as all hell broke loose. In an unforgettably beautiful shaft of green heavenly light pouring down from the cupola, a cascade of men in uniform – disordered, undisciplined, screaming – came tumbling down the cast iron spiral staircase. The bloody bodies followed, some few on stretchers but most wrapped in blankets and carried in the arms of their comrades.

Nobody noticed or questioned Uncle Thin. He found his way to the meeting room where he should have been an hour earlier. It was a utilitarian office, the type familiar to any boarding school boy or waiting room passenger in an English railway station. A notice on the dimpled glass door politely reminded passers by to be quiet: 'Executive Council Meeting in progress.'

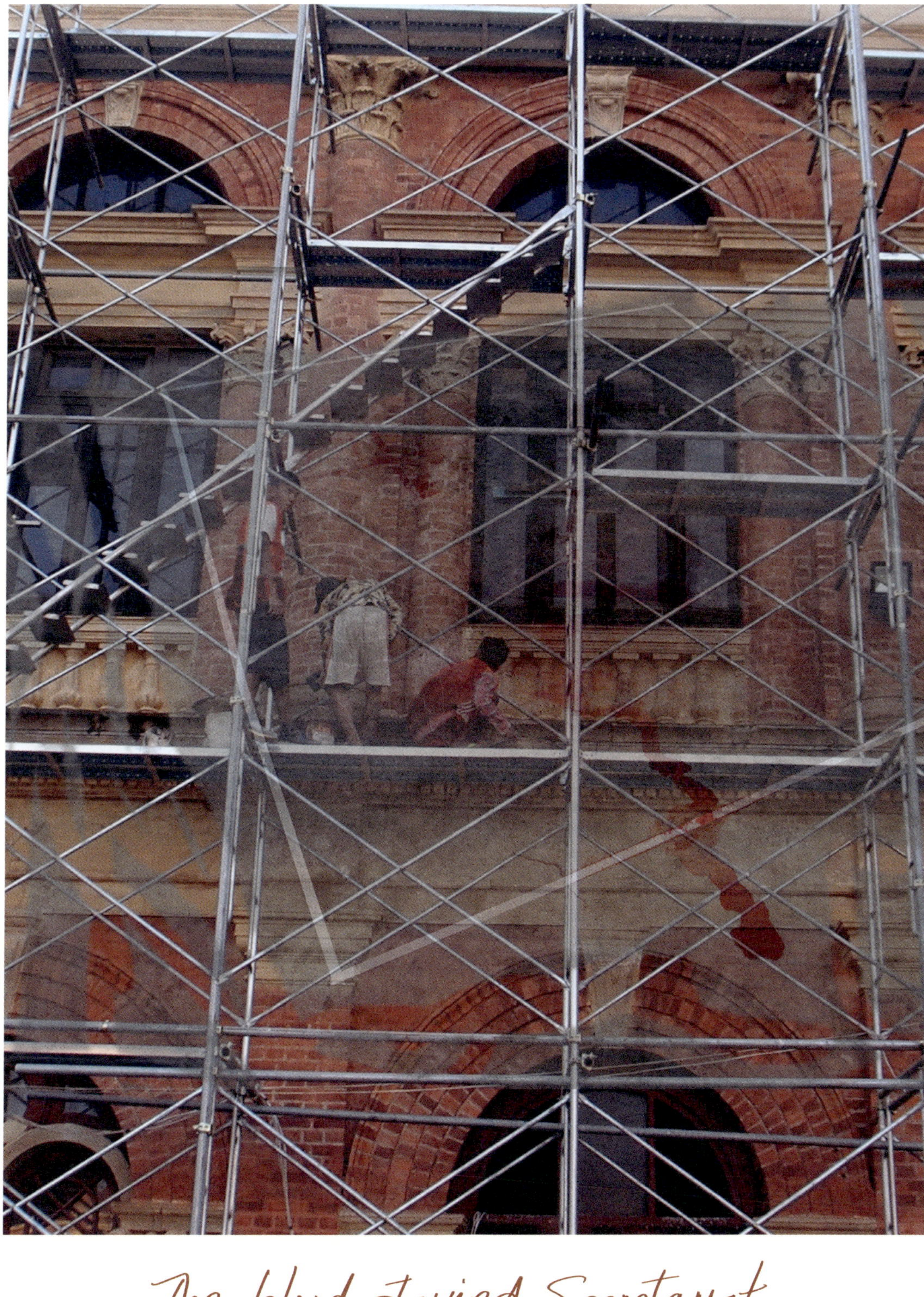

The blood stained Secretariat.
Colonial Administration office

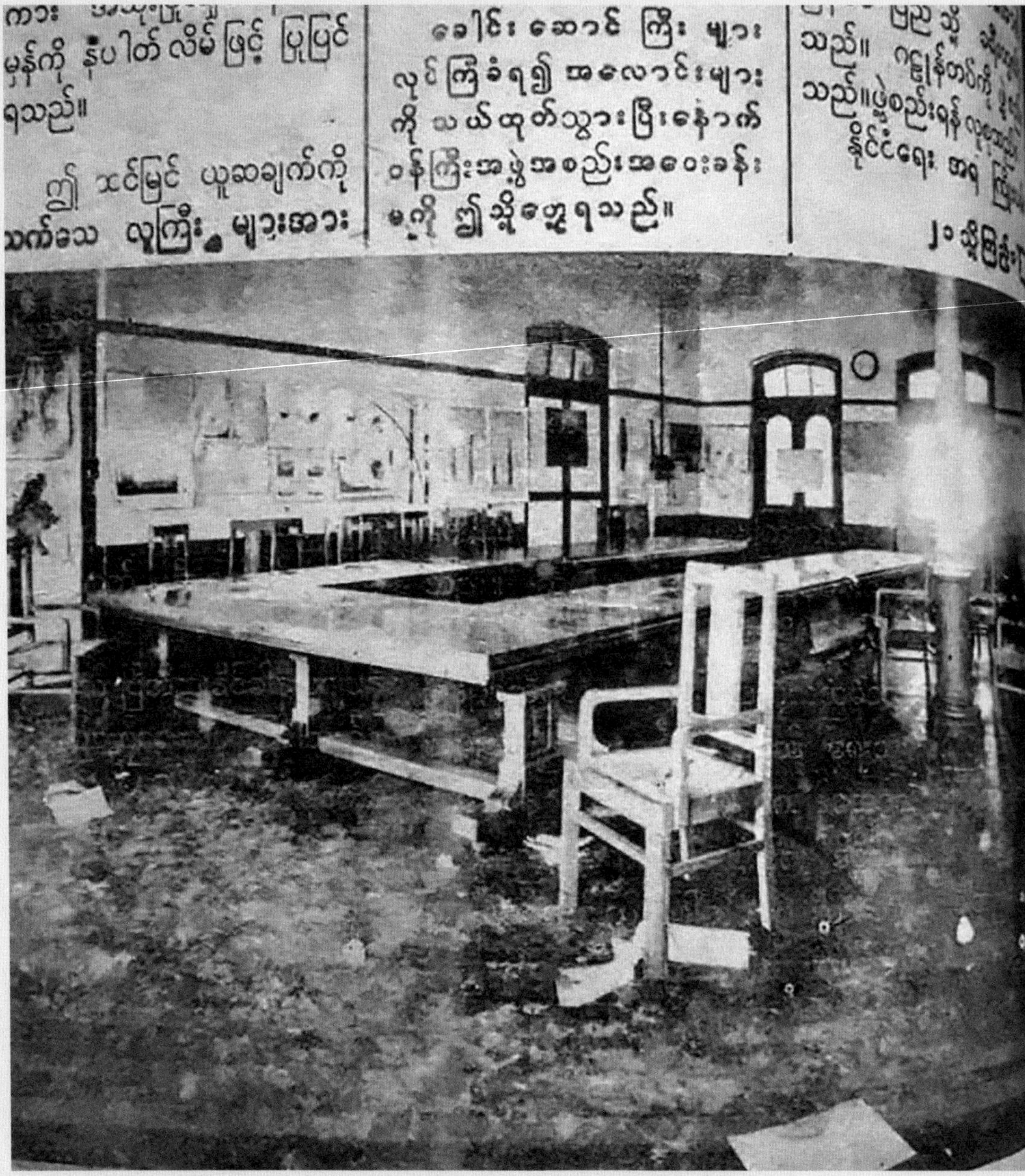

BURMA NEWS CLIPPING – ASSASSINATION – SECRETARIAT – RANGOON

Heavy wooden tables arranged in a horseshoe and square high-backed chairs remained in place on the linoleum floor. There were maps and charts on the wall as if prepared for an elementary geography lesson, but that was the end of anything that could be called ordinary.

The room was ripped to pieces, gun-smoke hanging in the air. Loose papers fluttering. Bullet holes sprayed across the walls and ceiling. All the country's best hopes for the future were assassinated on that morning: six government ministers, a secretary, a bodyguard and the charismatic leader, Aung San, with thirteen bullets in his body.

All this would be written up in the newspapers next morning. On 19th July 1947, Aung San was chairing a meeting of his Executive Council at the main Secretariat building in Rangoon when three gunmen with Sten guns burst in a little after 10:30am and opened fire. Aung San stood up when he heard the commotion outside and he was the first one to be felled by the hail of indiscriminate gunfire. He was thirty-one years old.

Many years later, when sometimes it seemed as if almost everyone of any merit had either died or emigrated for a better life abroad and the youth and strength of the country was drained away to foreign economies, Uncle Thin was one exception. He had spent time in prison and been released, he had navigated and survived all the difficult times and provided for his family. His wife was handsomely plump and his daughters elegant. At last he was left in peace to enjoy his children and play with his grandchildren, attending their university graduation ceremonies with pride. Sometimes, in the afternoon, if he answered the telephone, it might be a call from Aung San's widow, Daw Khin Kyi, requesting him to tune her piano. Uncle Thin would go up to the widow's house by the lake for tea and talk in her quiet sitting room. They enjoyed the late afternoon sun and the slight cool breeze from the open windows. He admired her family photographs and made her smile by singing the songs that hardly anyone except themselves remembered, and talked about the old days when their children were young and he made Suu Kyi laugh by carrying her on his back, pretending to be an elephant with a long trunk.

Your ever loving
Adaw Gyi

The Dawn Raid
1st February 2021
Narrator: *Linda Lewin*

Christmas – over. New Year – done and dusted. Aung San Suu Kyi and NLD ministers – elected. COVID-19 – year one over. COVID-19 – year two beginning. I decided to write a book, starting date 1st February 2021. It would just fill in the time nicely until the world returned to normal and travel restrictions were lifted.

My father rang me up.
'Darling, What news from Myanmar?'
'No news, dear Father. No news is good news.'
'Do you think there will be a coup?'
'Of course not, dear Father. Why would they? It's all going so well. The people have spoken.'

I sat down, ready to write on 1st February and in that instant my world and my book changed shape.
On 1st February 2021, Aung San Suu Kyi and NLD ministers were taken from their homes.
It was a coup.
Father was right all along.

On Facebook:
I recognise the locations. I scan the crowds for familiar faces and find them.

The young were not prepared. The old were not surprised.

I am relieved each and every day that nobody I know dies.

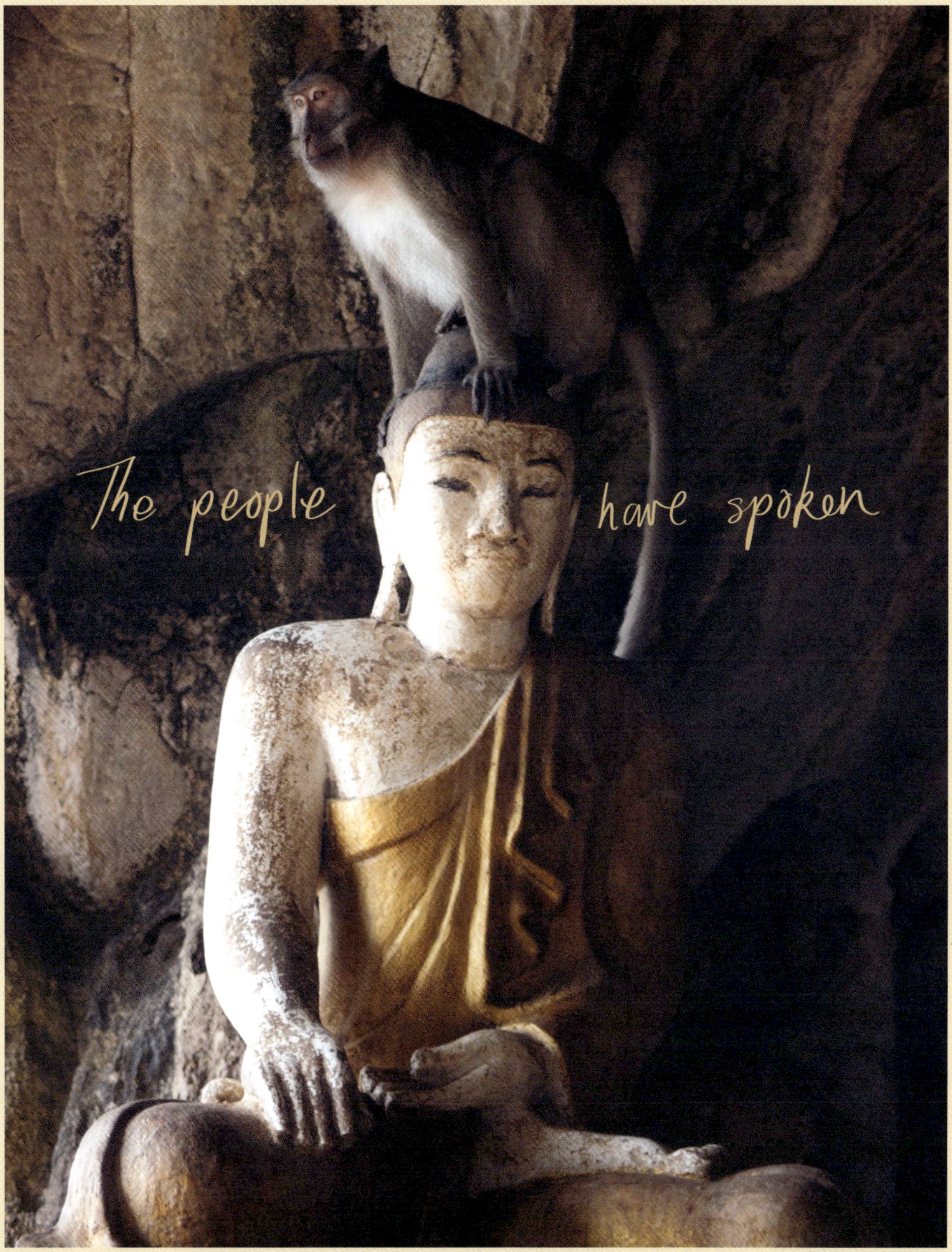
The people have spoken

Angels with Broken Wings
Narrator: *Linda Lewin*

'*A mind when tamed is conducive to happiness.*' Motto, Ministry of Religious Affairs and Culture, Myanmar.

Guide books inform us, one hundred and thirty distinct languages are spoken in Myanmar. This figure is widely quoted, including by Suu Kyi. However, many of these languages are dying as surely as the native forests where they live are being felled. When the minority indigenous people lose their lands to expoitation by international buinesses involved in mining, timber and industrial agriculture, they lose everything, including their community, their culture and their languages, but ethnic languages are not the only threatened form of communication in Myanmar. Censorship affects freedom of expression in all media, personal and public. Actors, film makers, journalists, musicians, artists, even beauty queens and fashion bloggers, everyone – and especially those with a public profile – know they have to be careful what they say and do in Myanmar. Censorship and self censorship are commercial decisions and a matter of survival, of life and death. 'I don't like it but I have to work with them' is a commonplace and necessary compromise.

In January 2019, I was lucky to hear a voice which The Generals had tried to silence. The censors seemed to relax their grip just for a moment and Myanmar artists bravely seized the opportunity by contributing their work to a contemporary art exhibition presented in the Secretariat Office in Yangon. By putting their signature to their work artists take responsibility for what they say and what they do not say. They make themselves vulnerable. I would like to say that artists cannot tell lies but that is not true. It would be more true to say when artists attempt or are coerced into telling lies those lies have a tendency to seep out on screens and on canvas in the form of nasty stains which look ridiculous to the public. Visual lies are easy to spot. Nothing in the exhibition looked ridiculous to me. It was the (rarely seen or heard in Myanmar) courageous truth.

The Secretariat is the former home of the British colonial administration in Myanmar. It is a pink brick building, a grand architectural fairy tale which lay mysterious and derelict for many years, surrounded by overgrown trees. This is where Aung San was shot and Uncle San Po Thin, with his usual good luck, avoided assassination. I had been waiting to see inside for a long time and at last my patience was rewarded when the doors were opened for an exhibition entitled *Concept. Context. Contestation.* The exterior of the building was beautifully restored but the internal spaces remained unfinished. The exposed brickwork and broken concrete floors were the perfect setting for the works of Southeast Asian artists including from Myanmar.

In 2019 I would have written this section in the past tense but since the events of 1st February 2021 I have changed it back to present tense. There were a very few years when censorship began to be relaxed but once more artists, poets, musicians and all kinds of celebrity figures are detained, whereabouts unknown. The military regime has made telling the truth a dangerous game in Myanmar, a contest between the artist teams and the censorship teams. To be a successful artist player necessitates speed and courage. Official permissions are required to show work to the public but the censors will probably not show up until a few hours before the gallery doors are due to open. Despite their lack of artistic credentials they are the final arbiters. If an individual censor takes personal offence to a black painting because he thinks it is too gloomy, it must go. If he takes offence to a white painting because it is too spiritual and inspiring or perhaps because it is the opposite of black and he thinks the artist is trying to play a clever trick, it must go. If he takes offence to a red painting because red is the colour of revolution, it must go. For some years black was recognised by both teams as a prohibited colour but the rules of the game, if any at all, are constantly changing. The self sacrificing individual who dares to paint the black and white truth for the public benefit is risking years of imprisonment,

I discovered the opening of the exhibition was exactly one year late because permissions had been refused in 2018 and true to form, the censors delayed permissions for the 2019 show until just twenty-four hours ahead of opening. The organisers had one short night to hang a major international exhibition but they were prepared. They succeeded in hanging everything except for the artist statements, which were left lying loose on the concrete floor. They had issued invitations to the powers that be but none showed up, which probably meant the artists and their guests had a lot more fun. I looked for the customary visitors' comments book but there was none. Health and safety at all times.

The opening began in the grand entrance hall with brilliant East-West fusion jazz music and carefully-crafted speeches. The crowd of foreigners and locals was clearly emotional. Little did they know this was to be a very short lived moment of victory. When the jazz musicians finished, a family of traditional village musicians with their babes in arms took over. Pied Piper fashion, they led us up the grand double-spiral staircase into the first floor exhibition halls. The raucous drumming and singing might have been loud enough to frighten away the old Nat spirits but somehow the simple country songs were overpowered by the high ceilinged, colonial rooms where the supporting Victorian columns were very familiar to me – cast iron, Made in Scotland.

A sombre atmosphere pressed down on all of us. The ghosts of old colonial history which hung around these derelict rooms made their influence felt but the artists were not afraid to confront them. They forced us to witness our worst nightmares, old and new horrors, including disappearances, death and torture, but the artists did not leave us without hope. Their works were fantastically varied. We were comforted by tender family memories, a box of old photographs printed on fragile tissue paper. I was invited to sit at a table and help prepare bean sprouts for cooking, talking and telling stories in the time honoured grandmothers' way. We were even given a DIY passport kit for stateless persons, an opportunity to create our own passports to a better future.

The artist Htein Lin showed a work entitled, *Recently Departed*. We city dwellers had no need to travel to military prohibited areas in the distant jungles to witness the truth because the artist brought it home to us, in the grandest old colonial building in the centre of Yangon. We observed the commonplace torching of a village home, the black corpse of a bamboo and matting house, entirely destroyed by fire. A skeleton of a padouk tree, surrounded by charred children's toys and broken cooking pots. Everyone in Myanmar has a village home. The powerful, silent sorrow emanating from the abandoned home and simple possessions, evidence of murdered family life, stopped viewers in their tracks. The sense of love, loss and longing was solid enough to negate the sound of traffic from the open widows. We were transported to the mountains and jungles where generations of families live in mourning and exile. It was a prayer for peace.

Halfway through the afternoon, the crowd parted to welcome a frail figure. A white-haired man, seemingly no more substantial than the stick he used to support himself. Younger artists respectfully shook his hand. In conversation with one of the curators, I learned that in Myanmar artists find performance and temporary installations are safer forms of expression than drawing and painting because the censor takes less notice of them.

The senior artist Aung Myint scattered rice on the concrete floor, one generous handful after another. Gradually, as he worked, the borders of Myanmar metamorphosed in gleaming rice grains. The life sustaining miracle which is rice has never been in short supply in Myanmar. There has always been more than enough for everyone. The artist illustrated his map with cheap plastic trinkets, cows in the countryside, plastic dolls representing Yangon, toy cars loaded with wood and gems, all rushing across the borders into China. When he finished his work we could see beautiful Myanmar overwhelmed with zero value plastic waste in exchange for its coveted natural resources. Aung Myint's installation, entitled *The Intruders*, exposed the plunder and exploitation of Myanmar by international business, in particular Chinese business. A depiction of unchecked commercial degradation, with no regard for anything but profit for the elite.

A little later, I spoke to the artist Kaung Su. He was standing in front of what appeared to be a jumble of rubbish strewn on the floor. When I asked for an explanation he said the tangled sticks and dirty rags were *Angels with Broken Wings*, his broken dreams of democracy in Myanmar.

Everything I knew about Myanmar fell into place in the moment I heard those words. The euphoria which had swept across the country when Suu Kyi was elected State Councillor in 2015 had dissipated and a resigned and tired disappointment had set in. Dismay and disillusion were the order of the day. Roads and cars for some, education for some, business opportunities but more for some than others, represent progress but they are not democracy. 2019 was the year I felt the weight of broken dreams pressing down on Myanmar.

Come the 2021 coup, Myanmar artists were in the first cohort on the streets, in the front lines of resistance and rebellion. Their speed and creativity, their wit and courage are remarkable. They have an arsenal of creative languages to evade the censor and communicate on social media. Many of their works are ephemeral, electronic and unsigned but they are part of Myanmar popular culture, viewed and shared by thousands. The more successful the artists' team are, the more dangerous the game becomes but creativity is not tamed, artists are not silent and they are not ever accepting their loss of freedom.

In Memory of the victims. Let one stand for many.

Phyo Zeya Thaw.
Born 26th March, 1981 – Died 23rd July, 2022
'Music can make us brave'

Hip Hop Artist and elected law maker.
Hanged to death. Age 41.

Nettie Thin and Suu Kyi: The Politician's Daughters
Narrator: *Linda Lewin*

Email from Nettie Thin:
My father took us to Suu Kyi's parents' house (now Aung San Museum) because we don't have home in Yangon. She was just a small girl. My father played with her. She addressed my father as Hsin Gyi meaning in English Big Elephant. We shared the same table under the same roof. After that the prime minister gave us a big flat. After staying there a few months my father was sent to jail because the insurrection broke out. After a year my father was out of jail because he was innocent. Since then we were very much in trouble. Suu Kyi was very much attached to my father because she lost her father since childhood.

I visited the Aung San museum in 2019, a couple of years after Aunty Nettie's death. It proved to be a lovely old colonial building with wide balconies in a quiet part of Yangon where great tropical trees hung over the garden walls. The lawns were well tended but the pond where Aung San's young son had drowned remained dismal green. The graciously proportioned rooms were simply furnished and the place was presented in a surprisingly low-key, minimalist way. My group were the only visitors.

In Myanmar General Aung San, popularly known as Bogyoke, pronounced Bojo, is credited for achieving independence from the British Empire, but perhaps independence was an idea whose time had come, part of an inevitable process. Aung San was a charismatic leader, the right man in the right place at the right time – that is, until he was shot. Bogyoke had two sons but as I learned from Aunty Nettie's email and as confirmed by my visit to the museum, one son died tragically young by drowning in the garden pond and the other lived in exile in America. Aung San had two daughters, the first died shortly after birth, the fourth child, his surviving daughter Suu Kyi, was destined to be his successor. I know very little about Suu Kyi's mother, Daw Khin Kyi, but let's say she had a loving heart and a straight backbone. Daw Khin Kyi understood her duty to her country, her husband and her daughter. Suu Kyi was too young to know her father when he died but she was educated to honour and respect his work and his spirit.

Aung San's emblematic military greatcoat was one of the few personal items on show in the museum. It was presented to him by the Japanese generals who trained him in military tactics and he liked to wear it with his hands stuffed in the pockets. He was a small man and judging by his portrait photograph, I thought he looked somewhat overwhelmed by the coat with its enormous lapels. I examined a few framed documents, longing to hear nonexistent ghostly voices. General Aung San's stern look followed me around the room but his full lips suggested he might have smiled a welcome in real life. I could find no physical trace of Suu Kyi in that house. There was a photograph of her two older brothers clinging to their widowed mother but Suu Kyi was not there. I know she was two years old at the time of her father's assassination, old enough to smile for the camera. Given that she is the most Notable Lady of the country I think the answer is surely yes, the Generals would prefer she is forgotten. Any other nation would leap at the chance to increase national revenue by selling thousands of tourists' mugs emblazoned with her portrait, but not here.

Personally, the most astonishing thing I discovered in the bland presentation was that my kitchen cupboard, which I had unwittingly picked out amongst all the junk in my local auction house in Scotland, was an exact match to the furniture in the Aung San home. Solid 1930-style teak made by the Rangoon and Bombay Trading Company. I took it to be a good sign but what it meant I am not sure, except perhaps, it confirmed my connection with this country where I felt so much at home.

Aunty Nettie, formerly known as Snow White, was born in 1937, so she would have been ten years old when Suu Kyi's father was assassinated on the 19th July 1947 and Nettie's own father, San Po Thin, was sent to jail not long afterwards. Although Suu Kyi had no direct memories of her father's assassination, in an interview she mentions her mother opened her home to an ethnic Karen family whose father was in prison and that is a corroborating link to Aunty Nettie's story. In her email, Aunty Nettie says that since then 'we were very much in trouble.' The not saying of exactly what is meant is a typical Myanmar safety precaution which Aunty Nettie learnt early in her childhood when she ran to her father at the garden gate. He instructed Nettie and her sister Rose Red to find their mother and sing their special song, 'If I Could Get You On A Slow Boat To China.' He disappeared into exile. Persecution of political detainees' family members is routine in Myanmar.

In fact, the whole country was in trouble. Aung San's dreams of independence came true but so did his worst nightmares, exactly as he prophesied just four days before he was assassinated. '*Unless and until there is unity between ethnic people and the national people, even if this country is independent, no matter which party and which government is in office, our country will remain a prostitute country.*'

By the *national people* he meant the Bamar. By the *ethnic people* he meant all the other nationalities, including the Karen. By prostitute he meant subject to foreign empires. Even at this distance in place and time I cannot avoid feeling uneasy about Aung San's use of language, the implied superiority of the word *national* over the word *ethnic*. Unity has never been achieved. The national army known as the Tatmadaw is predominantly Bamar and has persecuted vast numbers of ethnic people deemed to be insurgents. The so called insurgents, otherwise known as freedom fighters Shan, Mon, Chin, Kachin, Rakhine and Karen have died fighting for independence or they have been forced to flee to foreign countries. In 1962, fifteen chaotic years after Burma achieved independence from the British empire, General Ne Win staged a military coup and attempted to impose the Burmese Way To Socialism on all the peoples of Burma. The Generals grew fabulously wealthy but the citizens lost whatever little they had.

In the later years I knew her I wondered if the balance of Aunty Nettie's mind might be disturbed by age or by the tumultuous events of her life. She deliberately reduced herself to living in a village hut which may or may not have been, as she described it, a chicken house. I hope it was a figure of speech but really, at the time I believed it was the literal truth. I could easily imagine her nesting with the poultry, complete with straw in her hair. She forbade me to visit because she said it would be too much trouble to clean up for visitors. She preferred to see me in my hotel and she always made the effort to polish up nicely for the event. Eventually she gave away all of her possessions and refused medical treatment for her diabetes and failing eyesight because '*God must do his will.*' Adding all this together, over the period of the ten years I came to know her, her health slowly deteriorated. She found it more and more difficult to continue the active and helpful life she was accustomed to.

Age had the effect of loosening Aunty Nettie's tongue. She trusted me and was one of the few people I had contact with in Myanmar who felt free to say whatever she liked, pinning her faith in God for protection. Many of her stories were long and began in the middle or at the end. I found them difficult to follow because Aunty Nettie had learnt her English vocabulary so long ago from ancient history professors and Baptist preachers and had no opportunity to update her English language skills within the confines and reduced circumstances of Myanmar, and I had very little cultural or historical context in which to frame her stories, beyond my father's fairy tales. I had a lot of catching up to do.

Email from Nettie Thin. November 2009:
My Karen people are very ignorant, uneducated and poor. Most of the people in our fathers' village are very uneducated and poor. They have no understanding for the law and order of Myanmar.

Aunty Nettie joined the police force in 1960 to please her father and because he wanted her to help her people. Her 'introducing' portrait which she sent to me by email was a testament to how much she loved and believed in her work. It shows her in an immaculately smart uniform with a beaming smile. She said she always preferred to wear the trousers. Although she took early retirement from police work, she continued with her 'cases,' helping people because they had no concept of the law and order of Myanmar.

One evening, when I thought Aunty Nettie was definitely too old to make sense, I discovered why she had retired early from the police force. We enjoyed a family meal together on the balcony of a new downtown restaurant in Yangon. The family wanted to show just how much life in Yangon was improving. I looked up into the soft black sky, then down at my plate. The air was heavy and damp. As usual I struggled to eat because it was too hot and too late. I hated to be ungrateful. Nettie's favourite son Christopher sat at head of table. He was a pastor in the Baptist church but something had changed. Christopher's son had taken over the church work and Christopher was assisting the Karen tribes with mysterious negotiations involving a dam and hydro-electric power up in the Karen hills. On that night, wearing a brilliant white shirt and flashy watch, he glowed with new confidence. He said the government were prepared to negotiate with the Karens because the Karen army was strong, but I could see Nettie was worried.

When we left the restaurant she took hold of my arm because she said her eyes were poor. The street was dark. I tried to guide her safely over the broken paving stones and the accident-waiting-to-happen storm drains. In a mundane moment, walking close together, arm in arm to engage a taxi on the dimly lit street, caught between the car headlights and confusing shadows, Nettie recounted a memory I never wanted to hear. The story was quickly told. I bent my head to listen. Aunty Nettie had shrunk in size over the years. I wondered if I was dreaming but it must have been true because I could not have imagined such a horrific nightmare, not in my wildest dreams. I asked no questions for fear of the answers. I wondered if Nettie had ever shared this story with another person, her family or children? I still have no idea.

Quite why it slipped out at that moment I am not sure. I knew Aunty Nettie had survived two husbands. The first one had been shot and I knew she worried the same thing might happen to Christopher. Apparently his work was dangerous. I began to suspect that a surprising number of men in my Myanmar family had been shot and murdered. Much as I was fascinated to know how and why Nettie's husband had died that was not the story she wanted to tell.

The Burmese Way To Socialism had reduced Burma to one of the poorest countries in the world. Everyone's cupboard was bare. The government declared certain denominations of Burmese Kyat invalid, reducing people's savings to zero overnight. The atmosphere was volatile, riotous. Advised by fortune tellers, students in Rangoon chose what they thought would be an auspicious date, 8th August 1988, known as '8888,' to come out and protest on the streets, and the rest of the country followed suit. The army and the police were sent out to confront them. Aunty Nettie told me the protestors were children, other people's children, no different from her own. The orders were, no guns to point in the air – shoot to kill, execution style, a bullet straight to the head, regardless of whether the victims were neighbours, family or friends. It made no difference. Sources commonly say three thousand protestors died in the course of the demonstrations but I have no idea who was in a position to count. On the 8th August 1988 the military took command of the city of Rangoon by lethal force. Their soldiers occupied the hospital to prevent wounded protestors from being treated. They shot doctors, nurses, blood donors and innocent patients in their beds. That much is common knowledge but there was one thing in particular which bothered Aunty Nettie. The following morning she and her police officers were sent onto the blood soaked streets to pick up the bodies and burn them, dead or alive. That was the part which brought tears to her failing eyes. Not all were dead.

Nettie had lived with these memories more than half her lifetime. I do not know if she burned the bodies, dead or alive. She simply said she resigned her post. Half of me believed Nettie's story and the other half refused. I fought hard to forget I ever heard it.

Myanmar Now, English version. Sunday 11th April, 2021.
An eyewitness who spoke to Myanmar Now on the condition of anonymity on Saturday said that he had seen the bodies of several people stacked inside both Zeyar Muni pagoda and a nearby school compound on Friday.
The bodies of around 40 to 50 people had been seen near the pagoda's eastern entrance, but not all were dead, the eyewitness said. Injured people had been placed alongside those who had already died, and could be heard moaning from the mass of corpses.
'The bodies and the wounded people were dragged away by them,' he said, referring to the troops.
Soldiers were seen moving the bodies from the pagoda on Friday night at around 11pm, shouting in a way that suggested they were drunk, the eyewitness near Zeyar Muni said.
'Although I am not related to the victims, I was really hurt. I could do nothing, but I had to watch this. I want to take back the bodies of those young people who were still alive,' the witness told Myanmar Now.
By Saturday morning, the pagoda appeared as it had before the crackdown – blood had been washed away, the bodies gone, and occupying soldiers cleared out.

On Sunday 11th April 2021, sitting at home in Scotland at breakfast time, I read a report in Myanmar Now. An eye witness account of events identical to the ones Aunty Nettie described. Nettie's confession, which I received from her lips in Yangon, shortly before she died (of old age) was the absolute truth. Between the military crackdown on protestors in 1988 and the military crackdown on protestors thirty-three years later, I could find no difference. The truth was unequivocally, unavoidably rammed home. People were burned alive, people are burned alive, people will be burned alive. It goes on and on and on. That is the truth my father and Aunty Nettie lived with. A witness in the Myanmar Now report suggests the soldiers may be drunk. Myanmar people often describe the soldiers who callously shoot to kill as brainwashed military slaves. Surely it must be tremendously difficult to shoot a child, a child just like one's own child or the neighbour's child, in the head, even when drunk and brainwashed?

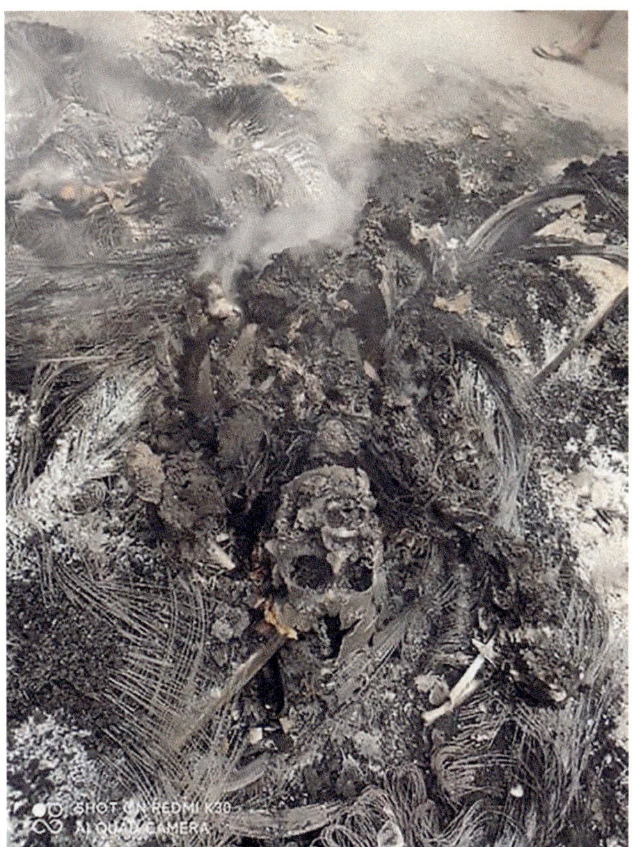

BURNED ALIVE – IMAGE TAKEN FROM SOCIAL MEDIA

Suu Kyi, the little girl who played elephant games riding on San Po Thin's back, grew up. She studied at Oxford, worked in New York and fell in love with an Englishman but she never forgot the lessons her mother taught her, or her dead father and his unfinished work in Burma. Before the wedding she told her husband that if ever her country needed her she must go back, and he accepted her condition as much as she accepted it, as fact, not choice. They enjoyed too few years together but long enough to bring two beautiful sons into the world. In August 1988 Suu Kyi travelled to Rangoon solely for the purpose of nursing her sick mother, leaving her husband and young sons in England. When she saw the riots raging through the city she was compelled, in the moment, to take her pre-destined place in front of the crowds at Shwedagon Pagoda. The people listened when she called out for an end to the riots and for peaceful protest. They trusted her and there was no going back. She was a beautiful young mother with flowers in her hair but she spoke with the weight and authority of her military father. She became the figurehead of the NLD, The National League For Democracy, Daw Suu Kyi, mother of the nation. At that time she could not have known what personal price she would have to pay. She did not know she would miss her sons growing up, that she would never see her husband again. She did know that whatever was asked of her she would willingly pay for democracy, her country and the future of its children. It was her duty.

The fearful and jealous Generals soon placed Suu Kyi under lock and key. She was forbidden to speak in public. Her only contact with her supporters was an occasional appearance at her garden gate but she was a stubborn woman. She played the piano, listened to the radio and survived fifteen years under house arrest. In all this time her popularity with the people did nothing but increase. In 1991 she was awarded the Nobel Peace prize, which her grown up sons accepted in her name. She became The Most Notable Lady of the country. People who know nothing else about Myanmar, somehow know something about the beautiful princess locked behind the high walls and mysterious garden gate of her mother's house beside the lake.

Email from Aunty Nettie Thin. Friday, 27th November, 2009:
The memorial of my parents, Daw Bu Ma and U Tun Hla.
The memorial of my parents started in our father's village since I shifted the remains from Yangon to Chaung Zauk because of the orders of General Khin

Nyunt. I felt so sorry because of this order. I prayed and shedded tears and mourned a lot while digging out the remains and cremated them at the village. Now where is the person who gave this order? Nowhere. God suffered on his thorns. We will see each other when we all get our passport visa to heaven.

In the aftermath of '8888,' The Generals consolidated their power and laid waste to the land. General Khin Nyunt, Chief of Military Intelligence, was a key player in the process. The 'orders' Aunty Nettie refers to in her email were to empty Kyandaw Cemetery in Yangon, which was the burial place of the nation's leaders and heroes, including the grave of Saw San Po Thin. The General's purpose was to turn the cemetery over to a construction company and develop the land for his own and his cronies' benefit. This was widely reported in the Myanmar papers as a scandal and insult to the people. For a long time, I puzzled over why Aunty Nettie associated this event with the idea of 'God suffering on his thorns,' but now it is obvious. Khin Nyunt was not only Head of Military Intelligence, he was responsible for establishing the secret police whose activities permeated every aspect of life in the country. They say he imprisoned and tortured thousands. In other words, he crucified his countrymen.

Khin Nyunt deliberately broke the students' power by relocating the universities out of town, where demonstrations were more easily controlled and less effective. Bit by bit, the entire education system was allowed to disintegrate, dislocated and broken by the weight of corruption, inept teaching and deliberate mismanagement. The students of 1988 still refer to themselves as '8888' survivors. My aunties and uncles, Nettie and her cousins and others of their generation spoke excellent English, a testament to the legacy of the old colonial education system. They had access to native English speakers and foreign institutions. Those who attended university after 1988, my cousins, distance learners who rarely attended lectures on campus, struggle to speak English. Their pronunciation is often poor and sadly, they are fully aware and embarrassed by their inadequacy. They are the ones who complain with a laugh that the system is staffed by unqualified teachers who can't even write a correct sentence on the board. They tell me that right up until the early 2000s education was so bad, university library doors were routinely locked in student faces, but they can't or won't say why. They feel personally ashamed and humiliated as a nation.

'We are '88 military regime survivors. They took the schools for a long time. That is why education is low. Now I must show the way for my new generation.' An '8888' student-cum-teacher on the occasion of the 2021 coup.

Eventually, in 2004 Khin Nyunt resigned from government for 'health reasons,' which I interpret as involvement in illegal activities, supporting drug traders, bribery and corruption which exceeded his powers even beyond the military's acceptable norms. Despite his resignation, the ingrained barricades of fear he engineered between the military and the people were not diminished until Suu Kyi was finally released from house arrest in 2010. She had spent so much time in what amounted to solitary confinement, with so little opportunity to speak to anyone in the outside world, it was a wonder she had any voice left, but no matter. The people only had to look at her to see truth, beauty and goodness personified. They were overjoyed. On my very first visit to the Shwedagon Pagoda a man approached. He wanted to show me something precious. With a shy smile, he revealed a miniature portrait of Suu Kyi and swiftly returned it to his pocket. After so many years of repression that small gesture signified release. It was an act of courage, and a celebration of freedom. Bystanders who caught a glimpse of our interaction nodded their heads in approval. At last they had found hope and pride in their mother, Suu Kyi. The respect of foreigners and the return of visitors to their country meant such a lot to the people on the street. Aunty Nettie said she had the honour of presenting Suu Kyi with a copy of her father's book and a copy of the Bible at Suu Kyi's own request. Aunty Nettie would have liked to introduce us to Suu Kyi but it was early days and she was afraid of attracting unwanted attention in our direction. Instead, we were proudly shown photographs of Suu Kyi at a family wedding.

The Generals' Glorious Dreams

Narrator: *Linda Lewin*

My Dear General,
You must know the children who lay their arms around your sweet scented neck are dead. Their cold flesh is your burden in this life and the next. All these haunted days and nights you must know where one seed of fear falls, ten ferocious branches grow.

The Myanmar army is known as the Tatmadaw, which means royal or glorious army, but this name seems rather out of place since the coup and the more popular term in Myanmar might be Sit-Tat – meaning military without reference to royal attributes – or Sit-Kwe – meaning dog soldiers who obey no one but their cruel masters.

The Generals' glorious dream is that they are the saviours of the people. They do not admit to having nightmares, but how could they not? Fear is a two-way relationship: the Generals suffer from it as much as they inflict it. I would speculate the ghosts of the poverty and destitution they have created haunt all of their private dreams, and if those ghosts are not the ones who haunt them, then that only leaves space for the nightmare of assassination. They have acquired so much wealth and privilege, caused so much pain and suffering, it must be impossible to sleep at night for fear of their victims' jealous and rightful rage.

Perhaps I made a fundamental mistake in my first assessment of The Generals' character role in the common story, good guys versus bad guys. Perhaps The Generals are not deliberately doing bad things, the reason being they do not know they are evil dictators. Sometimes I almost feel sorry for them. If dictators recognised evil traits in themselves, presumably they would not be dictators? In their attempts to control the country, The Generals appear to have modelled themselves on the old kings of Burma, who routinely murdered their rivals because it was their duty. The kings were prepared to beat their royal brothers and sisters to death inside velvet sacks, in order to secure the throne. The velvet sacks were a purely practical measure, respectful not to spill the royal blood, and at the same time, conveniently preserved the modesty of the superfluous princesses. When the last king, Thibaw, ascended to the throne the necessary murdering lasted a week. He attempted to distract himself from his unsavoury duty by hosting a fabulous party with drumming, dancing girls, and the loudest singing. There were so many victims the palace elephants had to be forced to trample the bodies into the ground.

By the time I arrived in Myanmar the Generals had been telling themselves and the nation lies for seventy years. Long enough to have forgotten the truth. Apparently, when foreign ships approached their shore in 2008 with relief supplies for survivors of Cyclone Nargis, The Generals assumed they were under invasion. Rumour has it they moved their capital from old colonial Yangon to Naypyidaw on the advice of fortune tellers. What we know for certain is that their city, Naypyidaw, The Abode of Kings, is a convenient, purpose-built, defensible bunker. It is a modern, architect-designed fortress for an old-fashioned purpose, a place where armies and their dependants could survive a siege. A place where protestors or insurgents cannot hide and where the roads are wide enough to be used as military airport runways. As a result of the latest 2021 coup, convoys of army families have been seen making their way to the safety of Naypyidaw with bags and baggage and truckloads of rice.

Fear equally affects The Generals and the army rank and file. Fear is escalated by the fact the army live their lives apart from the citizens, enclosed in military compounds with their own schools, hospitals and housing. Once you have signed into the system it's not easy to sign out. Access to information, freedom of movement, relationships and marriages, education and future careers of children are all tightly controlled within the military family. When it comes to election time, all military personnel are required to cast their votes within their compounds, or votes are cast on their behalf, like it or lump it.

It is noticeable that the Tatmadaw never fight anyone except their own citizens, the very same citizens they have vowed to protect. The atrocities the Generals have inflicted on the citizens are so extreme they are hard to measure by what I would call normal standards of atrocity, if indeed there were such standards. We know the ancient kings of Burma buried citizens alive to create protective spirits for their palaces and pagodas. Citizens are numerous and expendable and after all, they can be reincarnated to a better life if they make themselves useful.

When I think of The Generals' cruelty I think of Goya, of his painting of Saturn devouring his child. Spain was once regarded as the exotic primitive country of Europe, where myth, magic, religion and reality are one and the same, exactly as they are in Myanmar. Goya was accused of madness because he dared to paint his worst nightmares on his dining room walls but he was not mad. Goya was a witness to the universal horrors of war, firsthand in Spain.

After murdering his father and marrying his sister, Saturn devoured his infant sons because he was fearful of being overthrown by them. The Generals murdered their military father Aung San. They have imprisoned and massacred the youth of their country.

In time Saturn was deceived by his sister-wife, who managed to save one of their sons from being murdered. The Generals persuaded their military clan sister, Suu Kyi, to be their political bride in a hybrid government. Surely beautiful Suu Kyi knew this was a dangerous gamble but she has succeeded in bringing some of the benefits of democracy, especially education, to at least one generation.

Saturn was eventually murdered by his surviving son, just as he feared and just as he had killed his own father, just as the lion king was murdered by his son and turned into the Chinthe which guard the pagoda steps. I am optimistic. When the next Myanmar generation come into their own, as must be, they will act differently from their fathers.

The Generals' traditional justification for their existence is the need to defend national unity from ethnic insurgents, who could come from any of the unofficial or even the officially recognised races in Myanmar who are not Bamar. In addition they have more recently added defending democracy from election fraud, defending democracy from foreign undemocratic forces and defending democracy from the people's defence force as well as defending democracy from the shadow government, so they have a gratifyingly long defending-to-do list.

In order to defend the nation from foreign and ethnic dangers, The Generals have spent a huge proportion of the national budget on weapons. Their military and family based monopoly on business and trade gives them access to unlimited funds, literally taking the gems, the jade, the tungsten, the copper, the tea and coffee, the fish out of the sea and the rice out of people's mouths, and selling it at their pleasure and profit. Anyone who wants to build a business of any kind in Myanmar will sooner or later find themselves paying into the Generals' coffers. It cannot be avoided.

But the Generals' dreams are not all nightmares. The Pathein roundabout is a perfect representation of the Generals' more glorious fantasy – The Burmese Way To Socialism. I would prefer to drive past this golden lie with my eyes closed but it is strangely compelling. In the centre of the road, figures of armed military personnel are portrayed protecting prosperous peasants from imminent dangers, which we might imagine to be ethnic armed forces or interfering foreigners. The peasants are carrying scythes and hoes with bountiful baskets of produce. The tableau includes a well-dressed professional man who could be a teacher or an administrator, certainly an honourable person representing law and order and learning. The happy group are all presided over by a Buddhist goddess of plenty. A glorious dream.

Until now, the only place that national unity has been realised is in the ethnic theme park in Yangon, where different styles of imaginative wooden palaces are laid out within peaceful, neighbourly boundaries. These are supposed to be the typical homes of the eight official races of Myanmar. It might be uncomfortable for me to live in a Burmese village, but I would gladly live in any one of these show homes and so would anyone who belongs to the ethnic races.

They are all raised up on tall wooden columns, graced with large airy rooms and broad verandas, and the kitchens are filled with useful gadgets such as coconut teapots. The rooms are labelled in English for the convenience of foreign visitors although the place does not figure in any of the usual guide books. Hilary and I were the only foreigners on the day of our visit or probably any other day. Hilary was surprised to discover that all the houses boasted a virgin's room. There was that word again. Perhaps what they really meant was a young girl's room but, on the other hand, the Burmese can be very frank and practical people. Maybe virgin was precisely what they meant.

Every house had a lovely rail of clothes in a dressing room where visitors could try on different ethnic costumes, and Hilary and I were encouraged to have our photographs taken in Karen costumes. Luckily the traditional Karen dress is a simple tunic, not flattering but easy to slip into. The tunic was meant to be full length but it hardly extended beyond my knees.

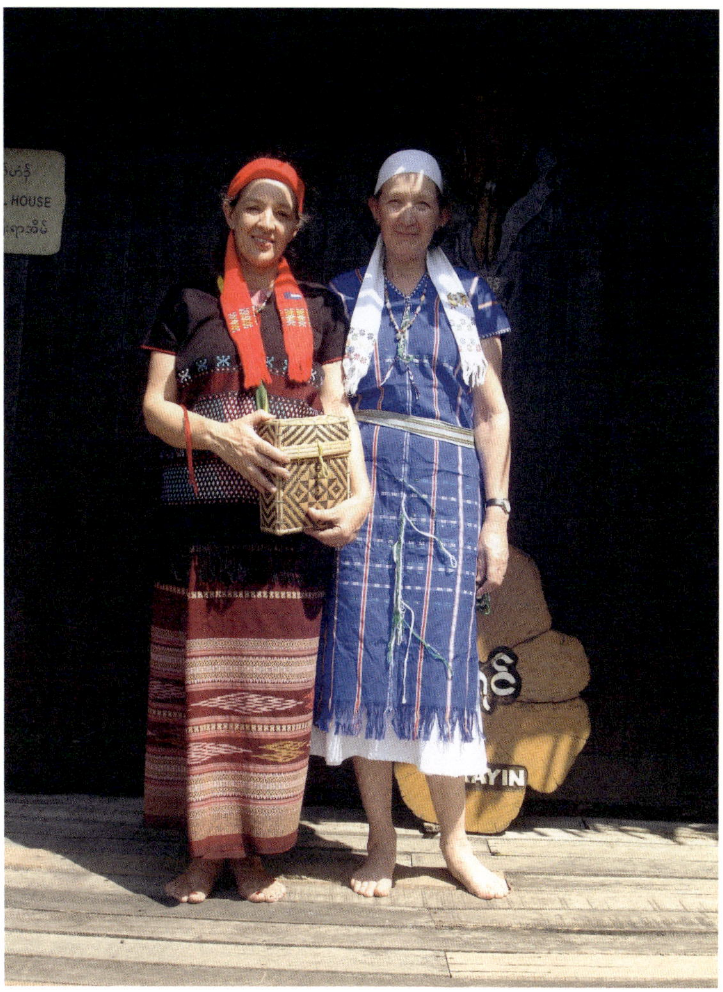

Hilary & Linda at the ethnic theme park

We looked like two oversize Karen baby dolls lovingly dressed by pretty little mothers. In retrospect, I would like to know why Hilary's outfit was trimmed with a very cute cane-woven handbag and mine was not.

As I walked from plot to plot with my Yangon cousin, she nervously whispered in my ear, 'This is not true.' I did not need to be told but I was impressed she had the courage to voice such thoughts. I got the strong impression the very idea of expressing an opinion which might be disagreeable to The Generals was a new kind of blasphemy to her. It felt dangerous.

What we did not see in the theme park were the flimsy, cigar-box huts people live in by the roadsides, evidence of the intimidation and evacuation of ethnic minority villages, seizure of land, fires, forced labour or any other of a long list of traditional atrocities. No sign of the vast numbers of refugees forced into exile.

The Generals must have done well in their past Buddhist lives because they have been rewarded with such luxury in their present lives but the problem I see is, where can they go from here? If they continue to be reincarnated on earth then really the only way is down. Perhaps a slug or a snail that can easily be trodden underfoot would be fitting. Luckily for them, they can easily afford insurance against any bad deeds they may have committed by buying merit. They make large donations to monasteries and pagodas, the Buddhist equivalent of paying for Christian indulgences in order to bypass purgatory and get to heaven more quickly. There are monks who are willing to sell guarantees of a better incarnation in exchange for state of the art glass lifts for their pagodas or a new jewelled umbrella to stick on the top. State-run media presents the Generals publicly receiving blessings from senior monks who invigorate nationalistic fears of Buddhism under supposed threat from foreign religions, Islam and Christianity.

The Generals have staged three coups in living memory but technically, if we believe the Sit-tat, (I find I can't bear to call them Sit-Kwe because it's an insult to dogs), the abduction of Suu Kyi and the elected leaders of the country, preventing them from taking their seats in parliament on the 1st February 2021, was not a coup because they were simply exercising the lawful powers enshrined in their very own 2008 constitution and it was all done for the benefit of the country and the people. I do wonder why the

Tatmadaw bullies who have all the money and all the weapons on their side are quite so bothered about the technicalities. Why do they need to prove their legitimacy when it is patently obvious democracy was never a reality, not even a partial reality, not even a work in progress? I remember saying to Aunty Nettie and Rose Red in the early, hopeful days, 'Why not change the constitution?' only to be met with a cliff edge of silence, followed by a skilful change of subject before anyone got hurt.

Our first trip to Myanmar in 2011 was marked by the arrival of the Arab Spring in Egypt. I sat watching protestors in Tahrir Square with my breakfast TV in the Golf Hotel, Yangon, wondering why The Generals permitted such things to be shown. It looked like an incitement to revolution. Excited reporters predicted that dictators would fall as a result of smartphone technology. They said a new kind of improved history was in the making. I am waiting.

People say The Generals can't speak English so I suppose they can't speak Arabic either. Perhaps they just don't watch TV or listen to the international news and were quite unaware of this new technological threat to dictatorship. But no one around me seemed to be paying too much attention. No one raised so much as one revolutionary finger, let alone a revolutionary fist, in solidarity. Breakfast continued peacefully, undisturbed.

It was true, on that first visit to Myanmar, that modern technology of any kind was thin on the ground. There were very few cars on the road and smartphones might as well have been made of gold and diamonds, although those are not in short supply in Myanmar. When I needed to make a call at the airport I tapped a complete stranger on the shoulder and he fell over himself with pure delight to show off his phone to a foreigner.

By 2014 all that had changed. Little children on the beach would skip up with smartphones in their hands, asking for a trophy photograph with a foreigner. Once the government relaxed the tax and import regulations, cars, motorbikes and smartphones proliferated. In one of our Pathein debating groups we discussed the pros and cons of Facebook. The verdict was that Facebook is an addictive waste of time that distracts students from their studies, but on the other hand Facebook messenger was the chosen medium of communication. Strangely, we never discussed security or surveillance except in the context of bullying. Of course we never dreamed of discussing Facebook in the context of a military coup. Who would have thought?

The Tatmadaw claim to support democracy but sadly their version is not quite as we know it in the West. Their version is Disciplined Democracy, which they deem suitable for the citizens of Myanmar. They say the 2008 Myanmar constitution which guarantees the Tatmadaw an unelected, controlling majority in the legislative assembly is designed to protect Disciplined Democracy. In addition the constitution includes prohibitions against anyone with foreign family members from becoming president. Suu Kyi told President Obama, although she was very flattered to have a constitution designed specifically with her in mind, it was not best practice and she would like to change it. Not just for her inconsequential convenience but for the wider benefits of democracy. Obama seemed to understand this and embraced her warmly when he heard her sweet words. He was also pleased to hear that the benefits of law and order would be equally applied to everyone in the country. The USA lifted sanctions and the Generals were delighted.

In 2020 The Generals were so confident of their impregnable moral position they were prepared to hold elections and agreed to abide by the results. It must have come as a nasty shock when true to form, Suu Kyi's NLD party won eighty percent of the ballot, equivalent to a slap in The Generals' combined faces. Suu Kyi and the people had an agreement and the electorate voted for her so many times you just have to believe they meant it. They agreed they wanted Western style democracy. The Generals turned an unhealthy shade of red and declared widespread voter fraud.

On the face of things The Generals need not have worried. The 2008 get-out-of-jail-free constitution card successfully allowed them to maintain control of events ever since they invented it. For reasons which are difficult to understand, Suu Kyi diverted international condemnation away from The Generals when she defended her country's purge of the Rohingya in Rakhine State. Perhaps she believed the Rohingya are foreign infiltrators, descendants of the despised Indians, and perhaps she was lied to about the atrocities because who dares speak truth to power in Myanmar puts life and limb at risk. Perhaps she thought it was a political trade-off necessary to remain in position and rewrite the constitution in democratic form. A price she had to pay.

So many plausible and implausible ideas have been floated to explain why The Generals chose to stage a coup it is hard to choose, but I believe The Generals, Min Aung Hlaing in particular, were shamed and angered by the election results. Over the years many people in Myanmar have told me they feel ashamed. Sometimes it is merely a politeness but it is also a common and keenly-felt emotion and I don't think The Generals are exempt. I do hope they feel ashamed. Although they have been shunned by the ungrateful electorate so many times, they never seem to understand why. They like to be seen welcoming patients to military hospitals, reopening schools closed by COVID-19 and being all-round generous good eggs, maybe even distributing some few eggs. From The Generals' point of view, they have been misunderstood and rejected by the country they have worked so hard to protect. They feel threatened and made foolish by a 'stupid' woman with flowers in her hair. Their representative used the word 'stupid' in a CNN interview. Since no other motives make logical sense, why not anger and shame?

Min Aung Hlaing has personal reasons for his illogical behaviour. He was too close to retirement to realise his ambitions for political power whilst Suu Kyi stood in his way. One of his very first acts after the coup was to repeal the law which Suu Kyi's NLD party put in place to force military men to retire. He can now claim a legal right to carry on as head of the army until he drops dead. He might even proclaim himself the people's President. After all, he has appropriated the presidential mansion for himself and his family. Which brings us to the usual considerations of money, power and inheritance.

Whatever the reason, once again Suu Kyi is incarcerated, whereabouts more or less unknown, charged with strange and childish crimes – owning illegal walkie-talkies, breaking lockdown rules by waving at her supporters and accepting golden bribes. If they could, the Generals would erase Suu Kyi from history and from the people's memory. She has already disappeared from the photographs in her family home and her image is tarnished in the world outside Myanmar.

General Liar and General Deceiver

General Liar and General Deceiver
cover their chests with buckets
full of gold medals.
General Liar is a shrimp, boiled head pink.
General Deceiver is an ass
fucking hole.
They review their troops
under the beautiful Fallen Stars.

Let's have no more heroes, no more need for heroes.
They all die in vain, in pain and tears.
I never knew I could cry so much for so many I never knew.
The aching arm and neck, swollen, broken bodies, beatings
It has been done too often.
Why does it make no difference.

They will smile and lie in your face
then turn around and burn you at the stake.

Make the page clean and blank.
Make the age clean and blank.

This page stands for all the fallen heroes, nameless
who were perfectly ordinary souls.
They wanted everything that was advertised for a better life.
Wedding gifts.
Motorbikes and pots and pans.
But mostly just a future for their children
and a peaceful place to sleep in the cool night.
May all your sweet dreams come true

a cruel little man with dyed
hair and too much jewellery

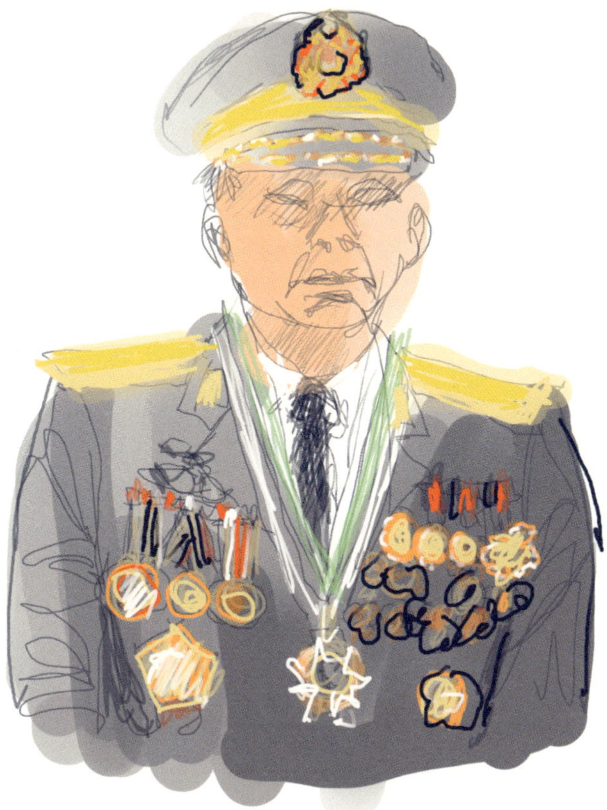

in love with himself

despot

Facebook. Funeral Book. The Every Day Coup Book

Narrator: *Linda Lewin*

Let fear be nothing more than a history lesson we teach our children in school. A Myanmar university professor on the occasion of the coup, February 2021.

Watching a coup unfold in real time on Facebook is a strange, novel experience. Facebook is my telescopic eye in the sky. I am physically immune to the violence but I experience all of the shocking emotions, even at this oceanic distance.

If you ever have the opportunity to drive through the Myanmar suburbs in the cool hour before dawn, perhaps on your way to an airport or a bus station, you will see the keep fit fanatics doing their morning exercises before the sun comes up. Min Aung Hlaing's coup was precisely organised for that same dark hour before dawn. A female fitness instructor in the administrative capital, Naypyidaw, unwittingly filmed herself as the light came up, against a bizarre backdrop of blacked-out army trucks on their way to steal Suu Kyi from her house. Suu Kyi, her advisors and ministers, mostly senior citizens, along with a carefully compiled list of journalists, artists and campaigners for change, were stolen away just a few hours before the signing in for the new parliamentary term. The keep fit video was a media sensation.

I find myself desperate for information, I check in online at short intervals. If I could stop to think about it I would know the events I view from afar are predictable, because it has all been done before. It just hasn't been done on social media before and I haven't experienced it before, but I am so shocked and horrified I can't stop to think. I just hope for miracles, watching the story unfold in seemingly slow motion on my screen, detail by detail. Airports are closed, night-time curfews are imposed. The immediate effect on the citizens is a kind of paralysis and disbelief. For a short moment, the entire nation lies prone, collectively punched in the gut, and I might as well be lying beside them on the floor, I feel so close.

People begin to react. At first by playing iron bucket, which means families and neighbourhoods banging pots and pans on the street and singing the old '8888' protest song, Kabar Makyay Bu. This is the traditional way to drive out evil spirits with loud noises. The drama is distilled and intensified by Facebook, which transports me directly to a hot night in Yangon. I see my cousin in her apartment. Her mother is washing the dishes. Minnie Mouse, as she has wisely renamed herself, is sitting on a plastic chair. Her face is wet and angry. She raises her fist. I have never heard her sing and she is terrifying. She is an '8888' survivor and the old protest song is familiar to her. I make a remark, 'When a woman starts banging pots and pans she must be angry.' Minnie Mouse brother replies. 'In Yangon' he says, 'there are two emotions, sorrow and anger.'

Brothers and sisters, unite for freedom and peace. History will be written in our blood. We await the final battle. Kabar Makyay Bu, the '8888' song.

Two strategies emerge: a practical Civil Disobedience Movement and peaceful protesting. Doctors and students lead the way, CDM spreads through the civil services, and there is a run on the banks. People refuse to pay taxes and electricity bills. Community groups promise to support the strikers and doctors promise home visits.

You Have Messed With The Wrong Generation. A Protest banner.

The Generation Z revolution begins with phones switched on and parties on every street corner. It is a social media festival. Protestors congregate in one place and avoid the police in another place, using their phones like a sixth sense. I watch them, like shoals of brightly-coloured tropical fish in my Facebook pond, quite unperturbed by the occasional stone being thrown into the reef, making peaceful and playful protest. Bare-chested body builders and handsome doctors with white coats and stethoscopes vie with Lycra-clad cyclists for top pin-up position. A well-groomed dog parade is followed by an exotic snake parade. Then the first bride appears on the street, negotiating her delicate way between cars wearing her wedding gown, on the arm of her gorgeous groom. They carry a placard with a slogan, *'The wedding can wait, this is more important.'* One bride becomes two brides and quickly a procession of brides and grooms. Girls in beautiful matriculation ball gowns swish by, and transvestites in full regalia. A group of young girls set up a pyjama camp by the roadside with a tent and teddy bears, and yet another group bring out their yoga mats. Everyone is in on the act.

Fearful parents, survivors of '88, watch their brave babies in amazement. Anticipating the worst, but full of admiration. Inspired by the brave babies, more serious, older commuters stage a car breakdown on the way to work. A bus is abandoned in the middle of a road. Vehicles mysteriously run out of gas and keys are lost. One man gets out a deck chair and stops for a relaxing breakfast cup of coffee in the midst of the morning traffic. Yangon comes to a standstill. The police can do nothing. The joke is on them.

On Friday 12th February, 2021, Myanmar Union Day, cousin Pandaw remarks: 'The good guys are in prison and the bad guys are on the street.' Twenty-three thousand, three hundred and fourteen prisoners have been released from the jails. It is not known what crimes they committed, but they look like poor men whose luck ran out long ago. Prisoners are routinely released on Union Day, for the sake of merit, as are caged birds in front of pagodas, but this is a bit different. The public assume the military are clearing jail space for political prisoners and there will be trouble ahead.

For the sake of 5000 MMK, which is less than three USA dollars, ex-prisoners are paid to break into people's houses, set fire to buildings, poison water supplies and even commit random murders with cheap kitchen knives. Once more, dacoits roam the streets and no one feels safe in their beds. The old fears, which had not disappeared but at least developed a thin skin in the years of supposed progress towards democracy, break open and bleed.

People do what they can to support each other. Neighbourhood vigilante groups are set up, and when they catch the released convicts they tie them to chairs with bits of old string. The ex-prisoners are not beaten or tortured but instead they are exposed on Facebook. Some even smile stupidly for the cameras. Then they are deposited at police stations. At this stage, citizens prefer to act honourably, even though they know the most likely outcome is that the police will release the prisoners back onto the streets. With all of this, and the banging of pots and pans to raise the alarm, no one gets any sleep at night, so they try their best to sleep during the day – but that doesn't help at all.

The military are totally paternalistic. A protestor.

Artists set up workshops and street exhibitions to raise funds. The people make their message clear, in Myanmar language and in English, because they want the world to take notice. Reject the military coup. Free our leaders. Creativity knows no bounds, especially when it comes to performance art with a twist of humour. General Min Aung Hlaing portraits are taped to the ground in attractive mosaic patterns, forcing soldiers to disrespect their leader by walking on his face. The soldiers remove the offensive papers but almost immediately the protestors up their game by spray painting the image with a template. So quick and easy to do, so tedious to remove. A woman hangs her underwear on the street, daring police and soldiers to risk their masculine powers by walking underneath. Good ideas are contagious. Suddenly, women's washing is hung in unexpected public places all over Yangon. Officers deploy embarrassed, genuinely frightened young squaddies with long sticks to remove bras and pants from overhead lines on the streets. Sometimes they have to climb on top of their army trucks to reach the offending garments. Finally, one woman strips off completely and walks down the road stark naked. I notice she carried her clothes in a plastic bag. She wasn't silly enough to risk losing them. Nothing could be more insulting than a naked woman who just doesn't give a damn. All part of the daily non-violent art and insult show.

Abolish the constitution. A protestor.

The protests break out spontaneously in all parts of the country, not just in the big cities. Every community and profession is involved. My favourite photo is of the elephants and their boys on the road with protest posters, and the beautifully decorated country carts with fathers proudly showing off their daughters in national costumes. Even the fishermen come out in their boats trailing floating banners in their wake. No one wants to miss out.

We are protesting knowing everything (the danger) because we have no choice. Thinzar Shunlei.

Witness To Courage
1st February 2021

My Love
They came to my door this morning
There is no law in a dictatorship
Rights can be made wrong in a dictatorship
Black can be made white in a dictatorship

Slowly, slowly clouds unfold
My song is sorrow
My drum is anger
Bring me my bow of burnished gold
Words are forbidden
History is stolen
To breath the air is to live a lie

My Love
Sing your deepest sorrow
A voice of iron
A stone from a sling shot
A sharp knife
The sharp knife which rips my heart open
Blood is boiling
A heavy weight presses down
It is the weight we carried for generations

Mother, sing when the harvest comes
Brother, leave the door open,
my sandals waiting on the step
Sister, make my place at the table
My father will not abandon me
Slavery will die when justice and democracy live.

My Broken Angel, My Love
The juice lies red on the ground
But I will sing when the harvest comes
The roots are strong
Your voice is the flowering of my soul
My mouth is full of sweet fruit

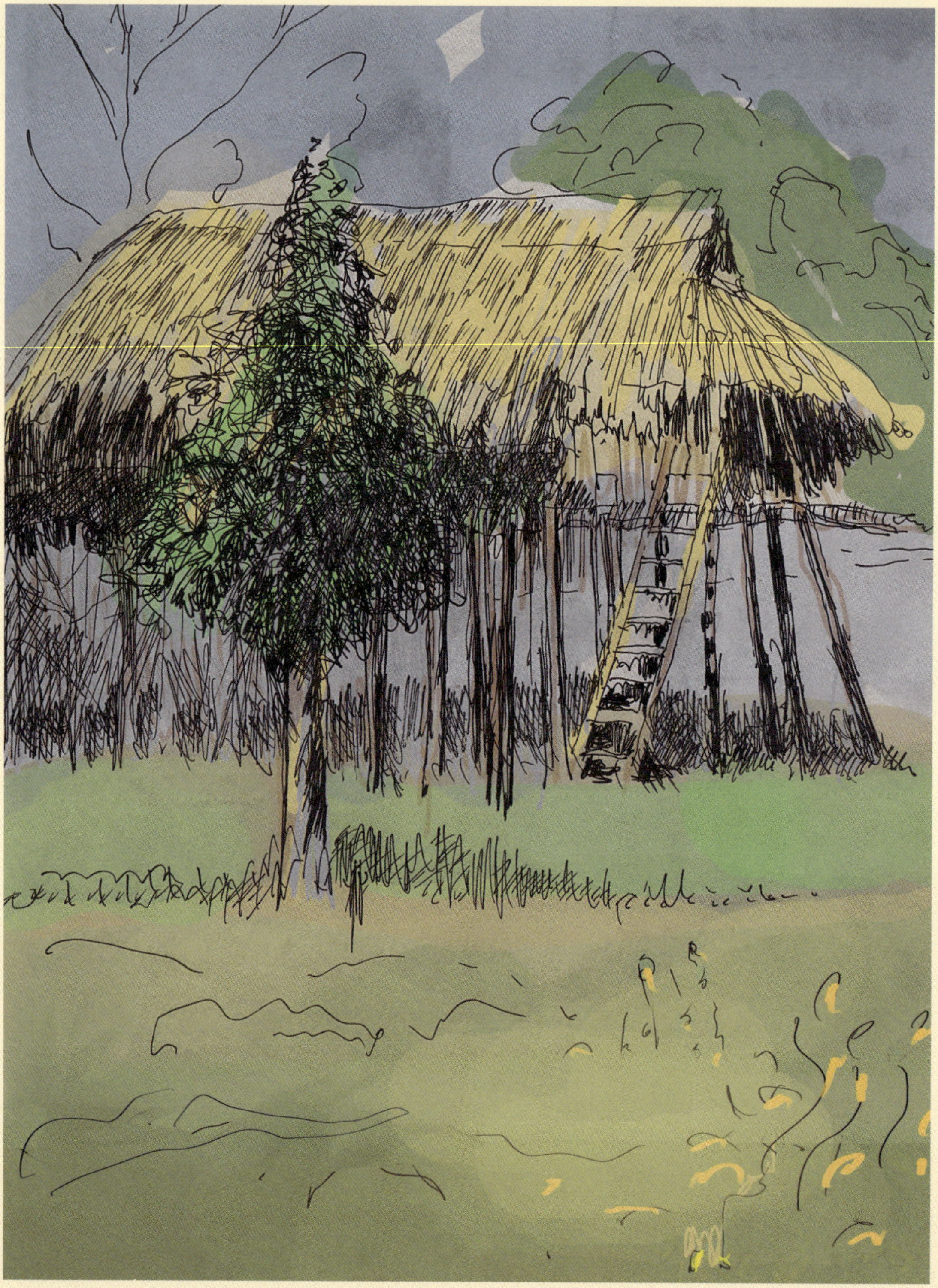

Loikaw. Please beware of the landmines

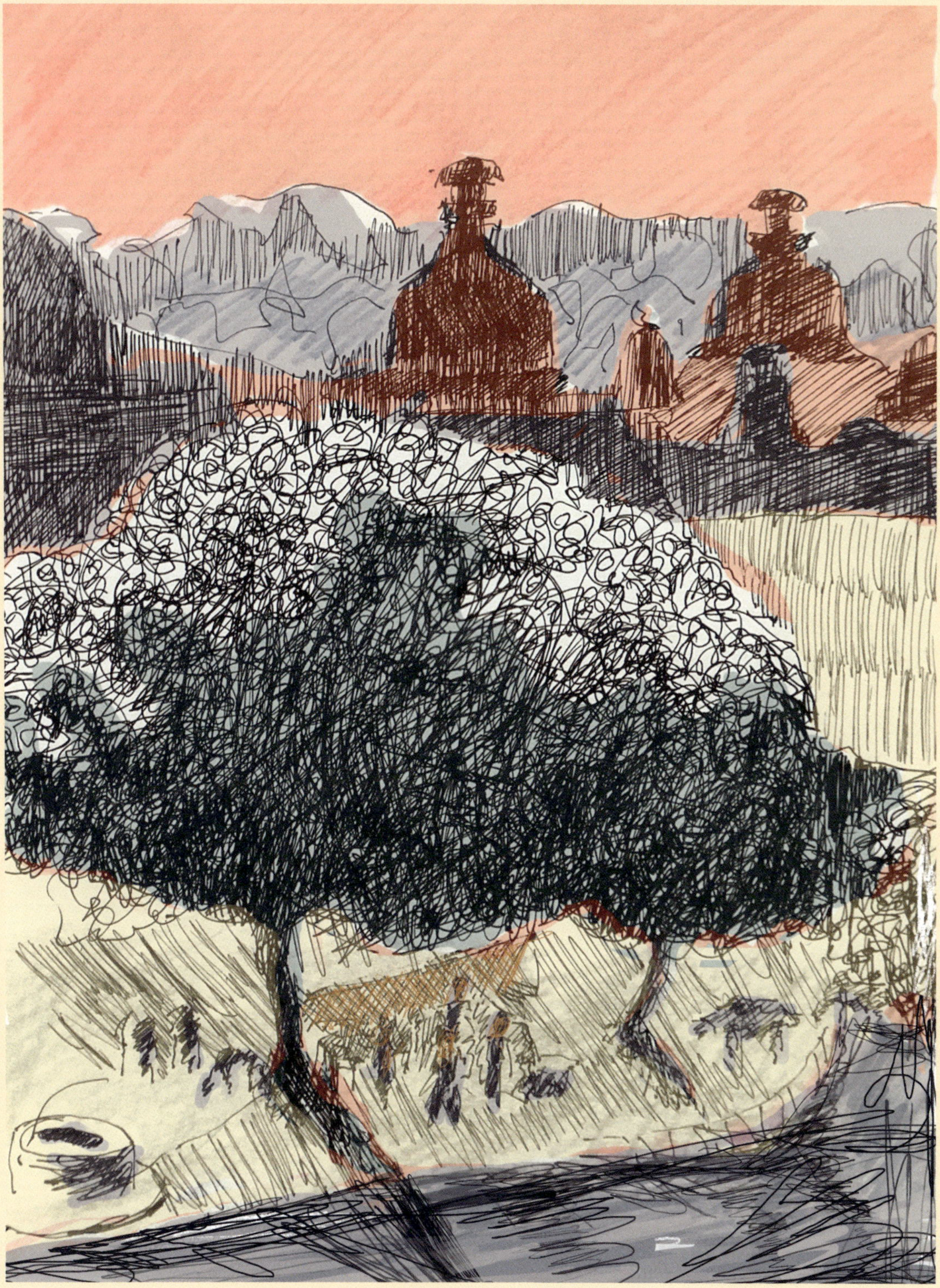

Mrauk U. Sunset. Boys playing chinlone

People say that this time around they want the real thing, no more sham democracy. They would rather die for democracy than live as slaves to the regime. I spot my 'granddaughter' with her best friend and student cohort on the streets of Pathein. She is an electrical engineering student and they are all wearing engineers' site helmets prepared with identical logos. A scored out figure 2008 demanding constitutional change. When I casually mention I have seen her on Facebook, she just as casually denies it was her. As is often the case, she is out without parental permission. When the student protesters go out they often leave a note for their families, husbands and wives or the lovers they never had time to know. Just in case.

At first the police on patrol appear unnerved by the unfamiliar disrespect and the three finger salutes of defiance. Not quite sure how to deal with bunches of flowers or Generation Z urban art and comedy attacks. But the tone soon darkens. When troops join the police on the city streets people tell each other they must be Chinese. They just can't believe these boys are Myanmar mothers' sons. There are lots of close-up photos of the eyes. Gradually, inevitably, the worst happens. These troops on the streets are the very same units which were used to commit genocide against the Rohingya, now deployed in the urban areas and city centres of Yangon and Mandalay.

In addition to modern armaments, old-fashioned weapons remain popular with Myanmar soldiers. Slingshots, knives, boots and metal batons. Every soldier seems to have a catapult in his pocket. It is an odd sight when the hatch of a tank trundling along like a bizarre armadillo on the suburban streets flips open, and a soldier fires off a couple of marbles or a handful of nuts and bolts from his catapult. Marbles are cheap and effective for breaking house windows and windscreens. They can also be used to disable CCTV cameras, but that requires a lucky shot. There is lots of aimless, jealous vandalism, smashing cars and motorbikes and breaking windows, alongside clips of police and soldiers stealing ice creams and bananas. The army doesn't feed them? A video of a boy with learning difficulties being beaten by a gang of police goes viral. The effect is that after only a few days, beating civilians with iron bars becomes routine.

There is another side. A policeman tries to protect a pair of protesters from army batons on a street corner. The army and the police fall to fighting amongst themselves. In broad daylight, a nun, Sister Ann Rose, drops to her knees before a phalanx of police officers with shields and batons, begging them to 'spare the children.' Some officers try to de-escalate the situation. They fold their hands together and pray with her, swearing their intentions are innocent. Minutes later a man lies dead on the street. Shot by a sniper.

When the army decides the people have tried its patience for too long, they set aside the rubber bullets and shoot real bullets to kill. Snipers pick off unarmed protestors as callously as they would chickens in a coop. Just the beginning of the daily slaughter. The snipers are ordered to aim for the head or the chest. Just like Aunty Nettie was. When the head 'blooms,' the injury is fatal and the corpses are hardly full grown. Citizens die on the streets where they walk to school and to work, where they do their shopping, sometimes shot through the windows of their own homes. The ethnic peoples are familiar with all of this – it is a way of life in the villages – but it is a shock on city streets. Generation Z make public apologies to the ethnic minorities, swearing that now they know the truth things will be different in future. I receive a message from a Bamar student, working in Singapore. She is upset, struggling to reconcile the history she learned at her elite military school with the evidence of personal experience. She honours my Karen identity by offering me her personal apology. I feel a fraud. This is the closest the country has ever come to unification, unwittingly brought about by the military, enemy of all the people. That must be a good thing.

You can cut all the flowers but you cannot keep spring from coming. Pablo Neruda. Protest light projection on a Yangon building facade.

As I write these words, tanks are rolling through the streets of Yangon. Like the kings of old, The Generals and their wives put on their finery and host a grim-faced party at the same time as their troops drop bombs and set fire to remote villages. Just as they have done so many times before.

Every morning I wake up wondering what the news is and hoping it is better than the day before.

9th February, 2021.
The first martyr was fatally shot at a bus stop, a twenty-year-old female student. Shot in the head from a safe distance by a middle-aged man with a similar aged daughter of his own. That was the beginning of daily slaughter.

Wednesday, 3rd March.
Angel, a nineteen-year-old ethnic Chinese girl who had proudly voted just once, NLD, received her father's blessing for the last time. He was a medical doctor supporting injured protestors so he knew the risks she was taking when she chose to go out on the protest barricades in Mandalay. She died from a sniper's bullet which entered her brain behind her right ear. Her body was lovingly laid out in a coffin surrounded by flowers and her hearse was modelled on a golden Chinese temple. Thousands of mourners followed her to her grave in the Chinese cemetery.

A May Sing, The Amazing Girl and I are watching Facebook. I can't believe my eyes but yes, she translates for me. Just a few hours after her funeral, Angel's body has been dragged fresh from her 'cave,' in the Chinese cemetery. Facebook relays more information. The watchmen were ordered to open the gates and threatened with terrible punishments if they told anyone what happened. About twenty men forced their way inside the cemetery. The next morning Angel's grave was discovered filled with cement, strewn with rubbish, including surgical gowns and plastic gloves. The flowers destroyed. Why? A May Sing says her friends are afraid it was because of powerful black magic. We agree we are not afraid of black magic because we don't believe in it at all, but is that the truth? National Myanmar media kindly explains what was done had to be done, for an autopsy, and it was all done with full permission of the family and the relevant authorities. The official autopsy revealed the bullet which killed Angel was of a type the Tatmadaw do not use. Could that be a kind of Black Magic?

Friday, 5th March.
Pandaw sends photos of exhausted protestors, mostly young men, but also women and older men, on the front line which is a street in Yangon. There are clouds of tear gas filling the air, mixed with smoke bombs and foaming fire extinguishers. Protestors are wearing plastic construction workers' helmets, or motorbike or cyclist helmets, anything they can find to protect their heads from police batons, including cheap snorkelling masks. Plastic barrels cut in half serve as shields. Some have wet rags, presumably to damp down the tear gas. A boy who is still at the growing stage, nothing more than a pair of long legs, has draped himself, exhausted, across a plastic chair. Pandaw says the military have cut off electricity because they don't want these scenes to be recorded on CCTV, but nothing escapes the

mobile phones. Pandaw wishes the protestors were enjoying their student days. Days that will not return.

A May Sing goes on to say the youths of her district have built a barricade across her street in Yangon. Right outside her window and they are prepared for battle. How does a normal family prepare for battle? Social media discussions reveal an essential to-do list.

Protestors' list:
Write your name and blood group on your arms and helmet before you go out.
Wear practical clothes and shoes, not sandals. Mask, gloves and shield if you are on the front line.
Do not provoke violence – they will beat you, especially boys.
If the police get hold of your phone, at best you could lose it or at worst they can use it as evidence against you and your friends. Take a disposable phone with contact numbers for lawyers and family.
Girls take sanitary pads, because stress can cause unexpected bleeding.
Otherwise they can be used as emergency medical dressings.
Take spare clothes you can easily carry
Take first aid and medication, for yourself and other people.

Householders' list:
Keep a neighbourhood night watch.
Sound the alarm with iron bucket.
Lock your doors and windows against forced entry.
Don't be frightened when you hear the sound of a gun.
Switch the lights off, stay away from the mirror.
Turn the phone sound down.
Stay below waist height.
Open your door to hide and feed protestors. They are children like your own.
Keep your suitcase packed and ready.
Keep valuables and documents in a safe place.
Make a list of essential contacts.
Write down essential medical information.
Keep supplies of first aid and drugs for yourself and other people.
Practise first aid for shock and bullet wounds.

Parents' list:
Children must be taught how to be safe.
Hiding behind a brick wall is best against bullets.
You can read familiar stories and play with familiar toys.
Do not send to school.

I realise my Facebook feed is full of parents weeping over dead children, whose faces look so similar to my students I must scan every one to check, but thankfully my students are unharmed, so far. In other places, other times, the pictures of bloody corpses might frighten protestors into submission, but in Myanmar it seems to have the opposite effect. The bodies are laid out in glass-topped coffins, smothered in flowers, transported through the streets in golden hearses just like in the Romeo and Juliet film. The people call them Fallen Angels. They are too young to know how much life they gave up, willing martyrs for freedom and democracy. Communities contribute to funeral processions fit for princes and princesses but sometimes they struggle to find the means. The offices of funeral charities have been broken into by soldiers and destroyed, the volunteer charity workers sent to prison. Poverty is all too cruelly revealed in glimpses of empty bare matting rooms, the homes of vacant-eyed orphans. Very often when protestors disappear into police and army custody, the bodies are not returned to the families. Rumour has it human organs are being sold to the Chinese. That may or may not be not true, but I am sure they would if they could.

In the '8888' revolution the slogan was, 'They die or we die.' The latest slogan is, 'They die or they die.' The protestors swear they will keep going to honour the memories of their fallen comrades. When one falls another will take their place. They have nothing to lose. They are the walking dead.

I receive a text message from Minnie Mouse in Yangon. She is plainly in shock. It is Sunday evening and normally she would be preparing her Monday morning Zoom lessons for COVID-19 home schooling. She tells me there has been live shooting on her street. The military occupied the local hospital and started shooting the public defenders with real bullets. There was one fatality. The only thing she could do was turn her lights off and lock the door.

It so happens, as I am remembering and writing, an erstwhile student, the girl who played Romeo, texts me a question. I remember her in class, shining with enthusiasm, asking permission to climb through a rather high balcony window to visit Juliet. Her present question is, how to compose an English birthday card for her brother. Life goes on. When I ask she tells me she is OK. She is at home and one day soon she hopes to return to work in town and study history at Pathein university. I wish my lovely female Romeo had chosen to study a technical subject. I don't trust those Generals with history. Nonetheless I persuade myself she will do well. She has such an original way of thinking she could do well at anything she chose, given half a chance. In reality she is unlikely to get even half a chance. The latest Myanmar news shows police rounding up students on a university campus. Demanding to investigate their phones, searching for incriminating evidence of goodness knows what under the beds. Perhaps it is safer if my Romeo never goes to university at all. Most likely she never will.

These days the army feel entitled to invade homes, hospitals and universities, helping themselves to whatever they fancy and the lovely, creative, peaceful party protesting seems like a lifetime ago. Cars are being stopped and searched on the streets, which means phones are a life-threatening liability. Martial law has been declared in parts of Yangon, which allows the military to apply the death penalty whenever they wish.

Suburban householders in ordinary streets summon courage. Middle-aged keyboard warriors are active, directing and warning the protestors on the streets. Social media punishment, the naming and shaming of CDM strike breakers, becomes a serious thing. From upper storeys, behind half-closed shutters, phone film evidence is recorded. Nothing goes unnoticed. Citizen cameras do not shy away from directly showing bloody corpses on the streets. They want the world to know. When the bullets come, straight through the skull, death is normally instant. There is no hesitation in showing comrades risking their lives to collect bodies, dragging them by the legs and arms, blood seeping across the road. Blood spreads much further and seemingly faster than I would have expected. Medics are ready and waiting to help, but they can't perform miracles.

At the same time as the slaughter continues, CDM grows firmer roots and the Junta retaliate by evacuating striking public employees from their tied homes. The railway workers pack hurriedly and depart, God knows where, with their arms full of plastic carrier bags containing personal belongings.

Their frail parents and random furniture are thrown into the back of pick-ups. An old man staggers out of his home attached to an oxygen bottle, supported by two younger men. They remain defiant, unanimously holding up three revolutionary fingers for the phone cameras.

In some of the quieter moments the citizen cameras record soldier boys walking in the evening, arm in arm as if to reassure each other, like nervous wildlife or country lads on their first visit to town, which is most likely the truth. Apparently unaware of the cameras they slink between citizen waste bins and parked cars, weapons in hand. Boys playing lethal games. It is a mystery to me why any one would join up to shoot their own people. I asked my student friend who is studying to be a priest.

In his own words:

The military government have been controlling information for more than fifty years.
There are military families.
They have many benefits awarded to their families.
They can do what they like.
The rank and file are afraid of them.
If they (the rank and file) leave they are killed so they dare not complain or go away.
Human rights are weak.
It is because the education is poor.
There are many conflicts between races.

He knows what he is talking about. The Tatmadaw have a track record of conscripting child soldiers with promises of food, education, wages. A sack of rice and beans for their family is all it takes. If that doesn't work, conscripts are threatened with penalties for violations of nonexistent regulations, such as not carrying identity documents. Once the Tatmadaw get the boys in their clutches, the young men are brutalised to the point where they say life loses its meaning. If any one of them steps out of line, the others soon learn the value of their lives is zero. Once they have been blooded by the pack there is very little chance of going back. On the streets the soldier boys bang their shields with heavy iron sticks, drumming up courage. The boys who joined up hoping for a motorbike of their own decide

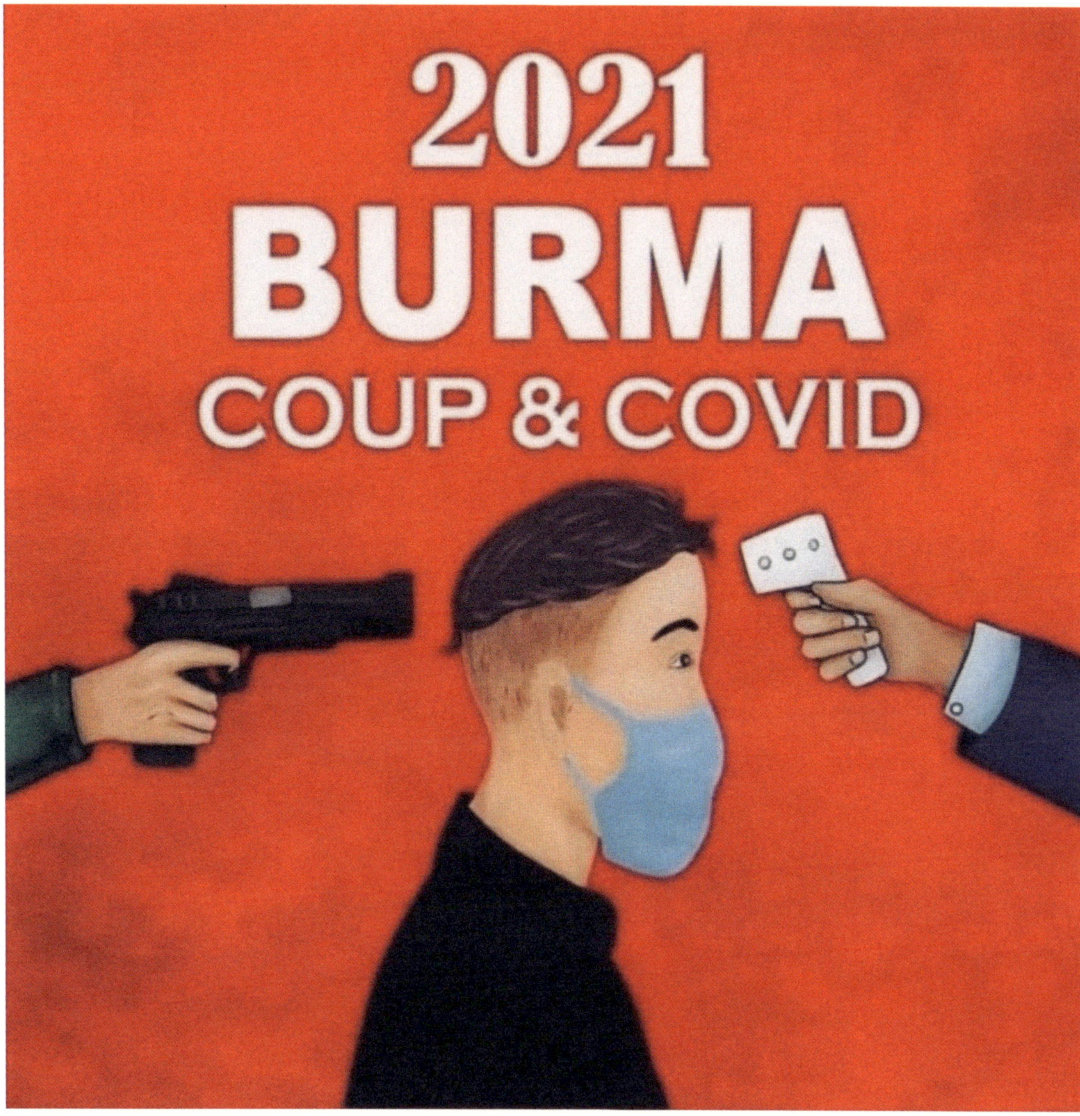

Keyboard Warriors – Social Media

to help themselves from those parked at the side of the road and go joy riding around town. It make more sense to steal them than to break them. A very few are brave enough to desert but know they risk their families' lives as well as their own.

The citizens, lacking weapons to defend themselves, have taken to burning soldier effigies in the pagodas. I can watch the little green and gold paper figures going up in smoke on screen. I find this fascinating but my Christian cousin finds it terrifying. Surely she doesn't believe but I think she protests too much – yes she believes. They say it was done, even by San Po Thin, years ago, but of course just out of interest, to help a friend, just as an experiment.

Articles online talk about people being caught between COVID-19 and the gun. It is extraordinary to see how much kindness and compassion exist within local communities. Volunteers devise a COVID communication system. Yellow flags and white flags can be hung out asking for help and the volunteers will try to source food and supply oxygen. There is no point trying to get into a hospital. The military have them all sewn up and are fighting the people for control of oxygen supplies. Drugs are hardly available. The female doctor who was in charge of COVID-19 vaccinations is arrested, along with her child and a friend who just happened to be there, and jailed for refusing to comply with military demands. When death comes to the COVID patients it is down to volunteers and families to remove the bodies, but there are not enough coffins so the bodies end up in queues at the crematoriums, wrapped in carpets and blankets. Young children porter parents and grandparents. The military solution is to reassure the people, not by building more hospitals or supplying oxygen, drugs and ambulances – they prefer to build more crematoriums.

On National Armed Forces Day, 27th March, which commemorates the Burmese resistance to the Japanese occupation in 1945, the Tatmadaw announce the great deeds of the military will be celebrated by building the largest seated Buddha in the world. I suppose the worse the sins the bigger the Buddha must be in order to compensate.

'There is so much crime against humanity [in Myanmar]. Poets in such situations live with tears in every single breath. Our poems are hordes of screaming children.' Anonymous Myanmar poet.

The military impose internet curfews. Gradually it gets more difficult but people are ingenious in finding ways around. Contacts are begging me to tell the world what is happening in their country but what can I do? It's heartbreaking. Making posts on Facebook and teaching English to refugees online is just not enough.

High Shrimp Mountain Road
Narrator: *Adaw Gyi*

December. The Sweet Year 2021.
Second Report: *Further loss of life expected but we are not defeated.*

My Dearest Darling Gazelles,

This is my final report. How can I say the situation? After the third military coup we no longer sleep well on High Shrimp Mountain Road, not friends, not family, not husbands, not wives, not students, not children. Not one. Our nerves are shattered. Fear floats from house to house, entering the open windows and doors as easily as the morning mist and smoke from evening cooking fires, but we must stay strong because this is our life. Any one of us can be imprisoned without rhyme or reason, including our children. Everyone is vulnerable all of the time but the worst time is morning time, before getting out of bed, counting who can and cannot be trusted. There are spies everywhere. We choose not speaking. Perhaps, in a dark night, walking arm in arm, one might dare say to another, 'We don't like it but we must live with it.' We stay strong.

At noon, the heat on High Shrimp Mountain Road weighs our shoulders down, heavy as the molten gold ancient kings poured into the throats of their enemies. We retire indoors. One idle waiter stands observing the street. A portrait of Suu Kyi is hanging on the back wall of his empty restaurant. That waiter is a tall man, fifty years old with tears running down his face like a child. The past haunts him, more real than the present, more solid than the back of his thin-skinned hand wiping away the tears. He wanted to be an engineer, not a waiter, but on the night of the four eights he and his friends set fire to their university and he would do it again. His name is on a black list. He might as well be in chains. He swabs a table. He sweeps the floor. He feels faint. He washes the dishes. Always, every day, he thinks of his child. What story to tell her? The version where he spent months in prison, the students who died, the torture? He cannot forget what others refuse to remember. Will he tell her that courage and sacrifice receive no reward? That nothing has changed, ever. He cannot bear to tell her the truth. When his daughter ties the blood red ribbon around her head and demands to join her revolutionary friends on the street, he silently removes the ribbon, strokes her hair and locks her in her room.

Our local administrator is a careful man. It is never easy to know how to be on the winning side but he can see, even when history proves that might is not right, it is most likely profitable, and in our country he thinks might is very much on the side of the military, so he must do the logical

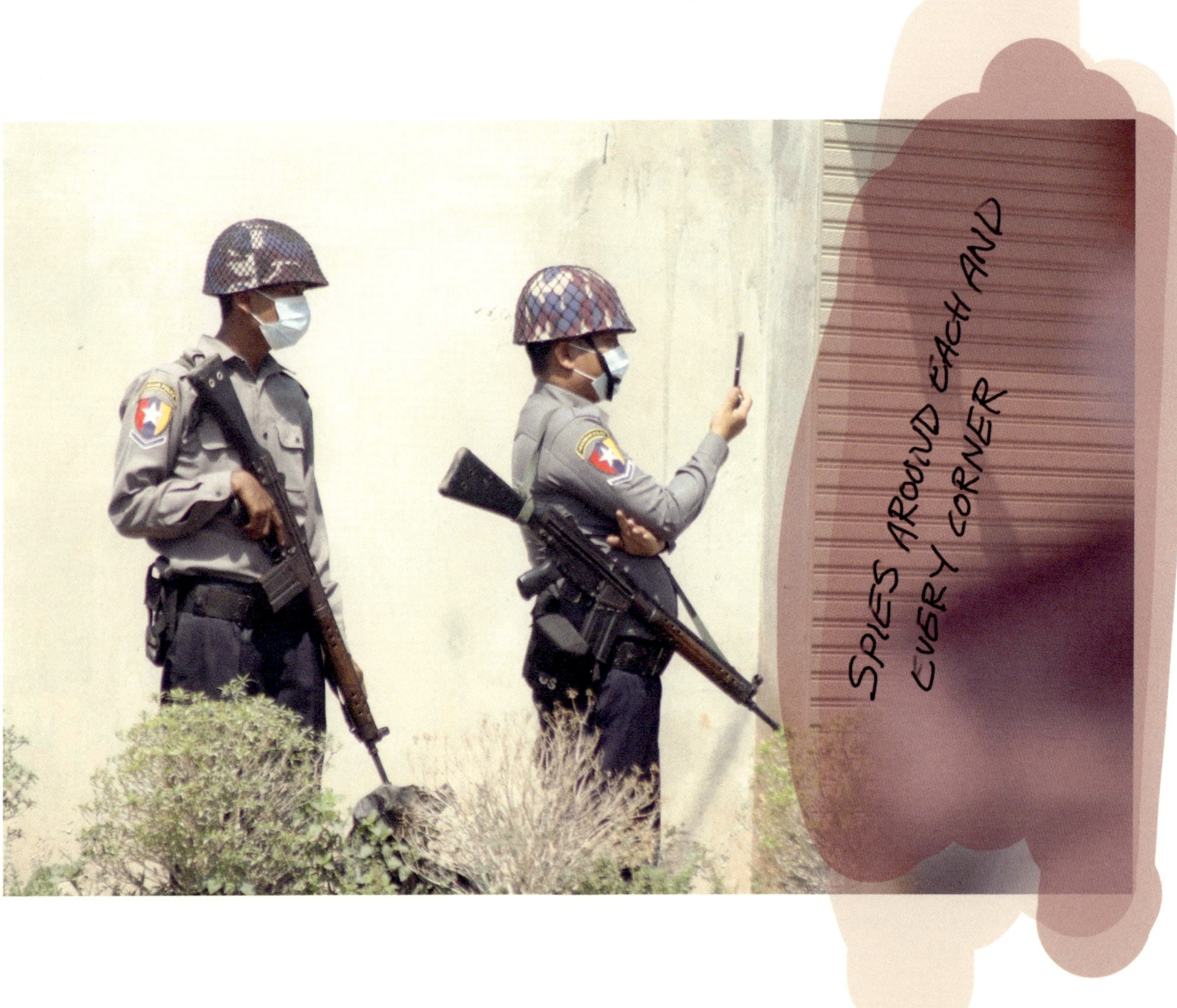

thing, which is to keep his eyes and ears open and report to the authorities as they request. He has several lists on the go. A visitors from out of town guest list, a children going to school or not going to school list, business owners lists, volunteer and charity workers lists, doctors lists, all useful and valuable information set aside for whenever it is required. Last week he purchased a well grown guard dog, which he keeps in his compound. Funnily enough, these sorts of dogs have become fashionable in town and his wife is pleased. She spends a lot of time at the pagoda, where she makes a big show praying for peace. Her friends will not speak but I think they are annoyed because she always sits on a chair for her prayers. She says it is because of her bad back but they think it is arrogant behaviour.

My neighbour is worried about her grandsons because the teenage boys have a maths problem to consider and they must get the answer right. The question is, how many boys can safely ride on one motor bike from A to B? Grandmother always helps the boys with their homework. She said the answer was two boys, on the way to and from work or wherever they wanted to go. Sometimes one boy rides alone but only if his parents are rich and all boys should remember to wear a helmet but rumours are spreading and word is that instruction leaflets will follow. Grandmother has heard that if the military see two boys on a bike they will shoot one boy and the left over boy will not be in good condition. If one man and one woman are riding a motor bike then the man must be the driver. If two men are riding a motor bike but one man is old then it is OK for two men to share a motorbike, but as far as old men are concerned, how old do they have to be? Thankfully girls are not mentioned. The boys had better not miscalculate this problem. It could be fatal.

The boys have found an answer and it's not maths, it's dressing code. They go to their sisters' cupboard, put on the girls' clothes and race about the town at night, two boy/girls per bike with flowers behind their ears and a cheerful song in their mouths. Beautifully, stupidly brave, but it's nothing to a young man who is not afraid of anything except growing old.

Your Grandfather has retired to the back room. We are worried about him but he is not worried at all because no one can tell him anything new. He says he tended his paddy fields in thunderstorms. He has survived fires, floods, plagues of rats and of course he has seen death, fair and foul. He has learned to be mindful and cool headed, never afraid. He survived independence and insurrection, he survived the first military coup and he survived the second military coup and at this point God will decide whether he survives the third military coup. He has got the ancient hunting rifle he inherited from the ancestors. We had it for generations, since the last true Burmese king sat on the golden throne, before the British put him on the boat for India. He kept it safe under the bed all these years. His father taught him how to fight and he says, 'Let the chicken brains in uniforms worry about boys on motorbikes. I am an old man but there is nothing wrong with my head.' He knows perfectly how to manufacture a homemade explosive, powerful enough to derail a train on the main line to Rangoon, and I am afraid he will do it. Tomorrow he will send number one grandson to buy a camouflage jacket at the market. The boy is respectful for Grandfather but he made me swear not to tell his mother.

In the cathedral compound life goes on as you remember. Mass is recited every morning in all our languages according to the day of the week. Sister Emerita has put on weight so it is hard to walk but the doctor says she must do it for her blood pressure, which is fit to burst these days. She makes her girls polish the pews until they shine like the sun. They still put vegetables out to dry on mats at the kitchen door and the pet dogs are fed. God requests us to maintain routine and prayerful order through all. That is our work. The senior priest sits in his office with his hair neatly parted. His smile is precisely adjusted, not too much, not too little, always perfect. Although he will not admit it, I know he is disappointed. He nurtured small optimistic hopes, not in the first year of Suu Kyi's release from prison, not in the second or third but gradually, over the course of the last ten years, he observed the young people in the congregation maturing and growing in confidence so his hopes grew more sturdy. He studied history and prayed God would reward his patience but now he believes change will not come in our lifetime. In this country life is complicated so we have our wars and we have our orphans. He knows because once upon a time he was one orphan himself. He feeds the people by conjuring rice and fishes out of the parishioners' paddy fields and distributing them wherever they are most needed. He is good at that sort of thing.

Mrs Golden Dreams is depressed. To be frank she has got fat and hates herself but she tries to accept it with a calm mind. In the afternoon she sits on her couch looking at her diamanté crown. She earned that crown by dieting to within an inch of perfection, attending dance classes designed for much younger chickens and squeezing her delicate feet into the highest heeled platform shoes, but she has lost heart for it. She employed the best artist with the most expensive makeup to paint her face and the best seamstress in Yangon to make the tightest costume imaginable. She remembers the night she won the crown. Thank God there was no swimsuit class like in the West. We would not know where to look. Mrs Golden Dreams came to life under the spotlights, by the cheers of the crowd and it all turned out to be a brilliant investment. These days she has a social media following worth good money. She has a smile that can sell anything to anyone but especially the rich men who admire her plump curves. She loves the stage, she could have chosen the political stage. She has all the right contacts in high places but who would want to take the risk? She thought film and beauty was a better and safer bet for her family. The Westerners call it soft power and she was satisfied with that.

She ran away from the first husband and married a film director who was not one of us, but he turned out to be a good man. The Tatmadaw have pulled the red carpet right out from under his feet.

The film director husband is Buddhist so she worships two religions because two is better than one and I think it is more safe to be a Buddhist in this country, but she is so easygoing about these things. Her hair is long and glossy, her skin is soft and golden like Western butter but she knows beauty is an asset that melts away in short years and how long will it be until things return to normal? One of the generals' wives has made a pet of her and so she goes with that wife to the pagoda. That is what pays bills, but not all – some are left over for another day. Mrs Golden Dreams lives in a gated compound with crumbling walls and a house she can't afford to maintain.

People gossip and say she has a bad attitude. Her own family say it is the truth but what can she do? Her husband loves her but he is an old man, growing tired. She worries about his health. She forbids her children to go out. They are unemployed in the safety of their own home. Her Cinderella sister does the housework dressed in rags. Mrs Golden Dreams says nothing to rock the military boat. She paints her face and turns it away from the horrors beyond the stage lights. She must do it because she is family breadwinner.

She sells lookalike Western products – jewellery, handbags, baby clothes. Little things that add Western comforts to life. It doesn't matter if they are the real thing or not since no one has the opportunity to visit the West and see for themselves.

She says if things don't improve she will go and sell wet fish in the market. I can see her sitting there, under an umbrella in the pouring rain with all the ladies passing by, holding up their skirts from the puddles. It smells so bad but this is better than telling golden lies to generals' wives. The water is dripping down her neck but no matter. She mops it with the dirty towel draped over her shoulder. She is squatting on the ground, her arms and broad thighs spreading wide for balance and an equally spreading smile. When a customer stops she holds the scales up high, metal weights balanced against a pan of flapping fish. They are not dead yet but they soon will be. The customer, a man shopping with his wife, pulls out some damp and dirty notes. He hands them over. I am happy for her. If ever Mrs Golden Dreams spies an opportunity to send her sons overseas she will take it, no matter if it breaks her heart. That is what the generals' wives do and she can do the same.

There are five teachers in our school on High Shrimp Mountain Road. Graceful girls who love the children, but these days the school is under armed police guard and we have no understanding if it is to protect or to intimidate. And now I will tell you the case of young Aung Thuka, eight years old. He arrived at school in a civilian vehicle accompanied by two guards. The vehicle did not belong to his parents and he did not return the following day. By witness statement, he was taken to the police station to be interrogated and his family have disappeared into the jungle. The young teachers choose to follow the good example and disappear before being disappeared. When the police are not looking they remove their uniforms and hang them on the school railings along with a note saying they refuse to teach the children 'Slave Education.' Every morning I pass by the green skirts and white blouses. They stir a little in the breeze, waving sad goodbyes to their owners. A pet dog rests in the shade of the school yard, waiting patiently for the return, but he is always disappointed. Nobody knows exactly where the teachers have gone with their school bags on their backs but we suspect their brothers are calling to them from the jungle. They must walk three days to the mountains.

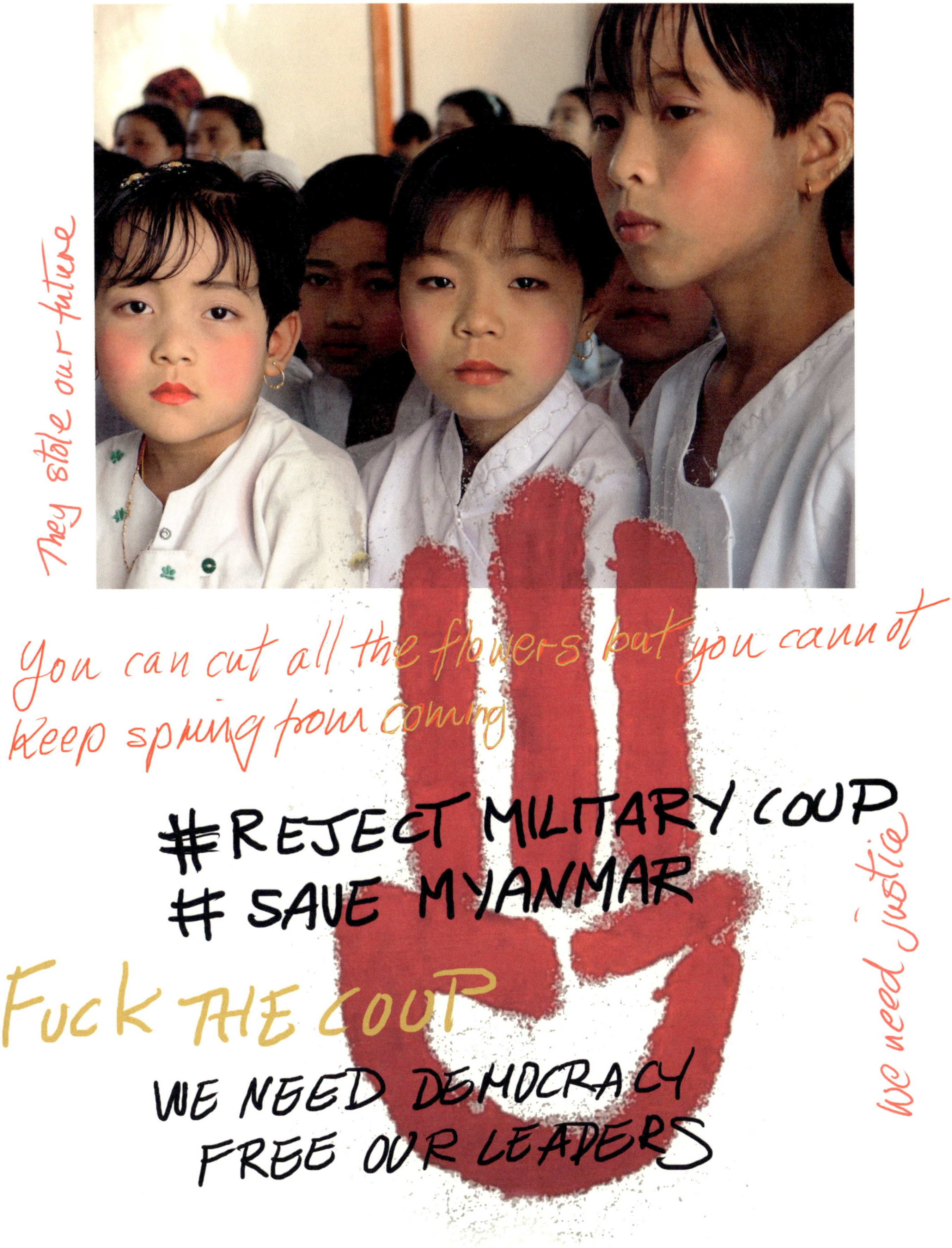
They stole our future
You can cut all the flowers but you cannot keep spring from coming
#REJECT MILITARY COUP
SAVE MYANMAR
FUCK THE COUP
WE NEED DEMOCRACY
FREE OUR LEADERS
We need justice

The teachers learn to crawl on their bellies in the mud and dress in branches from the trees to make themselves invisible. One becomes a military nurse. Some months later they will be captured by the regime forces, who force them to lie face down in the dirt and tie their hands behind their backs. Photographs are circulated. The teachers are wearing cute pyjamas with pictures of teddy bears which do not complement their scowling faces. As usual in this military situation, we do not know what happened to them after that but someone, unknown, took a pot shot at the village administrator, who had all of those valuable lists tucked away in his office. They wanted to teach him a lesson but I am sorry to recount that someone missed the intended target.

And so, my dears, I will finish my report here on a happy note. Your Uncle Char Ming has a new granddaughter. Our niece was so worried to have her baby in the military hospital because the public hospital was closed due to the war but she has been safely delivered at home, a beautiful baby girl called Snow White, after her grandmother. When the father saw Snow White he fell in love straight away and when she smiled her first smile he adored her beyond every other living person. When I see the love the fathers have for the daughters I am overjoyed and thank God for his blessings. I pray the mother and her baby will get some sleep when people stop banging the pots and pans at night.

But for now, my dears, I am tired and can hardly bear to write any more. Please remember those of us who live on High Shrimp Mountain Road. Pray for us to remain strong. We will do it. Your cousin would like a pair of gold earrings when you come to visit. We pray for you to be healthy and happy. You have great love for us and we have love for you because we are the same blood. God's work will be done.

Your ever loving
Adaw Gyi

Mirage of Snow
Narrator: *Linda Lewin*

The situation is the direct result of the failure to hold the military to account for their past crimes. Myanmar is a country awash in weapons with deep religious and ethnic divides where millions can barely feed themselves.
Thant Myint U.

Because I like to use pictures to inspire discussions, in my Pathein English lessons I very quickly realised that my Karen students were fascinated by snow scenes. True cold is something they have never experienced and a sensory experience I believe they cannot begin to imagine. To them snow must be as exotic as fabulous jewelled pagodas are to us: they see it as calm, pure and peaceful and they long to experience all of those things.

Snow or Snow Snow is a popular girl's name. They all aspire to having pristine white skin and Aunty Nettie was deeply insulted to be nicknamed Snow Black, the suggestion being she was a low-class person. I found it terribly upsetting when I realised beautiful young women in my English class were using caustic skin-whitening creams on their golden complexions. These aspirations are daily reinforced by Western lifestyle advertisements. One bizarre example floats on a hoarding above the wharf in Pathein, showing pure white milk on a white-topped Swiss mountain being consumed by white-skinned people. A truly surreal and totally inappropriate Western dream.

San Po Thin named his beloved twin daughters Snow White and Rose Red after the Walt Disney film. His fairytale wish was a peaceful and prosperous future for his beautiful daughters.

These days, my lovely, innocent Myanmar Snow White has grown up. I have met her so many times in so many different places but the last time I caught sight of her she was reincarnated as a crossdressing protest heroine willing to risk her life in front of the military guns. He may be fearful but

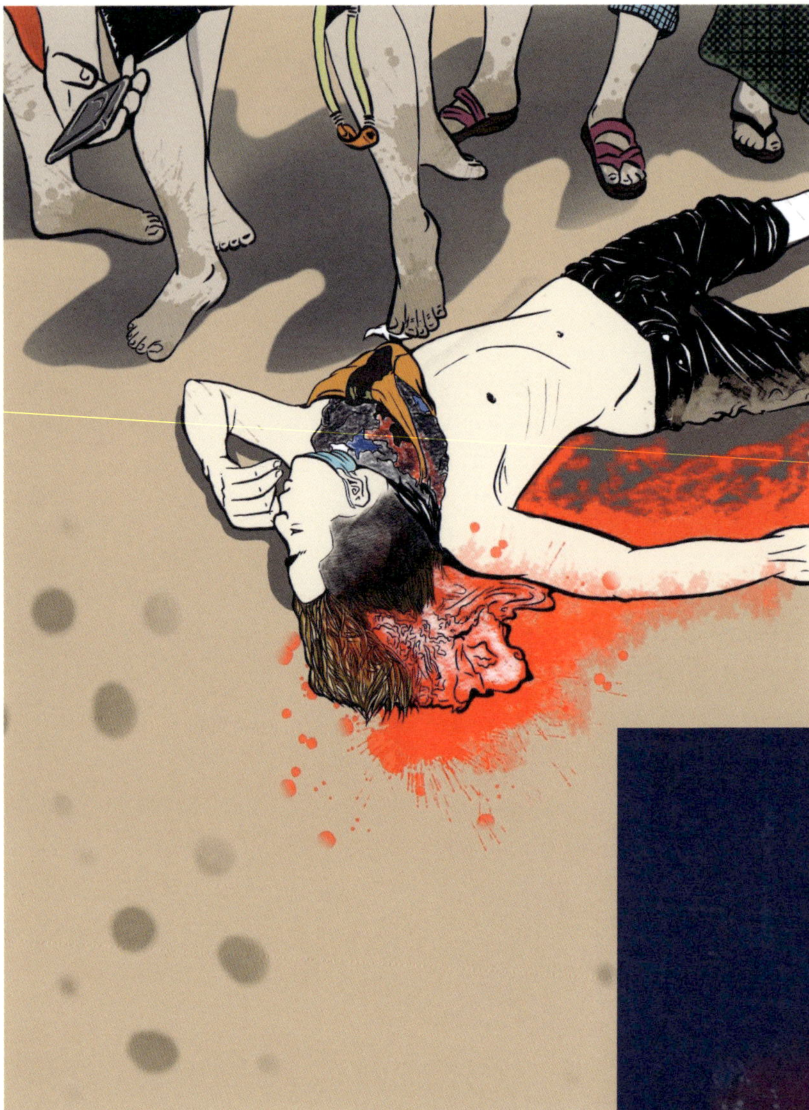

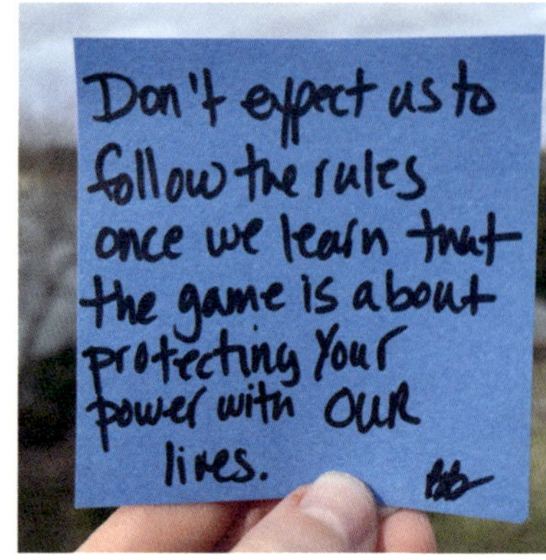

Gen Z.
Keyboard Warriors

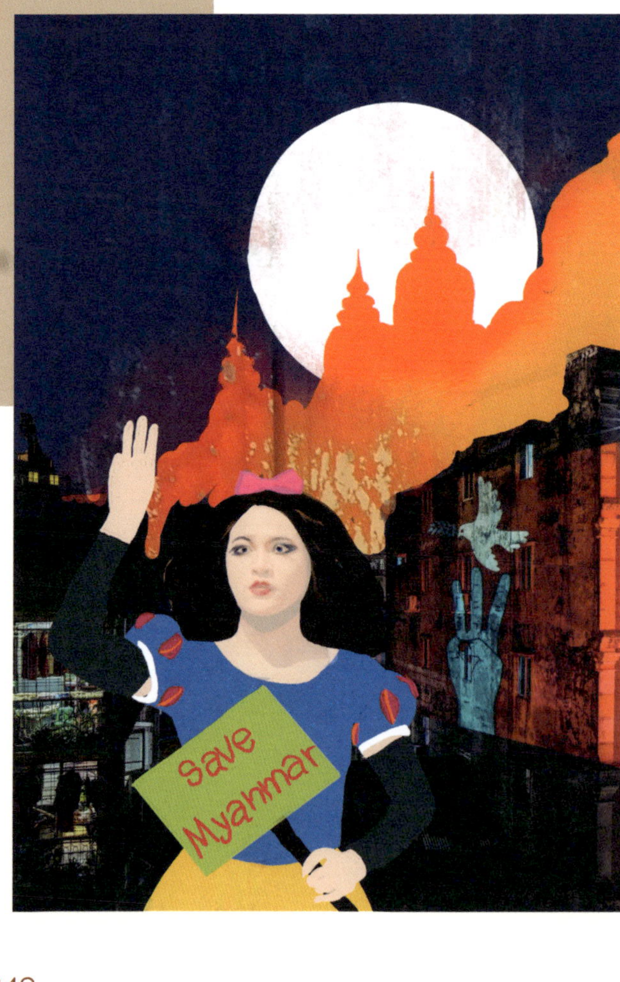

she is brave, marching along the street holding up a green placard with the words, 'Save Myanmar.' She is a little older than in the film but still beautifully dressed in her tight fitting blue bodice and billowing yellow skirt, although her expression has altered. He will not be manipulated. She will not be deceived. He knows the risks she takes. She is a film star who knows how to play to the cameras because everything Generation Z does is recorded by someone on their phone and they will find a way to share with the world, despite internet shut-downs. Her powers are youth, beauty, courage and imagination and he is using them to assert his rights to a democratic future for himself and Snow White's children.

Just like their parents and grandparents, Generation Z is committed to fighting the war in Myanmar for democracy and freedom from military dictatorship. Suu Kyi's father, Aung San, called for unity in his last speech before he was assassinated, but he believed unity would be achieved by force. He created the military machine which turned against his daughter and its own people, consuming them with a monstrous appetite which must be defeated because it can never be satisfied. Perhaps the difference is that Generation Z can imagine unity between different races and different religions. Perhaps they could even be persuaded to believe that race is no more than a divisive construct.

More and more buildings are going up in flames. Entire villages are going up in flames. The country is on fire, on screen, in front of my phone camera eyes. This is the reality of a civil war between the people and a dictatorship. The sad truth is that until now, peace and prosperity in Myanmar has been nothing more than a mirage of snow in a hot country but the fight goes on. Victory lies ahead, always tantalisingly close but never quite achieved.

I leave you with one last memory of Pathein in the fading light of a power cut. All too common in my far away country where it seems everyone and everything is broken. Pathein is not alone in the darkness. Lights are turning off in towns and villages across the land. Sweet Dreams of democracy will come True. Tomorrow but not today.

PUBLIC NOTICE PATHEIN.

Electricity will be cut off from 9:00am to 3:00pm in Pathein city.

Merchant road! Chinese school street! Bananas Road! Boots Street!
Market Road! Umbrella's street! Sweet sweet! Aung Thuka! Squeeze! Jail!
Mahabandula Road! Danish road! Myanu Road! Grocery street! Shwe Pagoda Road! The King's way! The road to the Macedonia! Beach Road! Hmbo's port!
Wedding Road! Latty Gold Rose! Field Street! Padinan Road! Kan Street!
Electricity will be cut off until 3pm.

The Ministry has high hopes and sweet dreams of Electricity but although the rain is falling they say the reservoirs are empty!

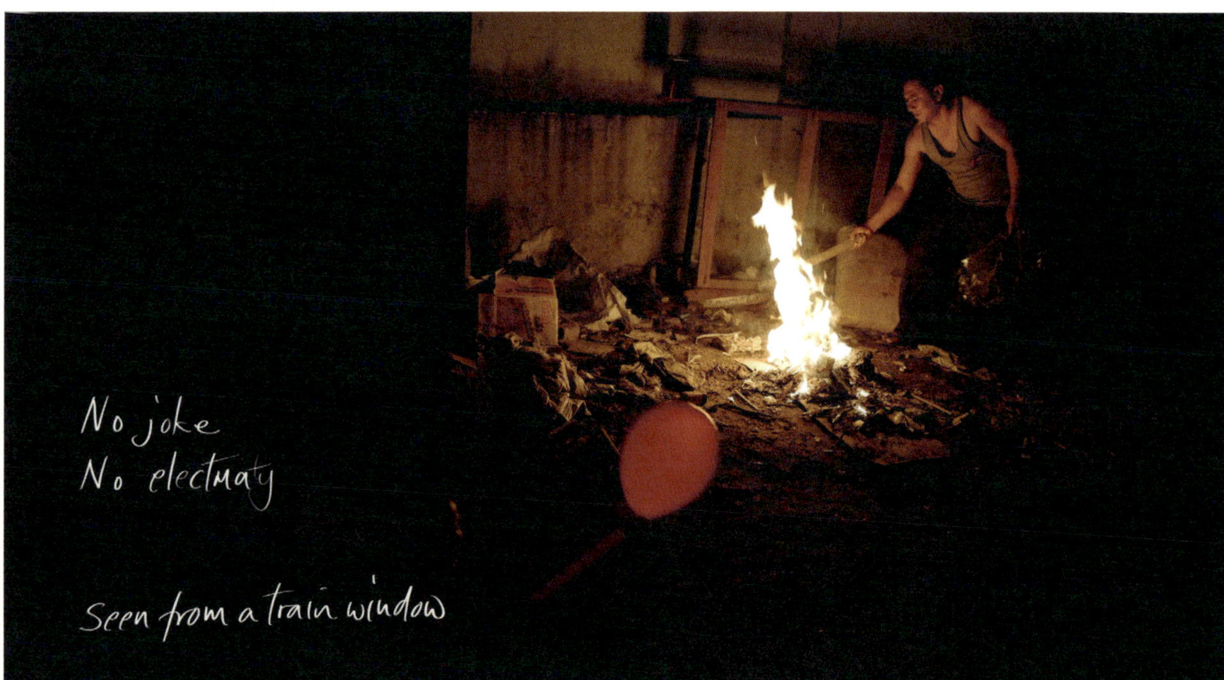

The farmers who left their villages before dawn have driven their trucks to the market by way of *Field Street!* and arrived on *Bananas Road!* where they unload their yellow hands, green and most delicious red.

The golden light of dawn on *Shwe Pagoda Road!* is a sight fit for *The King's way!*

The *Chinese school street!* children walk along *Danish road!*, splashing in the puddles. They disappear into dingy classrooms where daylight is sieved through dirty windows. They are not seen but heard all day long, chanting their lessons.

The prisoners in *Jail!* have been existing in the dark for days on end. No electric or living daylight reaches their cells.

Meanwhile, the *Merchant road!* keep their customers waiting while they search for long neglected but necessary goods in the far beyond memories of wooden warehouses.

On *Boots Street!* and *Umbrella's street!* the shopkeepers cook their breakfast on charcoal stoves. Oh, the smiling faces and *Sweet sweet!* smells.

Aung Thuka, take my hand and *Squeeze!* it tight, we must be careful crossing *Myanu Road!*, it is so busy these days. We will do our shopping on *Grocery street!* Will you have jam or margarine with your bread?

I want to visit the tailor on *Padinan Road!* The seamstress is so sad. Her sewing machine is silent and she cannot finish our order when there is no electric to light her lovely eyes. The temperature is rising high with the sun. *The road to the Macedonia!* is a long hot journey but my darling will arrive at *Hmbo's port!* today and our *Wedding Road!* clothes will not be ready in time.

If you are a good boy we will walk along *Beach Road!* past the statue of *Mahabandula Road!* We will watch the sun setting like a *Gold Rose!* on the blue ocean's waves.

The Further Adventures of Boh Lay
Narrator: *Adaw Gyi*

My Dearest Darling Gazelles,

Days become years and in my memories, years pass like days. At heart, Boh Lay remains the cheerful boy who had so many good things and so much love poured into him by his father, his grandmother and his family in Bassein, but in reality he is become an old man with children and grandchildren of his own. When he returned to Chaung Zauk many things remained just where he had left them. We sat in the church Grandfather built, ate a meal together and rested one last time on the hard wooden bed in his grandparents' house. It grieves me to tell you that, although he has never forgotten his native place and he remains in good spirits and good health past his ninetieth year, he will not come again because once more the men in uniform are waving flags and marching their armies across our land. The country is at war, burning to the ground, very much the same as on the night Boh Lay sailed away on the ebb tide.

When the foreigners speak about the Japanese invasion of Burma, if they remember at all, they call it The Forgotten War. Evacuation lists show that the majority who survived The Trek across the mountains and jungles to reach safety in British India were unencumbered single men. Boh Lay and his family were a unique case. Boh Lay is insistent he was never a refugee, he was an evacuee, but his escape from Burma was not much short of a miracle and he has his mother to thank for that. Boh Lay later described it as a Rolls Royce evacuation. Due to his mother's ingenuity, and I'm sure his father's planning, the young Master Desmond Lwin sailed safely around the Indian ocean on a coastal steamer, with his mother, brother and sister. Their journey took them from their home town Bassein, now known as Pathein, along the coast to Akyab, now known as Sittwe, and then across the ocean to India where they sailed up the Hooglie river to Calcutta, now known as Kolkata. Thanks be to God. It was only very much later that they heard the 'last boat' which they had missed because Mother was washing her hair had been sunk by a U-boat. It was a remarkable escape by a single woman and her three children from the chaos of a humiliating British retreat. It was the beginning of the end of the British Empire. As far as the 'white masters' were concerned the glory days had gone for ever. Their parting gift to us was a colonial legislative system which continues to enslave the people, ethnic divisions which have never been peacefully resolved and disputed borders.

Boh Lay did not get away completely unscathed. On arrival in Calcutta, he was sent straight to the military hospital and was treated for malaria by the wonderful Queen Alexandra nurses, whom he remembers wearing bright red capes. He was lucky enough to be treated with the new malarial drugs, which he swears were transported hundreds of miles across India specifically to save his life. He suffered from recurring bouts of malaria right up until the birth of his first child.

The family left almost all their possessions behind in Burma so they were forever grateful to the Calcutta Law Society, who supplied their immediate needs with an allowance for badly-needed new clothes and hair cuts – which I'm sure Lucienne appreciated. They were allocated a place in the evacuee camp, Almora, where records show they arrived on 10th March, 1942. Mother decided that there were too many U-boats lurking in the seas to risk another long voyage back to her family in London and she had a strong impression there was nothing left to eat in the home country, so she decided that the safest place for the children, until things returned to normal, would be boarding school in a healthy Indian hill station, and that is exactly what happened. Perhaps she had not given up hope of return to her husband and home in Bassein, where she left the man who I like to believe was the great love of her life.

Boh Lay was enrolled at St Joseph's, a Jesuit school housed in a grand palace in the Himalayan foothills, where there were plenty of fresh fruits and vegetables and he excelled in his studies as well as in sports. He resolved to be top of the class all of the time, which he achieved without any difficulty. Photographs of the students show a motley crew of boys who appear to have washed up from all parts of the Empire, lounging in typically cool 1940s style, but wearing clothes which are either too big or too small, and armed with fearsome knives which would definitely not be allowed on school premises these days. They were all young survivors of the war. Boh Lay kept the bayonet with him for a long time. It was a treasured possession which fortunately never had to be used in defence but came in handy for chopping kindling until eventually it broke.

There were very few reminders of the old life but Boh Lay was not the only boy from Pathein who was displaced by war. He says one day, idling by the roadside whittling a stick for want of anything better to do, he was delighted to see some boys from his home town marching up the road towards him. They had joined The Burma Rifles Regiment. He was honoured to be invited to take his place at the head of the table at a regimental dinner, for old times' sake.

His greatest sadness was that the letters he wrote to his father remained unanswered for many months, until at last the family received a letter from Bassein confirming his father's death, most likely from typhoid but to this very day the pork curry cooked by the unlucky sister is blamed by our family and Boh Lay remains very suspicious of undercooked pork meat. The family in Burma and the documents Lucienne carried in her suitcase supported San Po Lwin's children through their education but when Boh Lay graduated from the healthy, sporty school in the Himalayas he was forced to chose between his east and west families. Lucienne remarried and the children were invited to return to Burma, without her. Boh Lay made the only decision he could make but perhaps that was the hardest part of the whole adventure. He remained with his mother and his stepfather.

Lucienne was never idle. She earned her keep running a hotel in Lucknow, India. She loved to tell the story of entertaining the mountaineer Edmund Hillary on his way to, or perhaps his way back, from Everest. She remained in India until the death of her second husband from cancer. Her daughter Marie married an Indian army officer and made her home there. When Lucienne's youngest son, the baby of the family who never knew his father, left home to work in London she decided to join him, and returned to the city she had left as a young woman when her head was full of romantic dreams. Although by this time she was old enough to retire, she insisted on maintaining her independence by going out to work in a grand London department store, accepting a very similar sales position to the one she had left a lifetime before.

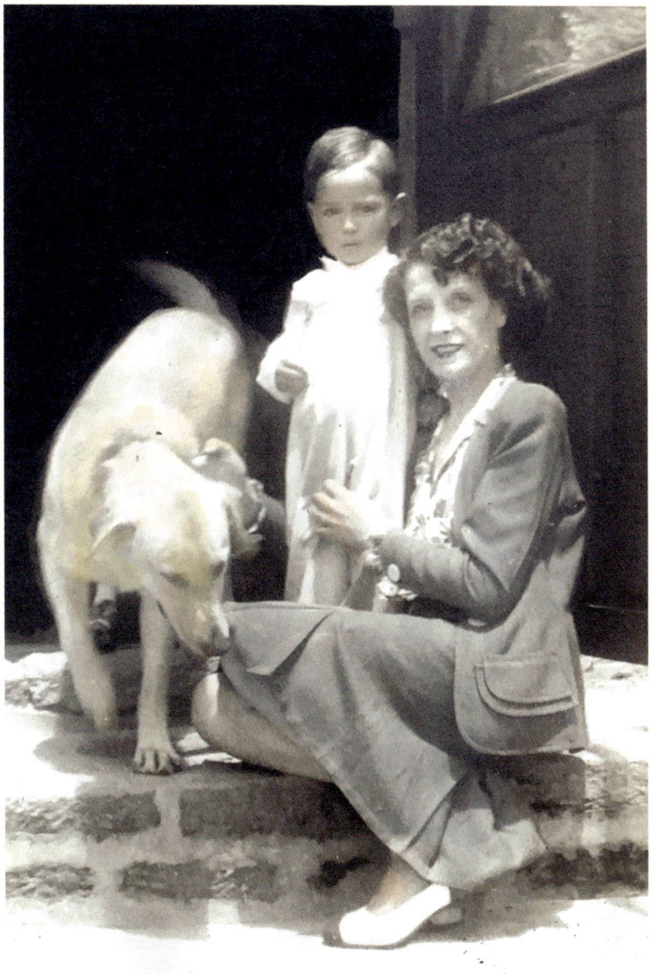

Lucienne, David and Simba in India

When Desmond, formerly known as Boh Lay was nineteen years old he followed his fathers example by travelling to England for the sake of his education. He was offered a place to study at Oxford but for unknown reasons his mother objected, so he accepted a place at Faraday House in London and he qualified as an electrical engineer. The World War, which had relocated so many young people all around the globe, was over and it was a wonderful time to be young and free. Desmond did his national service in the RAF, working as a wireless operator. He looked very handsome in his uniform. Soon after arriving in London, he met and married a blond-haired Scottish girl, to the consternation of the family on both sides. Desmond

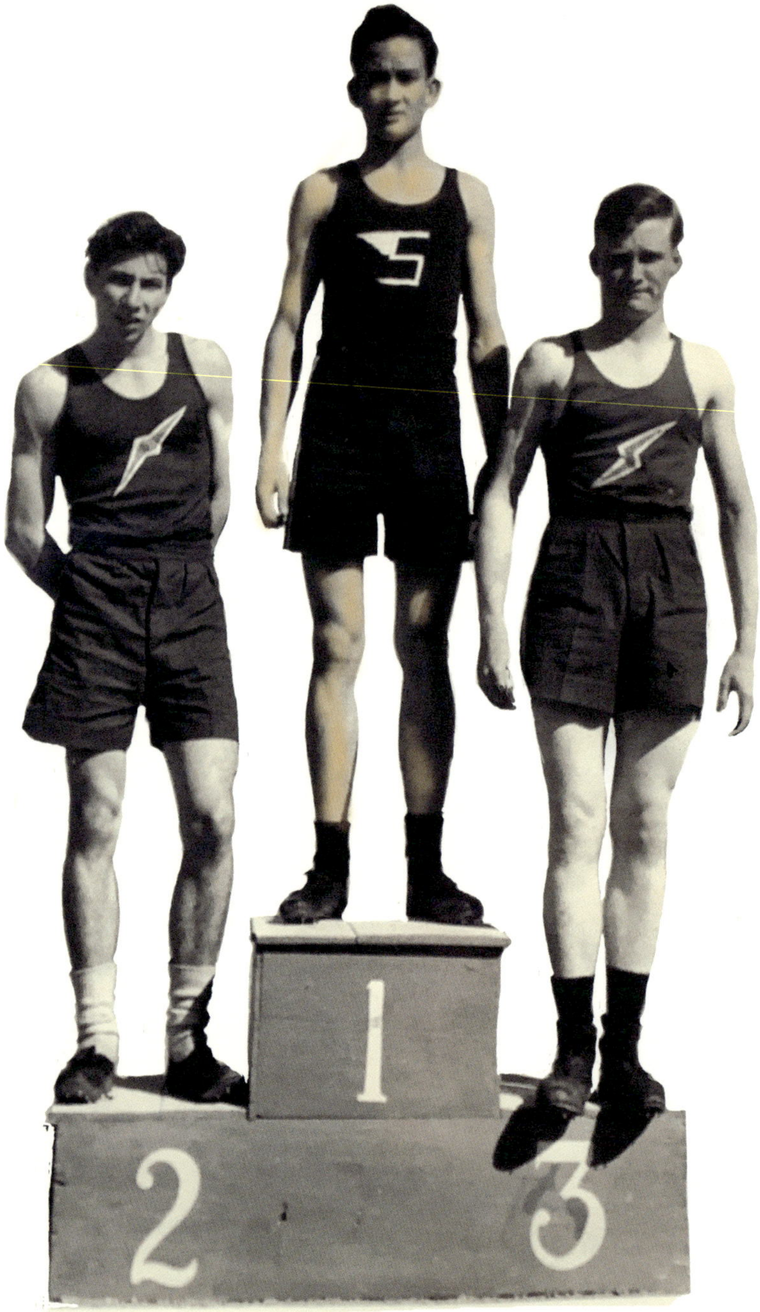

Bob Lay could jump 6 foot high

and Doris were considered to be a 'mixed' marriage in just the same way as Lucienne and San Po Lwin. It was only when Desmond and Doris's first child was born that the Scottish family was reconciled. Eventually, the young couple had a family of six children, who lived together as happily ever after as is possible in this world. Little sister Hilary continued in the family tradition of mixed marriages. The family held its breath when she brought her Japanese husband home to meet Father but Boh Lay rose to the occasion, vanquished the vicious little snake which had lain dormant but not dead for so long and forgave Kengo all his ancestors' atrocities. Everyone breathed a sigh of relief.

If ever you find your way to Chaung Zauk village, you might still see the fresh water ponds which San Po Lwin built and the church with its corrugated iron roof. Take a fishtail canoe at high tide and slip between the mangrove trees, searching for the wooden houses thatched with thorns and leaves. The church remains, but the tower is empty because the bell was stolen during the Japanese war. You might still see the astonishing green paddy fields which provide all that is good for the people who live there and you will be welcomed by the villagers, who will smile and say they remember my story. They will tell you it is the truth but you must go soon because the farmlands have been bought by foreign investors and factories are devouring the land. Fresh water has turned to salt in the magic rice bowl and the storytellers are leaving their paddy fields for ever.

Daw Bu Ma's brave spirit lives on. It continues to fly with her grandchildren and great grandchildren all around the world. Somehow I do not think she would be surprised. I am sure she would be pleased. Many of them are artists, including Bo Lay's eldest daughter, who metamorphosed into a writer.

'I grew up in a terraced house in Glasgow where very occasionally my father would tell us stories of his childhood in a mysterious place where "even the stones on the road could be rubies or sapphires." Fairy tales, or so we thought.'

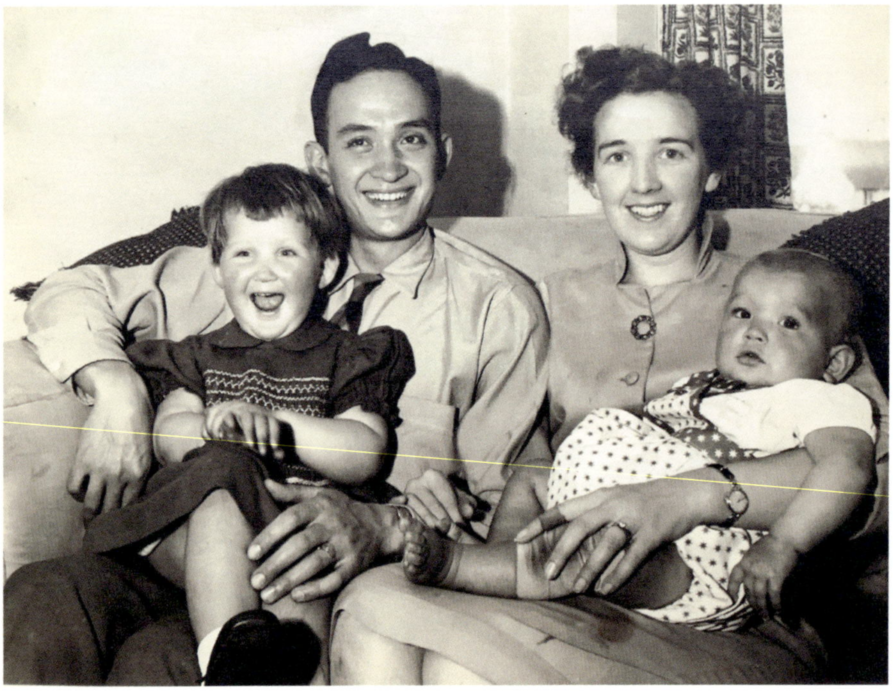

Desmond, Doris, Linda, Paul, 1956

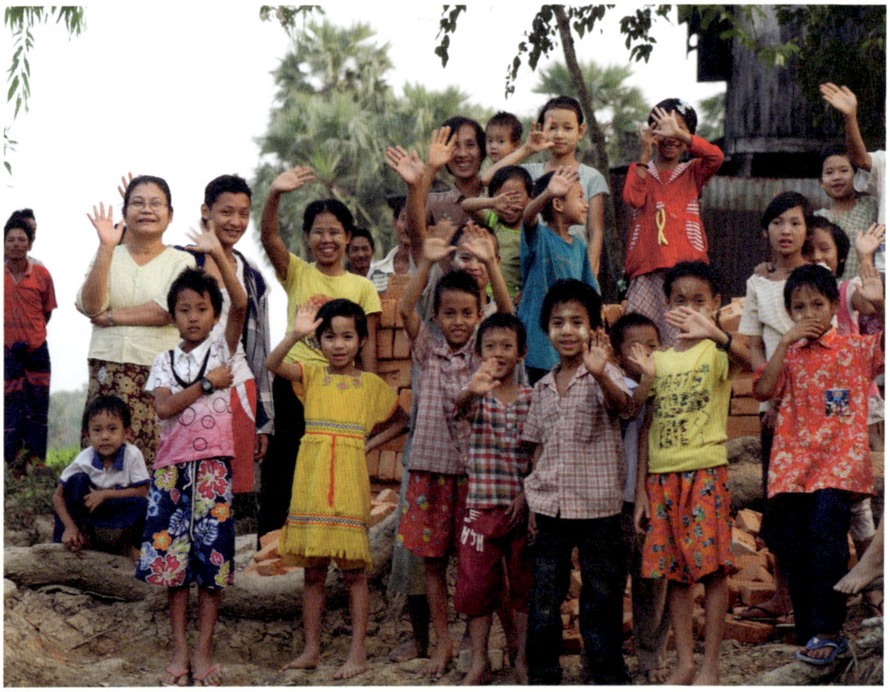

Farewell from the village

My Dear Gazelles,

I have not told everything but I hope I have told enough. There were many things I did not know when I began writing this book. I did not know it would be a farewell to places and people I will never see again. I did not know fairytales are the truth, the best and the worst of whatever we can imagine. I did not know just how closely the past, the present and the future are entwined in endless repeating circles and what a struggle it is to break free. I swear, I did not fully understand who Adaw Gyi was until I arrived here, at the end of my tale, where I discovered that Adaw Gyi and Linda Lewin are one and the same person. I have learned the value of being neither one thing nor the other, not from here or there but from somewhere else which is hard to define. I have grown up.

Today, through my window, I see Scottish hills shining green and amethyst in the pale silver sunlight. Sheep and Easter lambs are appearing in the fields. I know I will never stop longing for tropical sun, hot enough to dry peppercorns and chillies by the roadside, strong enough to cook flesh through to the bone, but my old grey horse is waiting to be fed. It is time to resume my normal routines, the precious daily interactions which stitch our lives together.

My love and respect go out to all those courageous individuals, Daw Bu Ma, San Po Lwin, San Po Thin, Lucienne, Boh Lay, and Aunty Nettie, that difficult but admirable woman who devoted her life to 'helping her people.' All of those including the Strange People who are forced to explore the world right up to the dangerous edges, gambling everything precious in life for survival. There are good people in the world who never give up hope of making the future a better place for our children. When Angel, the ethnic Chinese girl sacrificed her life for freedom and democracy in Myanmar, she was wearing a black and white t-shirt with the motto, 'Everything will be OK'. You may say she is a dreamer but she is not the only one.

Your ever loving Linda Lewin
Formerly known as Adaw Gyi

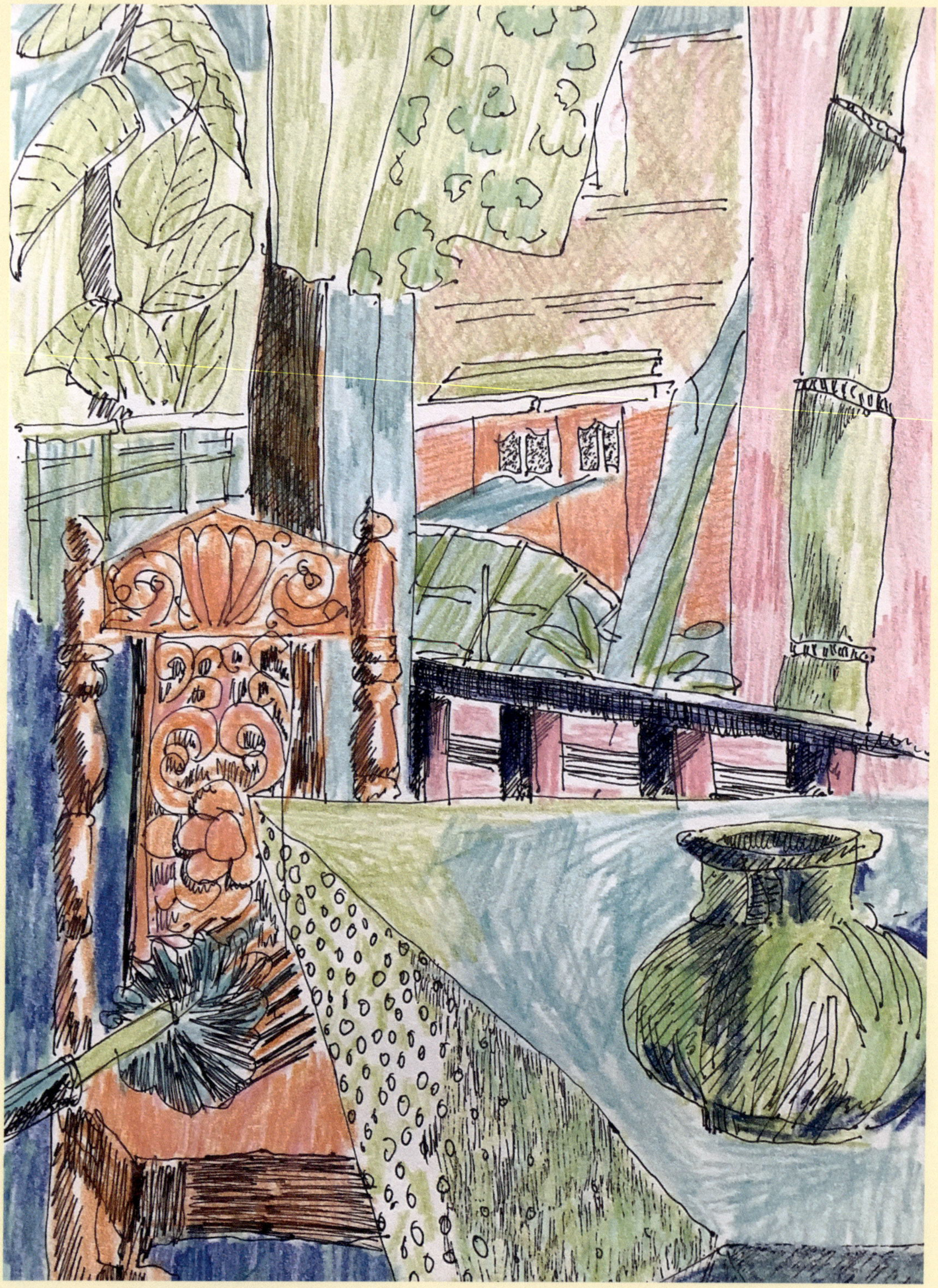

Remembering rats under the veranda

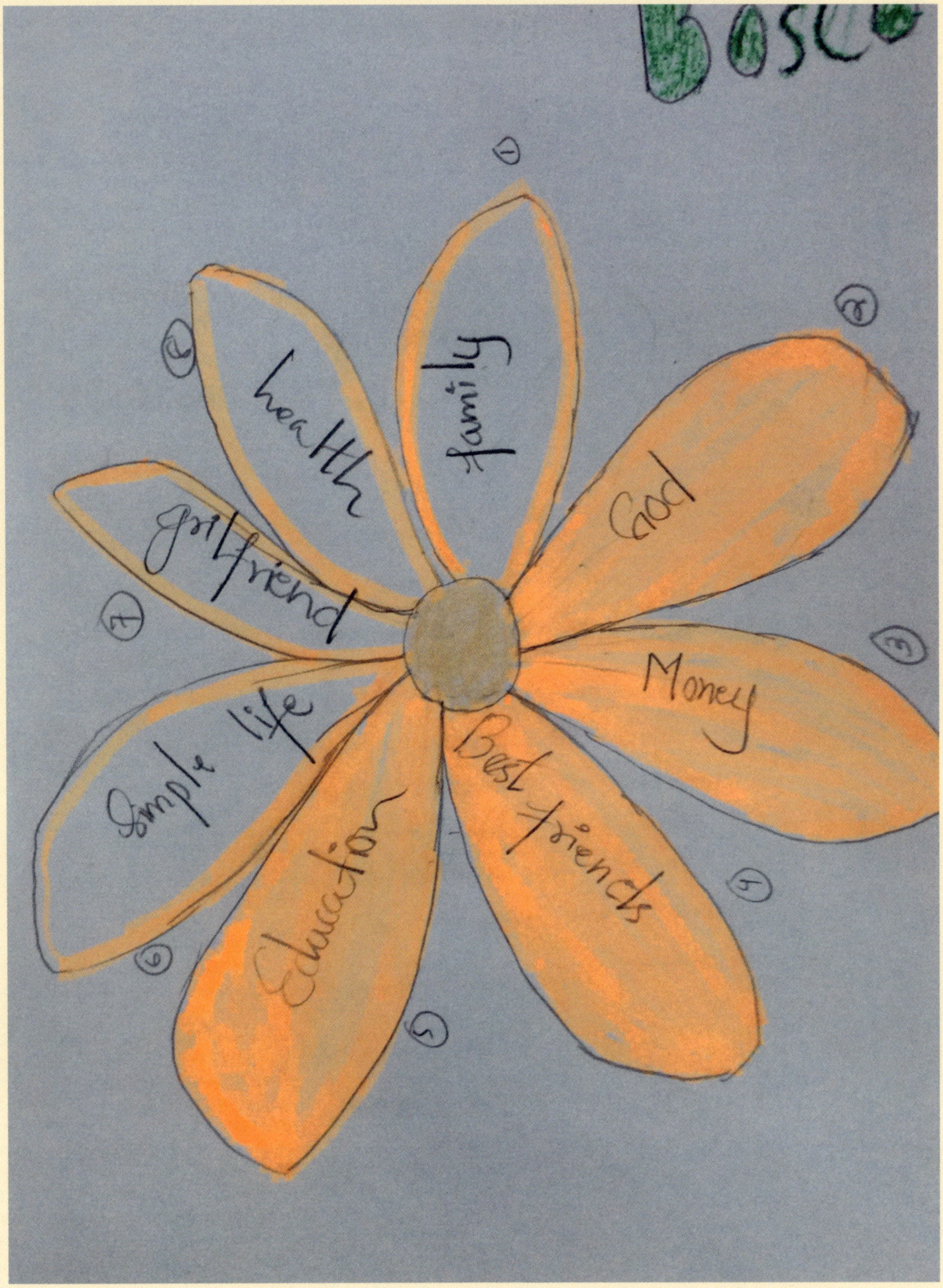

Amen to that xx

Burma = Myanmar

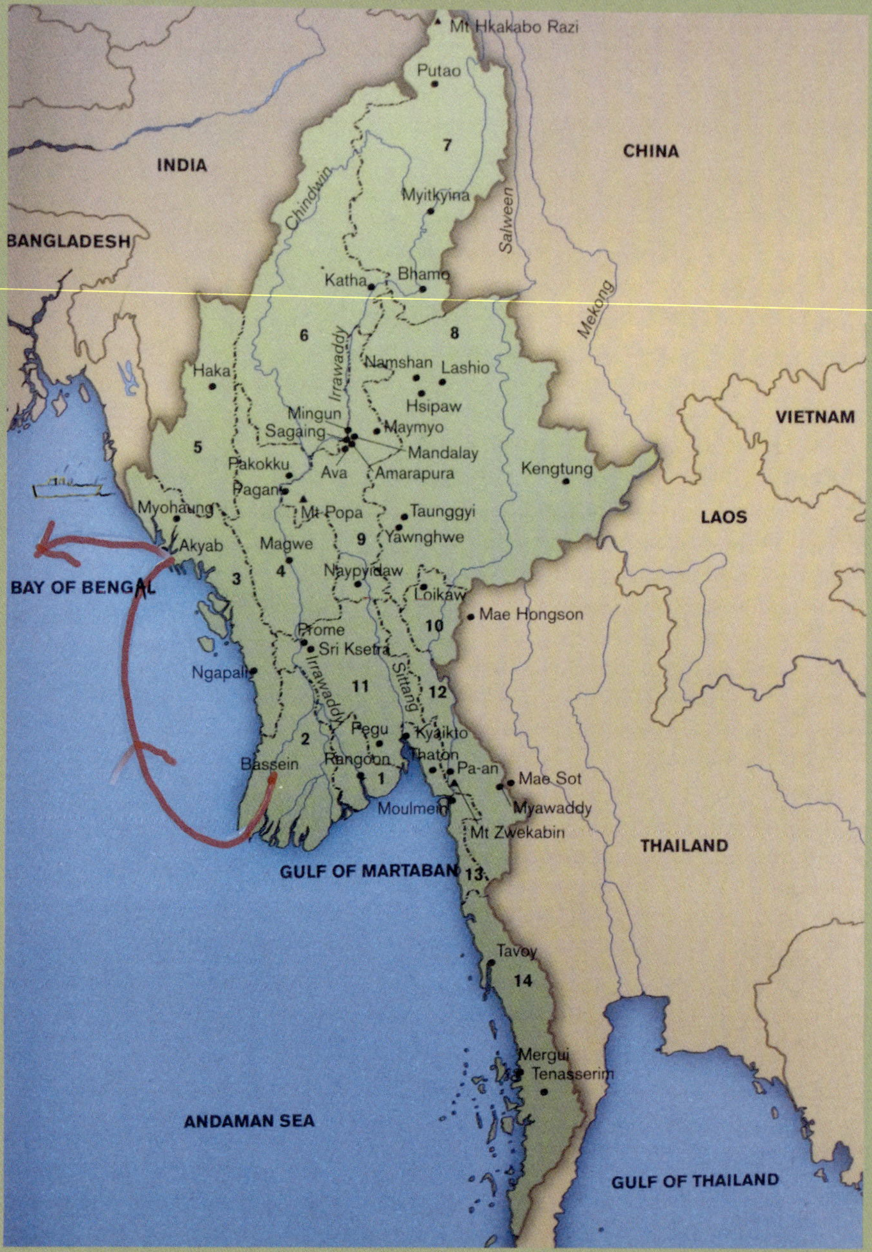

Calcutta = Kolcata

Bassein = Pathein
Akyab = Sittwe

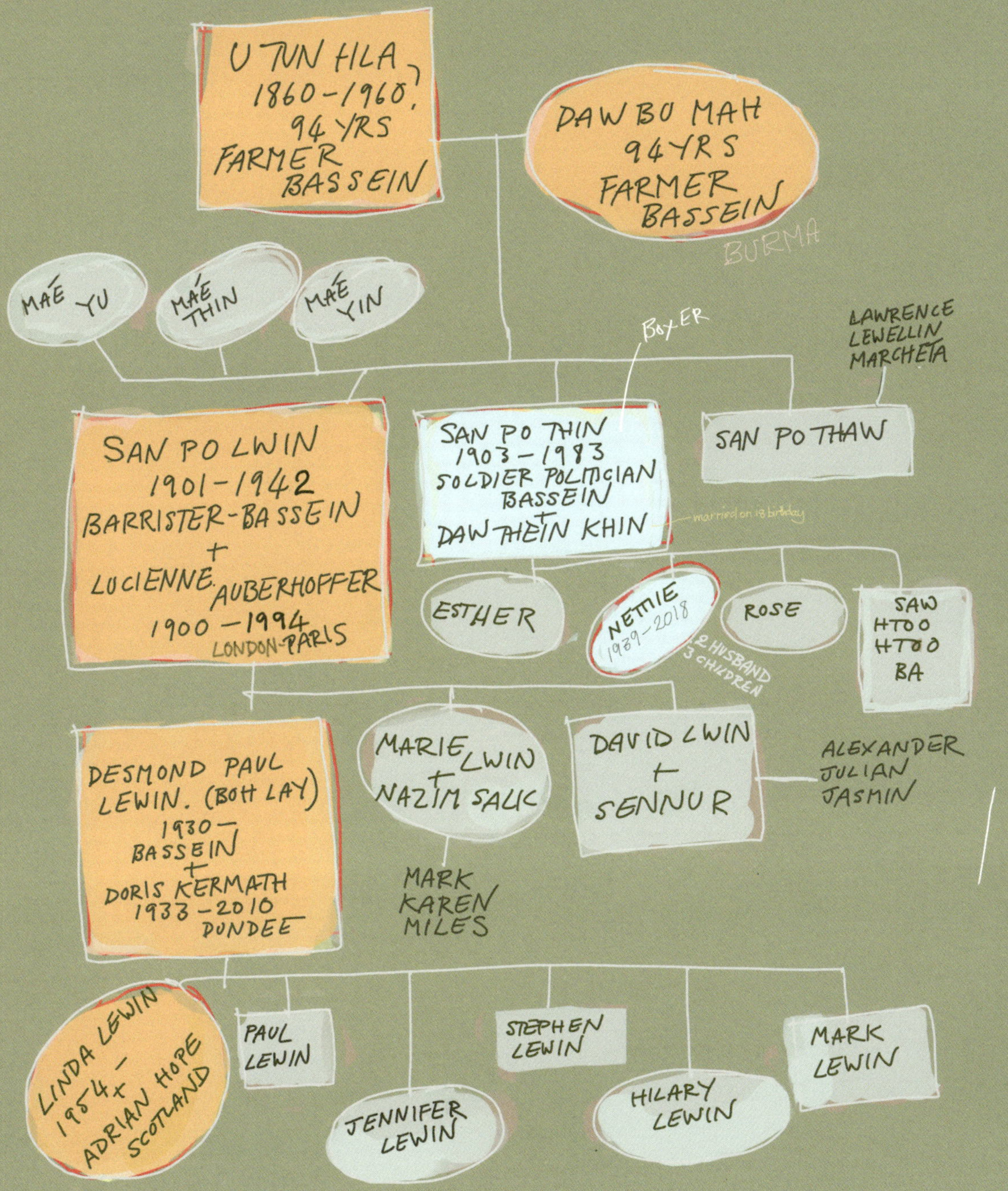

FAMILY TREE

SCOTLAND - IRRAWADDY DELTA

3 GENERATIONS

My Faraway Country: Myanmar

Written and illustrated by Linda Lewin

First published in Great Britain by
Golden Hare in 2023

A catalogue record for this book is
available from the British Library

ISBN 978 1 83840 655 4

Designed by James Brook,
www.jamesbrook.net

Printed and bound in Great Britain
by Gomer Press, Wales

Golden Hare
68 St Stephen Street,
Edinburgh EH3 5AQ
Scotland, United Kingdom

Find out more about Golden Hare
from www.goldenharebooks.com

Supported by Luminate
Scotland's Creative Ageing Organisation